Silent Visions

Discovering Early Hollywood and New York Through the Films of Harold Lloyd

John Bengtson

Foreword by **Kevin Brownlow**

SANTA
MONICA
PRESS

Copyright ©2011 by John Bengtson

All rights reserved.

This book may not be reproduced in whole or in part or in any form or format without the written permission of the publisher.

Published by: Santa Monica Press LLC
P.O. Box 850
Solana Beach, CA 92075
1-800-784-9553
www.santamonicapress.com
books@santamonicapress.com

Printed in Canada

Santa Monica Press books are available at special quantity discounts when purchased in bulk by corporations, organizations, or groups. Please call our Special Sales department at 1-800-784-9553.

ISBN-13 978-1-59580-057-2

Library of Congress Cataloging-in-Publication Data

Bengtson, John.
 Silent visions : discovering early Hollywood and New York through the films of Harold Lloyd / by John Bengtson ; foreword by Kevin Brownlow.
    p. cm.
 ISBN 978-1-59580-057-2
1. Lloyd, Harold, 1893-1971—Criticism and interpretation. 2. Hollywood (Los Angeles, Calif.)—In motion pictures. 3. New York (N.Y.)—In motion pictures. I. Title.
 PN2287.L5B46 2011
 791.4302'8092—dc22
                                    2011003279

Cover and interior design and production by Future Studio

To Edla, Linden, and Arden

Contents

Acknowledgments—"Today" Photo Credits

This book was truly a collaborative effort. While I am sincerely grateful to all who have assisted, these colleagues were especially generous in sharing their time, talents, and expertise:

Paul R. Ayers is an attorney, historian, and archivist, who made many discoveries here, and for my prior books. Photos: 54 all; 67 r, lr, bc; 144 all; 145 all; 188 ur; 189 bc.

Jeff Bridges is a Los Angeles-based artist, illustrator, photographer, and amateur local historian. Photos: 45 ll, lr; 48 all; 132 ur; 149 c; 153 lr; 154 ur; 173 lr; 183 ur, lr; 184 ul.

Jeffrey Castel De Oro is a visual effects artist, and vintage film enthusiast, who also assisted greatly with my prior books. Photos: 20 ul, lr; 23 lr; 35 ul; 43 ll, lr; 70 cr; 81 b; 97 lr; 109 bc; 115 ur, lr; 120 lr; 156 ur; 167 lr; 174 bc; 211 ll; 213 ll; 215 lr; 285 ll.

Lon Davis provided invaluable editorial assistance, is author of *Silent Lives: 100 Biographies of the Silent Film Era*, and with his wife Debra, author of *Stooges Among Us*, and *King of the Movies: Francis X. Bushman*, all available from BearManor Media.

Annette D'Agostino Lloyd (no relation) is the author of four books on Lloyd, including *The Harold Lloyd Encyclopedia*, from McFarland, and *Harold Lloyd: Magic in a Pair of Horned-Rim Glasses*, from BearManor Media, both of which I referred to constantly.

Graceann Macleod who provided invaluable editorial assistance, and blogs at http://silentsgirl.wordpress.com/. Her husband David is the author of *The Sound of Buster Keaton*.

Piet Schreuders is an award-winning graphic designer, author of *The Beatles' London* and *The Paperback Art of James Avati*, re-creationist of the musical scores of Hal Roach Studios composer Leroy Shield, film location expert (*e.g.*, *Mr. Hulot's Holiday, The Red Balloon*), and editor of *Furore* magazine—www.PietSchreuders.com. Piet graciously created all the maps in this book, depicting the streets of L.A. and N.Y. Photos: 160 all; 175 bc; 182 all; 273 all.

E.J. and Kim Stephens, E.J. is author of *Early Warner Bros. Studios*, film-series host of *Flickers at the Junction*, and blogger of *Deadwrite's Dailies*—www.deadwrite.wordpress.com. Kim is a docent for the Warner Bros. Museum, and, along with husband E.J., works closely with the Santa Clarita Valley Historical Society. Photos: 84 ur, lr; 85 ul, ll; 87 ll; 191 lr; 192 lr.

Marc Wanamaker owns Bison Archives, the foremost source of images and facts relating to the development of the American film and television industries, is a founding member of Hollywood Heritage, the Beverly Hills Historical Society, and the L.A. Conservancy, and is author of many books, including *Location Filming in Los Angeles*, *Early Hollywood*, and *Early Beverly Hills*, all available from Arcadia Publishing.

Also deserving of special thanks is the *Speedy* camera crew, who took all of the contemporary New York photographs:

Tom Dannenbaum is a graduate of the Brooklyn College film program, and a life-long fan of silent films. Tom has contributed to works on Stanley Kubrick and Francis Coppola, and lives in New York City. Photos: 202 lr; 254 lr.

Beth Goffe is a systems analyst, an ardent student of American, New York City, and film history, and an accomplished bird/nature photographer—www.pbase.com/bgoffe. Photos: 244 lr; 245 lr; 257 all; 263 lr; 265 ur; 266 b; 267 l; 268 lr; 270 all; 271 all; 274 lr; 275 ur.

Hooman Mehran is co-editor of two books about Charlie Chaplin: *The Dictator and the Tramp*, available from the British Film Institute, and *Limelight and the Music Hall Tradition*, available from McFarland. Photos: 217 lr; 236 ur; 237 lr; 238 all; 239 lr; 252 lr; 253 ll; 256 lr; 279 bc; 283 lr; 284 r; 286 lr; 287 ll.

Nick Rumaczyk is a filmmaker and vodcaster, who has a particular fondness for silent comedy. Photos: 234 lr; 241 lr; 242 ll; 243 ur; 248 all; 249 ur; 250 ur; 278 ur; 280 all; 281 ul; 290 ur, ll.

Lastly, special Thanks to the following for sharing their photographs: [Note flickr below=www.flickr.com/photos]

Ray_from_LA:flickr /15132846@N00/: 31 lr; **Ron Reiring**: 42 c, 192 ll; **Patrick Rohe**: 47 lr; **Alan Light**: flickr /alan-light/473855192: 50 lr; **Eli Pousson**: flickr /elipousson/4243558814: 55 lr; **Curt Gibbs** (ExperienceLA): flickr /experiencela/98771917: 66 ll; **Eileen O'Shea**: flickr /osheas/3694884780: 66 lr; **Bruce Perry**, California State University, Department of Geological Sciences: 67 ul, 190 ur; Tony Barraza, 73 ll, 79 ll; **Michael Elson** of Los Angeles Helicopter Tours, 82 ll; **Bryan Norwood**: flickr /movementofexistence/3076045767: 113 lr; **Martin Schall**, 107 ul, 110 ul, 114 ur, lr; **John C. Mills**: 128 ul; **Doug McClintock**, 130; **Alec Ananian**, 134 ul; **Bernard Wee**, 150 lr; **John Morgan**: flickr /aidanmorgan/3324489207: 172 ll; **Joanne Shimada**: flickr /lapie/3075727057: 172 ll; **Chris Eason**: flickr /mister-e/198394941: 177 ll; **Nancy B. Reimann**, 177 lr; **Linden Bengtson**: 180 cr; 181 ur, ll, lr; **Theron LaBounty**: flickr /notanyron/361314245: 190 ll; **Dave & Margie Hill / Kleerup**: flickr /the-consortium/3062160639: 197 bc; **Alexander Konovalenko**: flickr /alexkon/52316532: 197 lr; **Tomas Fano**: flickr /tomasfano/2708640016: 200 lr; 278 lr; **Tim Schapker**: flickr /albany_tim/3468656897: 201 top; **Romina Facchi** 201 lr; **Tamsin Slater**: flickr /offchurch-tam/3984134235: 203 ur; **Josh Hallett**: flickr /hyku/2930739373: 206 lr; **Missy S.**: flickr /listenmissy/2319444375: 231 lr; **Ian Wilson**: flickr /foolstopzanet/483128239: 239 ur; **Alan Strakey**: flickr /smoovey/3524813779: 249 ll; **Peter Radunzel**: flickr /radunzel/3740626035: 249 bc; **Boris Miller**: panoramio.com/photo/18272532; 251 lr; **Lasse Petersen**: flickr /hyp_/4014227522: 274 ur; **Alan Cordova**: flickr /acordova/1456419072: 282 ll; **Paula Soler Moya**: 289 lr; **Julius Yang**: flickr /lordjulius/1543030325: 295 lr; **David Sameth**: 296 all.

Introduction

All Harold Lloyd fans will agree that this is a most remarkable book. The conception and visualization of the stories, and how they came to life as Harold's movies, is laid out in exceptional detail.

In the time that I was with my grandfather he would explain how shots were done, but never in such incredible depth as what John Bengtson has researched and included in this book. Even after all this time, I have a new appreciation as to how these films were made.

Harold used Los Angeles and New York like his own personal playgrounds, and that can truly be understood in this book. Harold's dangerous stunts always put him in peril, but they worked largely in part thanks to his gifted team of writers, cinematographers, set designers, grips, and the rest of the remarkably talented crew. They had none of the technology or experience that modern day filmmakers have, but this book helps show how these pioneers used their ingenuity and creativity to craft Harold's beloved films.

My grandfather would be so pleased and grateful to John for taking the time to share all this with his fans.

SUZANNE LLOYD

Above, Suzanne Lloyd with her grandparents "Mimi" and "Daddy," on the grounds of their Greenacres Estate in Beverly Hills, Suzanne's childhood home. Mildred (née Davis) and Harold appeared together in 15 films, beginning with *From Hand to Mouth* in 1919. They began dating in 1920, and were married a few weeks before their final film *Safety Last!* premiered in 1923. Mildred played a few independent movie roles after marriage, before settling in to motherhood and family life. Together Mildred and Harold raised three children, Gloria, Peggy, and Harold Jr., and years later would raise Suzanne as if their own daughter. Mildred and Harold were married for 46 years, until Mildred's passing in 1969. Harold died in 1971. Today, Suzanne serves as Trustee of The Harold Lloyd Trust, and is a tireless champion of Lloyd's enduring legacy.

Foreword

Harold's disastrous inaugural drive in his new car, from *Hot Water* (1924), filmed at 3rd Street and Broadway in Santa Monica, which is now the site of the Santa Monica Place shopping center.

Much as I admire John Bengtson's books on Keaton and Chaplin, I have been looking forward most eagerly to this one. As I hoped, he has surpassed himself. Admittedly, Harold Lloyd used locations more prodigiously than other comedians, but that doesn't mean one could identify them all, let alone provide such fascinating details. Once again, we needed detective work of a very high order.

In giving us precious Los Angeles history through the prism of Lloyd's comedies, Bengtson does a valuable service for film preservation. The more evidence of the past a film contains, the more likely it is to be preserved. When the proofs of this book arrived, I was about to go to New York, and the book made the trip much more interesting, enabling me to explore some of the *Speedy* locations.

Bengtson has been aided by modern technology, but Google Earth is only helpful when you have an idea where to look. I sometimes think Bengtson must be psychic—does he lay out his photos on a Ouija board? I can appreciate his achievement particularly because in a small way I have practiced his craft. While David Gill and I were making *Harold Lloyd—the Third Genius* in 1989, we had to identify the buildings used in the *Safety Last!* climb in order to film them.

Two experts were immediately helpful; Hollywood historian Marc Wanamaker told us where the first stage of the climb had been filmed, and a friend of Lloyd's, director Rich Correll, drove us down. We discovered the building had gone, to be replaced by a parking lot. The most prominent structure in the background was still standing; however, in 1922, it bore the sign "BLACKSTONE'S California's Finest Store." The sign had been painted over, but the paint was peeling and we could just make out ". . . est store" in the original '20s lettering. As we walked along the street, comparing frame enlargements to the reality, we noticed that although a few buildings had been added and one or two demolished, the majority of old Broadway remained intact. The big department store in the background of the middle section of the climb was now BF Robinson's; in 1922 it was the May Company. By working out where the camera had been placed, we pinpointed the building with the clock to have been 908–910 Broadway, originally occupied by the Western Costume Company. It should have been a historic building of California; instead it was boarded up, awaiting demolition.

The demolition company was unwilling to let us film from the building in case we proved its historic value and they were prevented from wrecking it. But, as always, money talked. We returned with our camera equipment and a hefty tip for the security guard. It was a 12-story hike, since the elevators were out of action. The roof was covered in water. A rusty ladder was fixed to the next level. We clambered up and the first emotion that hit me was triumph. There was no doubt, the view matched the frame blowup almost precisely.

The next emotion was terror. There was no protection at this level. On three sides was a 12-story drop. You had to watch where you walked—one slip could be fatal. My palms sweated and I clung miserably to the tripod, begging David not to keep stepping into thin air to take snapshots of the crew. Nothing could have persuaded me to climb a structure at this height, no matter what protection you offered. And even though I know how it was done, whenever I see the sequence, I break out in a cold sweat.

We had read the details of how they did the climb, but what still surprised us was the fact that the set had been built across the street from the store. When you see the film it seems impossible to believe that when Harold is hanging from the clock, he is not hanging directly above the street, alongside the store. (Special effects like these would never work in 3D.)

Consider what Lloyd and his team were up against. Any alteration of speed, to make his movements more nimble, would become apparent because of the unnatural pace of the traffic and the pedestrians below. Shadows restricted the time it was possible to shoot. It was high summer, baking hot anywhere in Southern California, but insufferable on rooftops. Lloyd had to wear a three-piece suit. And he was doing all his work, clinging to the set, with only one complete hand. His right hand had been shattered by a property bomb three years before.

We managed to find one person who was present on that rooftop during filming, Alf Goulding Jr., the son of a Hal Roach director.

"It was physically very strenuous," said Goulding. "He hung on to the hands of the clock, I can never forget that, for long periods of time. And you'd hear them say 'Cut' and there was no relief. Harold would still hang there—he put his toes in the bricks, to relieve the total pressure."

From this, one can deduce that Lloyd's injured hand was wired to the hand of the clock. For the scene in which he grabbed the rope, he had to hang with all his weight on his incomplete hand and how he did that I cannot imagine.

Goulding recalled that when they were ready for another take, the crew would get behind the set and move the hand of the clock up—pulling Harold up, too. "And that went on for a long time."

How gratifying to find that nearly 90 years after Lloyd filmed from it, that building is still standing! I would love to think it was our film which made someone realize its historical importance, but in the harsh world of California real estate, there is bound to be a more prosaic explanation.

There were people who felt, then as now, that once the climbing technique was revealed, it would ruin the illusion. Not too many members of the public got the hang of it. But for those who did, quite the opposite happened. They admired the breathtaking brilliance with which it was achieved, and it made the scene all the more astonishing.

While Lloyd had to do many of his stunts himself, no one would have risked his doing anything too dangerous since the entire picture rested upon him. Stunt doubles were the answer.

Stunt man Harvey Parry told us that he did the climb on *Safety Last!*. He did work for Harold Lloyd, but actually, his climb was on *Feet First*. It is not impossible that he did a day's or so work on the earlier film. But it now seems certain that a human fly named Bill Strother, who co-stars as Limpy Bill, did all the long shots. (It would be helpful if television documentaries could have footnotes!)

On top of all the hard work involved in tracking down the locations, and the events that happened there, Bengtson reveals an uncanny knowledge of silent comedies. He acknowledges the experts who have contributed to this knowledge, but he is nonetheless a phenomenon. I have been studying this period twice as long as it lasted, and I could never have told you that when Chaplin sticks his head out of a tall building in *The New Janitor* (1914), he is on the periphery of a future Lloyd location. And who would have guessed that another Lloyd location would have featured battling robots from *Transformers* (2007)?

I guarantee you will end this book with an increased admiration for Harold Lloyd, for his amazing co-workers . . . and for John Bengtson.

KEVIN BROWNLOW

Following his first screen persona Willie Work, Lloyd's second characterization was Lonesome Luke, deliberately patterned after Charlie Chaplin, only in opposite form. For example, whereas Charlie's clothes were baggy, Luke's clothes were tight, and so forth. The story goes Lloyd overheard an audience member say, "Oh, there's the fellow that makes like Chaplin," convincing Lloyd he had to create a character uniquely his own, leading to the development of Lloyd's "Glass Character" persona. The scene to the left, from *Luke's Movie Muddle* (1916), was filmed at the Hollywood Theater (spelled out on the tile floor), at 6764 Hollywood Boulevard. The theater appears to the far left, above, where it is playing the movie *Detective Craig's Coup* (1914). The surviving theater building is now home to the Guinness World Records Museum (far left).

Author's Note

Harold Lloyd reigned as the box office comedy king throughout the 1920s. More prolific than Charlie Chaplin and more popular than Buster Keaton, Lloyd sold more tickets during the Golden Age of Comedy than any other comedian. As befitting the energetic and hard-working characters he portrayed, Lloyd produced a torrent of first-rate comedies that audiences eagerly lined up to see. Lloyd learned early on that quality productions were the key to success, and he employed the best writers, directors, and technicians in the business. Lloyd also pre-viewed his films extensively, trimming scenes here, adding jokes there, until satisfied they were ready for general release. The results speak for themselves. I attended a ten-week Lloyd festival as a young adult, and cannot recall another experience where I heard such joyful and sustained laughter.

Lloyd's idea to create a screen persona who wore glasses was a stroke of genius. The glasses immediately drew attention to Harold, setting him apart without distancing him from the audience. Lloyd's "Glass Character" rejected the oversized slapshoes and outlandish makeup of his contemporaries, and eschewed physical affectations such as Chaplin's bowlegged shuffle and Keaton's frozen face. Lloyd's persona was not an outcast or a sphinx-like stoic, but someone far more natural and, dare we say, normal. Audiences might empathize with the Little Tramp's sorrows, or marvel at the Great Stone Face's unflappability, but Harold Lloyd played someone we actually wanted to be: fun, daring, and resourceful.

Hollywood was woefully shortsighted when it came to preserving its heritage. The studios saw little value in silent films following their initial theatrical runs; the highly flammable nitrate film stock used was difficult to preserve, and obsolete film was often destroyed simply to retrieve its negligible silver content. Even stars who could afford to preserve their legacy were vulnerable. Lloyd lost nearly all of his early Willie Work and Lonesome Luke productions (filmed prior to creating his Glass Character) during vault fires in 1938 and 1943. Thus, much of Lloyd's early development as a comedian and filmmaker can no longer be appraised.

Ironically, while the great majority of silent movies have been lost forever, today there are more silent films publicly available, through digital media, than ever before. For this we owe a tremendous debt of gratitude to the dedicated archivists, historians, and preservationists who worked so hard to rescue the history of silent film from complete oblivion. By preserving the history *of* silent film long enough for digital media to catch up, the history *in* silent movies can finally be studied and told. Hidden in plain sight for decades, the landscapes preserved in the background of these marvelous films can tell us much about our common heritage; we simply needed the ability to pause the films long enough to look.

Lloyd's enthusiastic, go-getting persona, with his dapper clothes and straw boater hat, was unapologetically a man of his times. As such, who is better suited than Lloyd to guide us through the Roaring Twenties as captured on film? Lloyd's elaborate chase sequences provide some of the best photographic documentation of silent-era Los Angeles and New York ever recorded. His antics on New High Street, once part of the early Los Angeles Civic Center, may be the only surviving film record of that now lost street. Lloyd's so-called "thrill" pictures capitalized on the decade-long building boom, incorporating high-rise construction sites into the plots while capturing Los Angeles' constantly evolving skyline in the process. Los Angeles' burgeoning growth is particularly evident when comparing Lloyd's final two thrill pictures, *Safety Last!* and *Feet First*. During the eight-year span between filming, six new skyscrapers appeared, including the Spanish Gothic United Artists Theater Building—once the tallest commercial building in town—and the Zigzag Moderne masterpiece, the Eastern Columbia Building.

Lloyd's movies also capture priceless glimpses of everyday life—from shopping and riding the trolleys and subways, to attending ball games and long-vanished amusement parks. Like pixels on a screen, these individual images converge into a broad and detailed composite view of Los Angeles and New York during the 1920s. Preserved for posterity, Harold Lloyd's remarkable body of work leaves behind an incomparable legacy of laughter, and silent visions of the life and times in which he made his classic films.

JOHN BENGTSON
John@SilentEchoes.net
http://SilentLocations.WordPress.com

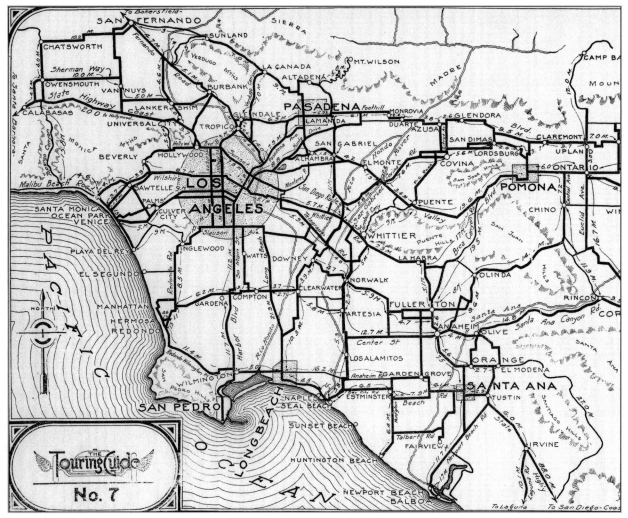

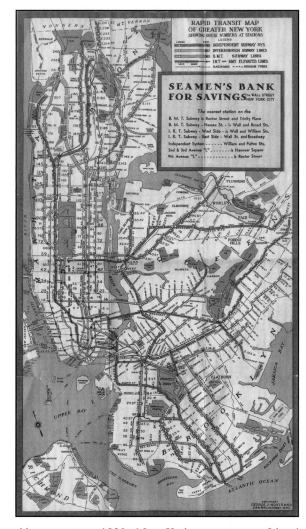

Above, Southern California in 1920. Aside from filming *Speedy* (1927) on location in New York, and filming football scenes from *The Freshman* (1925) in Berkeley, California, Lloyd stayed close to home for his shoots. Lloyd filmed on Santa Catalina Island and at Santa Susanna (both not pictured), Chatsworth, San Fernando, Altadena, Ontario, Malibu, Santa Monica, Ocean Park, Venice, Manhattan Beach, Palms, Culver City, Westwood Village, Beverly Hills, Hollywood, the Lasky Ranch near Universal City, Tropico (Glendale), Pasadena, Chinatown, Downtown Los Angeles, and Long Beach.

Above, a circa 1930s New York transit map. Lloyd filmed scenes for *Speedy* at Yankee Stadium in the Bronx, at Coney Island and near the Brooklyn side of the Brooklyn and Williamsburg Bridges, and throughout Manhattan; including the Hebrew Orphan Asylum, Amsterdam Avenue, 5th Avenue from 16th Street up to 57th Street, Sutton Place, Times Square/Herald Square, Pennsylvania Station, Washington Square, Union Square, Fulton Street, the Coenties Slip, and Battery Park.

The Rolin Studio

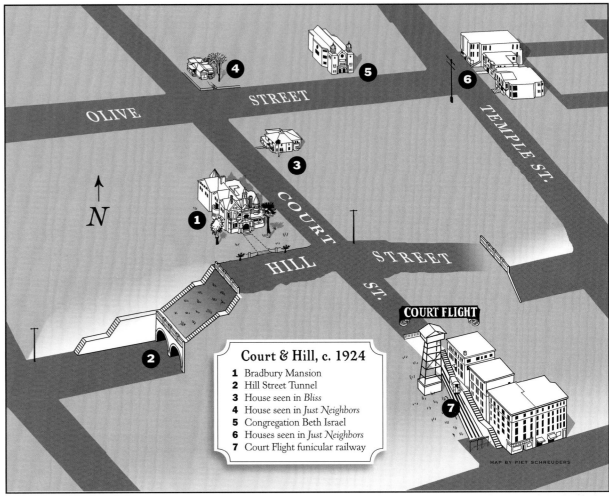

Court & Hill, c. 1924

1 Bradbury Mansion
2 Hill Street Tunnel
3 House seen in *Bliss*
4 House seen in *Just Neighbors*
5 Congregation Beth Israel
6 Houses seen in *Just Neighbors*
7 Court Flight funicular railway

MAP BY PIET SCHREUDERS

The Bradbury Mansion (1) atop Court Hill was one of the finest homes in all of Los Angeles. It was completed in 1887, but fell into decline as the city's elite began moving to the outlying suburbs. The mansion was first leased for film production in May 1913 to a studio run by J. A. Crosby. A year later, nascent producer Hal Roach formed the Rolin Film Company with partner Daniel Linthicum (RO from Roach and LIN from Linthicum), incorporating in July 1914, and taking space in the mansion later that year. Roach hired his friend Harold Lloyd (the two had met in 1913, working as extras at Universal) to appear in the Rolin Studio's earliest comedies. The first Rolin-Lloyd comedy sold for theatrical distribution was the April 19, 1915, release *Just Nuts*, filmed on Court Street and on the mansion grounds. Charlie Chaplin's Essanay Studio comedy *Work*, also filmed at the mansion, was released in June that same year. At first Rolin struggled to survive, but after fits and starts, and interim stays at other facilities, the company and Lloyd returned to the Bradbury Mansion in 1917, and would stay there until 1920, when Roach built new facilities in Culver City named the Hal E. Roach Studios. The mansion was situated above the Hill Street Tunnel (2), an important filming location discussed in later chapters.

Overleaf: A circa 1899 view of the Bradbury Mansion atop Court Hill.

Lloyd described the Bradbury Mansion's large, drafty rooms as "pneumonia hall." Before it was demolished in 1929, the mansion was used for apartments and artist's lofts. It also contained a restaurant frequented by the Superior Court judges who would take the Court Flight Railway (7) up for lunch from the courthouse below. Built in 1905, the city's second funicular railway bypassed the 140-step staircase from Broadway to Hill Street. Half as long, and considerably steeper than Angels Flight (discussed later), Court Flight was said to be the world's shortest railway. An observation tower stood at the top of the hill, offering some of the finest views in town. Sam Vandergrift ran the railway single-handedly for nearly 28 years. After his death, his widow Annie struggled with it for several more years, until she received permission to abandon the franchise in 1943. Flames destroyed the line a few months later.

Lloyd was quite superstitious. For example, he would insist upon always exiting a building from the same doorway as he had entered. When the Rolin Film Company (renamed Hal Roach Studios) moved to Culver City in 1920, during the production of *An Eastern Westerner*, Lloyd continued to drive to the Bradbury Mansion, where the production had started, to apply his make-up before filming, and did not use the Culver City make-up facilities until after the movie was completed.

To the left, the Rolin "PhunPhilm" Company in 1915, providing a glimpse of the Bradbury Mansion interior. Bebe Daniels is seated in the center on the floor, behind her is Harold Lloyd—dressed as Lonesome Luke—to the right of Harold, his early partner, the mustachioed Snub Pollard; to Snub's right, Earl Mohan; and above Harold, the boss-man Hal Roach. Everyone in the photo is formally dressed, or in costume, except for Roach, appearing without a tie, in his shirtsleeves.

This panoramic scene from Charlie Chaplin's *Work* (1915) (*above*) was filmed by the Bradbury Mansion front steps, as was this scene from Lloyd's 1915 comedy *Just Nuts*.

The house at 425 Court Street (3), behind the Bradbury Mansion (*left, box and arrow*), appears to the right.

Bebe Daniels flirts with Harold near 425 Court Street (3) in *Bliss* (1917).

At left, Harold is by the mansion's front walk in *Count Your Change* (1919). Below, Harold and some original Rolin actors beside the mansion side porch on 406 Court Street.

Snub Pollard races toward 425 Court Street in *Are Crooks Dishonest?* (1918).

Vivacious Virginia "Bebe" Daniels (*above*) played opposite Harold for four years, appearing in 144 films. She started in 1915, when she was but 14, and Harold was 22. "Boy" and "Girl," as they called each other, soon fell in love, and they became known off-screen for winning numerous dance contests. In 1919, Bebe was offered a lucrative contract to play dramatic roles for Cecil B. DeMille. Harold did not ask her to stay, and their relationship ended, perhaps to each person's secret regret. Bebe went on to become a major star in her own right.

A reverse angle view of Harold in *Just Nuts* (1915), standing on Court Street. 425 Court Hill is off screen to the left, the Bradbury is off screen to the right.

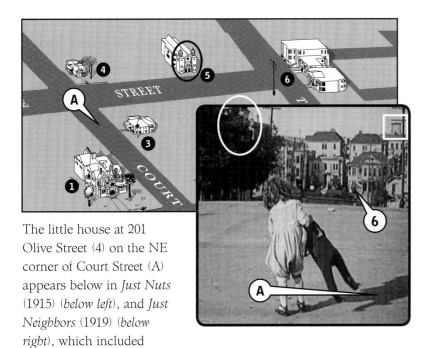

To the left, this view looks up Olive Street, towards the Beth Israel Congregation (5) (*oval*), beyond houses along Temple Street (6), to the clock tower of the original Los Angeles High School in the far distance (not pictured on map). Built in 1873, the school first stood at Temple and Broadway, and was relocated to Fort Moore Hill in 1886, where it survived until 1950, when it was razed to make way for the Hollywood (101) Freeway.

The little house at 201 Olive Street (4) on the NE corner of Court Street (A) appears below in *Just Nuts* (1915) (*below left*), and *Just Neighbors* (1919) (*below right*), which included cringe-inducing scenes of a little girl sitting in the middle of busy traffic.

Above, the Beth Israel Congregation (5) and Los Angeles High School.

In 1955, the Hill Street Tunnel was demolished, and much of Court Hill was excavated. If you were to stand on Hill Street today, the Bradbury Mansion site (1) would be several stories above your head! The former corner of Court and Olive (A) now sits in the middle of the Civic Center Mall (1966) (*right*). The mall rests above a large underground parking lot, and is bordered by the Los Angeles County Superior Court on First Street, to the left, and the Kenneth Hahn Hall of Administration on Temple Street, to the right. Today, the downtown Los Angeles Civic Center boasts the largest concentration of local, state, and federal government buildings of any city outside of Washington, D.C.

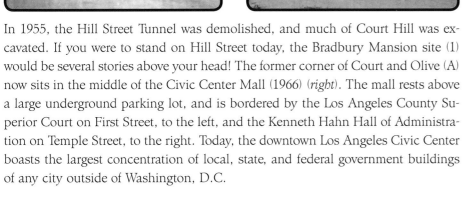

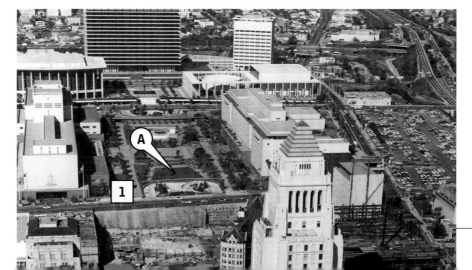

Bumping Into Broadway

(1919)

The Trinity appears in two other Lloyd films. In *His Royal Slyness* (1920), (B) below, Harold's brother Gaylord (intentionally made up to resemble Harold) appears before the building, while in *High and Dizzy* (1920), (C) below, inebriated Harold and Roy Brooks try to sneak past a cop. The former Pickwick Apartments stood next door. In real life, Lloyd was a teetotaler.

Bumping Into Broadway was the first two-reel comedy featuring Lloyd's "Glass Character." Under his contract with Hal Roach, Lloyd was now receiving half of the profits from his films. At the lower left, Lloyd ponders his next step standing across the street from the extant Trinity Auditorium at 851 S. Grand Avenue. The box in the modern view below matches the Lloyd frame to the left. Charlie Chaplin strolled past this building (*upper left*) in his 1915 Essanay short *The Bank* (A). Completed in 1914, the Trinity housed a three-tier 2,500 seat auditorium, as well as the Trinity Church, and a 330 room men's dormitory. The building has been vacant for years, but may some day be converted into a hotel or apartments. More settings from this film appear in the *Visions of Bunker Hill* chapter.

Harold keeps a watchful eye over Bebe, who has been asked out by an unsavory man. This scene was filmed on Weller Street, an unusual diagonal street running from 2nd and San Pedro Streets, to 1st and Los Angeles Streets. Weller Street pointed directly toward the Los Angeles County Court House (*ovals*) on Pound Cake Hill. The court house is discussed further in the chapter about Lloyd's 1919 comedy *Ask Father*. Although none of the Weller Street buildings survive, a row of similar vintage buildings stands close by on E. 1st Street, across from the Miyako Hotel and the Japanese Village Plaza Mall.

Both views below look north up Weller Street. When City Hall opened in 1928, becoming the tallest building in town, it completely blocked the view of the court house from Weller Street (*below right*).

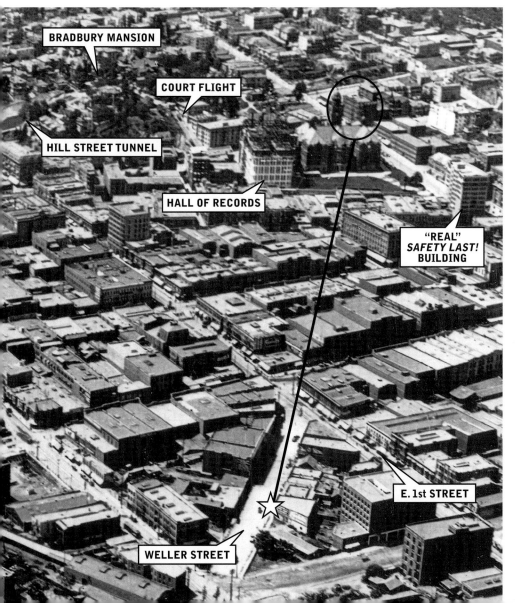

BRADBURY MANSION

COURT FLIGHT

HILL STREET TUNNEL

HALL OF RECORDS

"REAL" SAFETY LAST! BUILDING

E. 1st STREET

WELLER STREET

Today, Weller Street is a pedestrian walkway in the heart of Japantown. It is named Astronaut E.S. Onizuka Street, and is informally called Weller Court. Ellison Onizuka was the first Asian American to reach space, and was later among the crew who perished in the 1986 *Challenger* Space Shuttle disaster.

From Hand to Mouth

(1919)

Presaging themes from Charlie Chaplin's *The Kid* (1921), downtrodden Harold befriends a hungry young waif played by Peggy Cartwright, who would later appear in the earliest Our Gang comedies. After Harold and Peggy innocently attempt to pay for food with counterfeit money, a wealthy heiress (played by Harold's future wife, Mildred Davis, in her first Lloyd film appearance) intervenes on their behalf. Harold returns the favor by later rescuing Mildred from kidnappers, and delivering her to her lawyer's office in the nick of time to claim an inheritance.

Many exterior scenes (1–8, *below*) were filmed along sections of New High Street, an irregular five block street that once ran from Court Street to Alpine Street, and roughly parallel to Spring and Main Streets. The southernmost block of New High (not pictured) was demolished in 1927, as part of the new City Hall construction, and the next block was lost to the U.S. Court House and Post Office Building completed in 1936, and then the freeway. The third block (3-5) disappeared when the streets surrounding the Plaza de Los Angeles were reconfigured. Only two blocks (1-3) remain, from Cesar Chavez Avenue (Sunset) to Alpine Street.

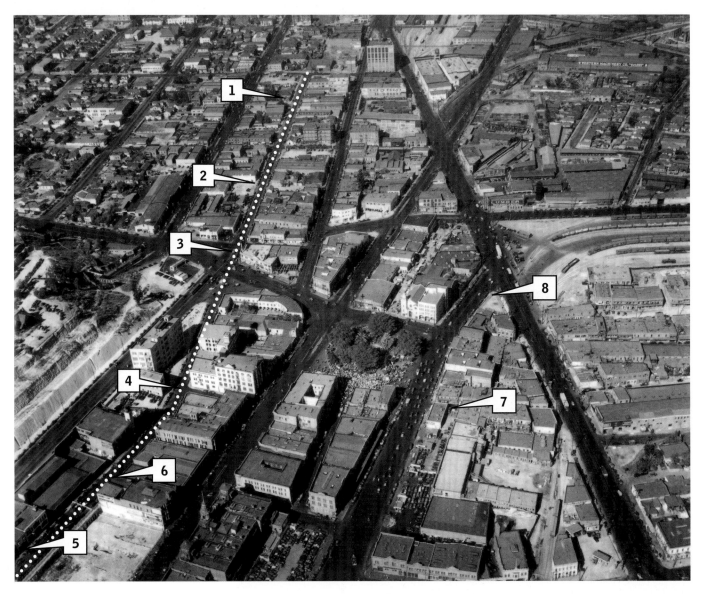

Above, Harold is chased towards the "T" intersection at Alpine Street. The arrow (1) on the aerial view to the right marks his position.

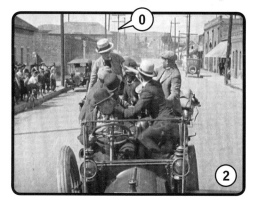

Above, Harold lands in the thugs' car, near the arrow to the right. The building on the corner of Ord Street, (0) above, still stands. A modern view up New High Street appears below.

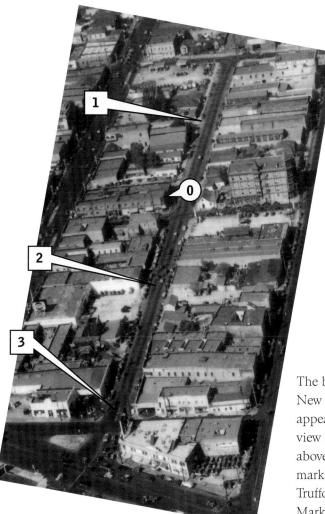

The Truffo Market appears below in the Douglas Fairbanks film *The Mystery of the Leaping Fish* (1916).

Below, Harold runs south down New High towards the thugs' car (3).

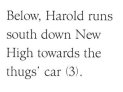

The building Harold passes at 618 New High still stands (*box, above and below*).

The building at 618 New High (*box, right*) appears in this aerial view below. The star above and below marks the former Truffo & Truffo Market.

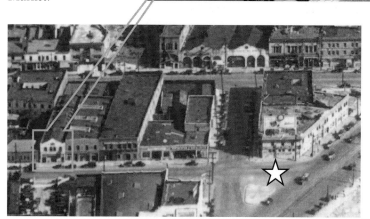

Scenes (4) were filmed at the corner (*star, left*) of New High Street and Republic, a very short block that connected New High to Main Street. To the left is a view down Republic towards the extant Pico House Hotel (*box*) standing on the Plaza de Los Angeles at Main Street. The house was built in 1869 by Don Pio Pico, the last Mexican governor of Alta California before the land was surrendered to the United States in 1847. The Pico House was the city's first three-story masonry building, and the first hotel to offer bathtubs with running water. The Banning stagecoaches running from the port at Wilmington would stop at the Pico House, and the first street car line in Los Angeles also had its terminus at the hotel, running south down Main Street.

This 2005 view above matches the movie frame to the right from the opening of Charlie Chaplin's *A Dog's Life* (1918). The view below was taken some time after Union Station was completed in 1939, as the station clock tower appears in the back, center. The gas tank to the back, left (*below*) appears in *For Heaven's Sake*.

The corner of Republic and New High (*star above and below*) is subsumed into a parking lot and no longer exists (circa 2005). The three-story building nearest the star is now also demolished.

The tall building in this 2005 photo (*right*) is the Brunswig Drug Co. Building, built in 1888. It has since been restored to its original grandeur, and will be part of the LA Plaza de Cultura y Artes.

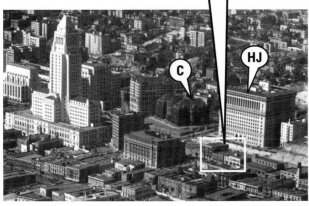

Scenes (5) and (6) were filmed on the block of New High that was lost in 1936 to the U.S. Court House. At left, Harold rushes to thank Mildred for getting him out of trouble. Behind Harold is the office of tobacco wholesaler Philip Herbold, at 337-339 New High Street. The 1906 Sanborn Fire Insurance Maps identify the upper floor "ROOMS," pictured here (see sign above Harold's head), as "FB" (Female Boarding), the map company's euphemism for bordello.

The tracking shot below, scene (6), shows Harold walking south down New High, directly across the street from scene (5). The addresses 350 and 348-346 New High, below, are also designated "FB" on the 1906 maps, as is 327-329 (FB) on the upper-left photo. All of these establishments were but a block north of the County Court House (C) (*left*), and just around the corner from the former county jail—replaced by the 1925 Hall of Justice (HJ)—to the left. We can see the 344 address on the doorway (*oval, right*). The detail view to the lower left comes from the circa 1924 aerial view to the lower right, also showing the County Court House (C) and Hall of Justice (HJ), as well as the International Bank Building (SL), that Bill Strother climbed for the Harold's classic feature *Safety Last!*

New High Street	350	352	348–346	344

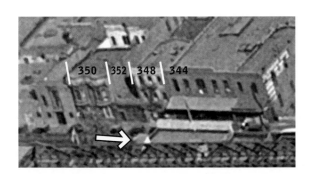

350 352 348 344

350 352 348 344

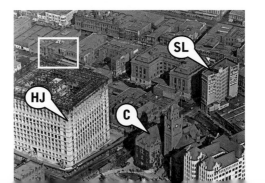

Harold's hiding spot behind a parked car (*near right and circle, below*) is revealed when the car pulls away. A street sign for Ferguson Alley (*oval*) appears at back. Ferguson Alley stood at the SE corner of the Plaza

de Los Angeles, running from Los Angeles Street to Alameda Street (A), perpendicular to Calle de Los Negros (Negro Alley). The center view above is from the Dorothy Gish drama *Gretchen the Greenhorn* (1916). It looks west towards the Cosmopolitan Saloon (C) (*box, above*), the former, and now-restored, Plaza Firehouse (1884), the town's original fire station, on Los Angeles Street. The upper-right view from *The Mystery of the Leaping Fish* looks east down the alley towards Alameda (A) as Douglas Fairbanks steers his checker-board patterned car. The extant Pio Pico House (P) and the Brunswig Building (B) appear below. Scene (8), discussed on the next page, takes place at the narrow intersection of Alameda and Los Angeles Streets, marked at the far left, below.

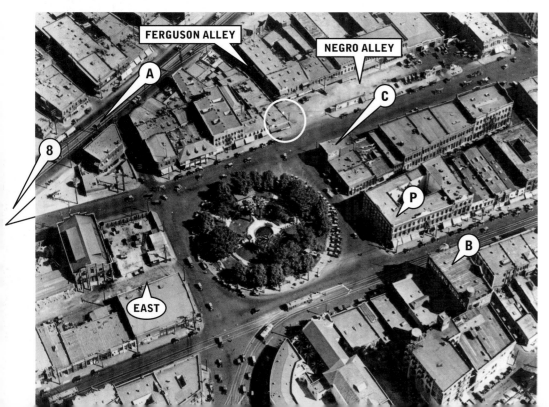

The middle view to the right looks north up Los Angeles Street, towards the Ferguson Alley sign (*oval*), the same sign (*oval*) in the three movie frames at top. Despite protests, all of the buildings between Los Angeles Street and Alameda were demolished, at first to provide a nice view of Union Station from the Plaza, and then to provide a cloverleaf entrance on to the Hollywood (101) Freeway, pictured above.

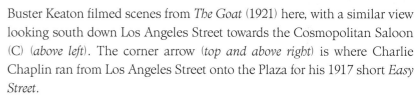

The circa 1920 view above looks south down Los Angeles Street, with Alameda Street intersecting from the left, towards the Plaza de Los Angeles (where the trees are) and the Cosmopolitan Saloon (C) (*above and below*). Harold filmed scene (8) at this unique corner (*left*), as did Larry Semon in *Frauds and Frenzies* (1928) (*below left*), and Hank Mann in *The Janitor* (1919) (*below right*).

Buster Keaton filmed scenes from *The Goat* (1921) here, with a similar view looking south down Los Angeles Street towards the Cosmopolitan Saloon (C) (*above left*). The corner arrow (*top and above right*) is where Charlie Chaplin ran from Los Angeles Street onto the Plaza for his 1917 short *Easy Street*.

The 1884 Fire House No. 1 facing the plaza closed in 1897, and became a saloon (C). The saloon's upper floor was also labeled "FB" on the 1906 Sanford maps. The building was restored in 1960, and is now a firefighting museum (*far right*).

Harold Lloyd filmed a few, and possibly several more, of his early Lonesome Luke comedies at or near the Plaza de Los Angeles. We'll never know, as only about a dozen of his 67 early Luke comedies are known to survive. Scene (A) above from *Luke's Shattered Sleep* (1916) was filmed in front of the HIA LUNG general store at 429 N. Los Angeles Street (A) below. The 1906 Sanborn map reports that the 425 address two doors down (O) was an opium den. Scene (B) from *Lonesome Luke on Tin Can Alley* (1917) was filmed looking south down Negro Alley by the utility pole (B) below. Scene (C) from *Young Mr. Jazz* (1919) was filmed looking north up Negro Alley by the utility pole (C) below, which stood before the Rescue Mission Inn. Negro Alley was the most notorious part of town, overrun with saloons, sporting houses, and opium dens. It was also the site of a terrible tragedy: the Chinese Massacre of 1871, when the accidental shooting death of a white policeman prompted an angry mob to murder 19 Chinese men and boys, most by hanging.

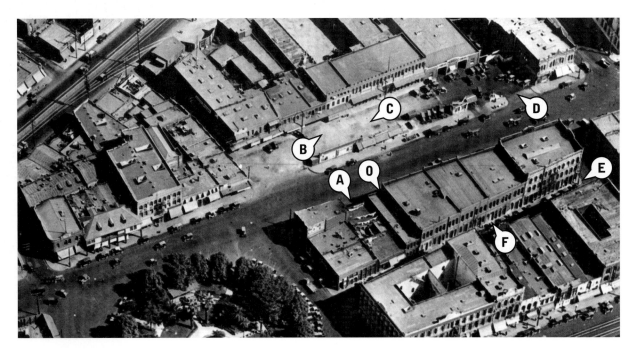

The area around the Plaza de Los Angeles was a popular place to film. Buster Keaton knocks out a cop with his boxing-glove-turn-indicator from *Cops* (1922) at the intersection of Los Angeles and Arcadia (D), and is led by a cop from Arcadia onto Sanchez Alley, past the corner of the Ville de Paris Hotel (E) in *Neighbors* (1920). Meanwhile, Charlie Chaplin picks the pocket of the thief robbing him in the middle of Sanchez Alley (F) during *Police* (1916).

Haunted Spooks

(1920)

Harold outraces one rival to ask a millionaire for his daughter's hand in marriage, only to lose her to another suitor. Heartbroken, Harold decides to end his life. After several failed suicide attempts, Harold meets Mildred and her lawyer, who explains she will inherit a Southern estate if she can find a husband to live with her there for a year. Instantly smitten, Harold agrees to the plan. The couple arrives on a dark and stormy night, not knowing Mildred's scheming uncle has secretly "haunted" the place, hoping to scare the couple away in order to claim the estate for himself.

A

Lloyd filmed at the extant Milbank Mansion tennis court and gardens, located at 3344 Country Club Drive, where he returned to film scenes for *Dr. Jack* (A).

Midway through production, Lloyd was severely injured in a life-threatening accident that nearly ended his sky-rocketing career. On Sunday, August 24, 1919, Harold posed for a gag publicity photo of him lighting a cigarette with the sputtering fuse of a fake bomb. Somehow the prop bomb brought from the Rolin Studio had a real charge, discharging moments after Harold lowered the bomb away from his face. The explosion ripped a hole in the 16-foot high ceiling of the photo studio, and put Harold in the hospital for over two weeks. The accident temporarily blinded Lloyd, who lost half of his palm, and the thumb and index finger of his right hand. For a time it was uncertain whether he would ever appear in films again. When production of the movie resumed in January 1920, Lloyd compensated for his injury by wearing a tightly fitted glove over a prosthetic thumb and finger. He also cleverly staged scenes to favor his left hand, filmed mirror reflections of his left hand as his "right," and used hand doubles for certain close-ups. Although the accident was news at the time, Lloyd worked hard thereafter to preserve the illusion that he was not injured. Undeterred by this setback, Lloyd never took for granted the good fortune that had spared his life.

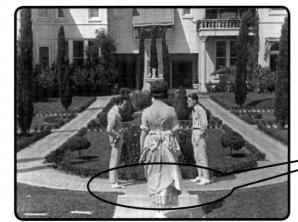

TENNIS COURT

Fail! The deceptively shallow water thwarts Harold's suicide attempt at Lincoln Park, located at N. Mission Road and Valley Boulevard, a few miles northeast of downtown.

Harold's attempt from the much higher, arched bridge at Hollenbeck Park fails (*below center*) when he lands in a passing canoe. The park and bridge (*below right*) are discussed in further detail in the *Girl Shy* chapter. The lower left frame, filmed before Harold's accident, clearly shows Lloyd's intact right hand resting on the bridge railing (*below left*). Charlie Chaplin filmed scenes from his Keystone film *His Trysting Place* (1914) (*right*) at the park, before the original low-arched bridge that stood at the narrow part of the lake was replaced by a bigger bridge, seen here.

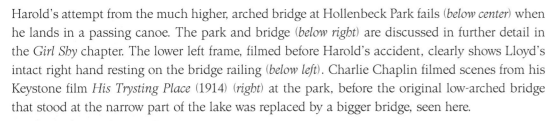

Although Lloyd had the most haunted-looking, real-life mansion in all of Los Angeles to work with, the studio dressed up the front of the Bradbury Mansion to look like a Southern mansion instead (*above*). The most likely explanation for the story being set in the South, especially considering the racially insensitive double meaning of the title, was, unfortunately, in order to portray an entire house-staff of scared black servants for comic effect.

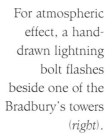

Harold and Mildred arrive beside the Bradbury Mansion retaining wall (*left*). The extremely ornate woodworking and trim appearing in the interior scenes (*below*), suggest that they were filmed within a real mansion, most likely the Bradbury Mansion itself. Close inspection of the mansion scenes shows that Harold is now clearly wearing his prosthesis.

For atmospheric effect, a hand-drawn lightning bolt flashes beside one of the Bradbury's towers (*right*).

Visions of Bunker Hill

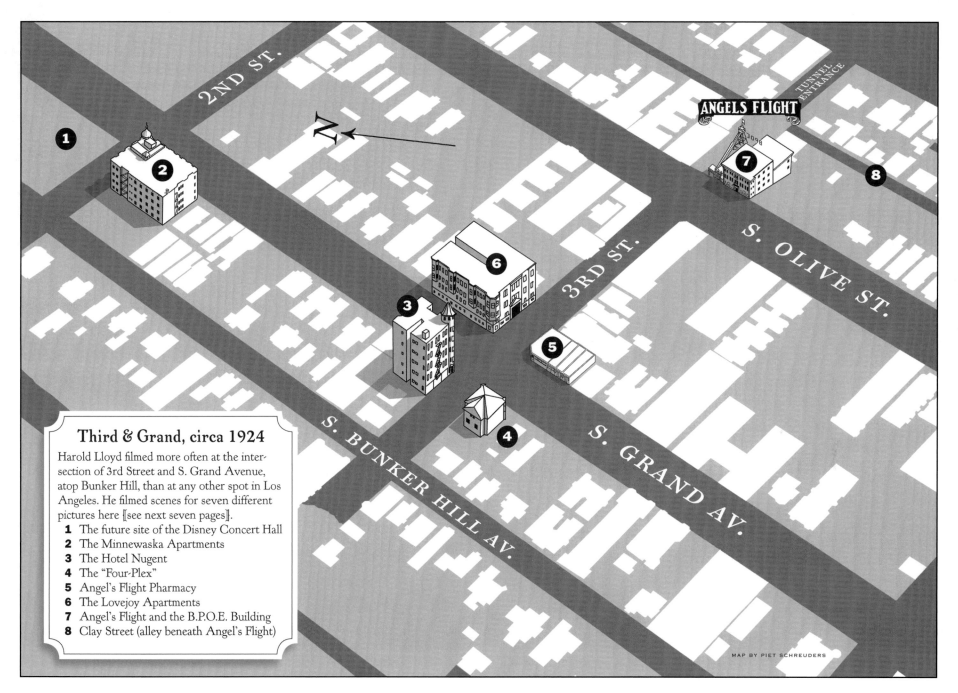

Third & Grand, circa 1924

Harold Lloyd filmed more often at the intersection of 3rd Street and S. Grand Avenue, atop Bunker Hill, than at any other spot in Los Angeles. He filmed scenes for seven different pictures here [see next seven pages].

1 The future site of the Disney Concert Hall
2 The Minnewaska Apartments
3 The Hotel Nugent
4 The "Four-Plex"
5 Angel's Flight Pharmacy
6 The Lovejoy Apartments
7 Angel's Flight and the B.P.O.E. Building
8 Clay Street (alley beneath Angel's Flight)

MAP BY PIET SCHREUDERS

Overleaf: The intersection of Third and Grand (*circle*) on Bunker Hill, as City Hall (1928) nears completion. Lloyd filmed scenes for *Bumping Into Broadway* (1919), *An Eastern Westerner* (1920), *High and Dizzy* (1920), *Never Weaken* (1921), *Girl Shy* (1924), *Hot Water* (1924), and *For Heaven's Sake* (1926) at this location.

Looking up 3rd towards Grand today.

During *Bumping Into Broadway* (*above*), Harold hitches a ride in a trash cart while grabbing the back of a car (*above*), arriving in front of the Lovejoy Apartments (off camera) to the right (6). This view looks up 3rd Street towards the Four-Plex (4) that is obscured from view by the car.

In *High and Dizzy* (*above*), Harold and Roy Brooks stagger by the corner of the Lovejoy Apartments (6) at 3rd and Grand, with the Hotel Nugent (3) behind them.

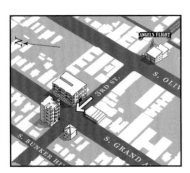

This composite view looking NW up 3rd Street towards Grand, depicts, from left to right, the Angels Flight Pharmacy (5), the Four-Plex (4), the Hotel Nugent (3), and the Lovejoy Apartments (6).

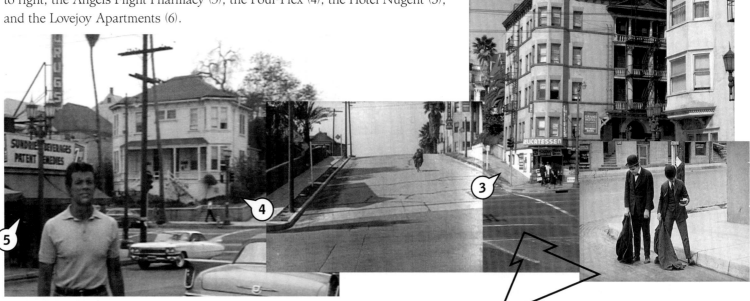

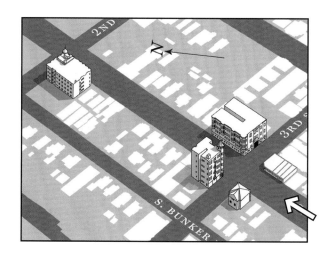

The three scenes on this page all look NE up 3rd Street towards the intersection at Grand. During different scenes from *Girl Shy*, filmed from the same vantage point, Harold first races down 3rd Street, and then back up along the same stretch of 3rd Street as he commandeers a horse wagon (*above center*), sending the angry owner to the ground (*far right*). At the site of the Hotel Nugent (3) now stands the Grand Promenade apartment towers (*above right*). Further up 3rd Street stands the ultramodern Disney Concert Hall (1), also pictured at the lower right.

This brief scene from *An Eastern Westerner* (*below*) looks up 3rd Street, past the Angels Flight Pharmacy (5) and the Lovejoy Apartments (6), way back to the onion dome of the Winnewaska Apartments (2).

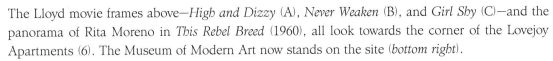

The Lloyd movie frames above—*High and Dizzy* (A), *Never Weaken* (B), and *Girl Shy* (C)—and the panorama of Rita Moreno in *This Rebel Breed* (1960), all look towards the corner of the Lovejoy Apartments (6). The Museum of Modern Art now stands on the site (*bottom right*).

A prominent Bunker Hill landmark, the corner onion dome of the Winnewaska Apartments (2), appears to the lower left, and in the Hal Roach–Sunshine Sammy comedy *Non-Skid Kid* (1922) (2A) (*below*).

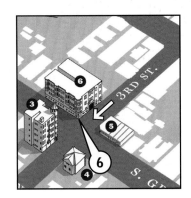

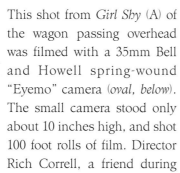

This shot from *Girl Shy* (A) of the wagon passing overhead was filmed with a 35mm Bell and Howell spring-wound "Eyemo" camera (*oval, below*). The small camera stood only about 10 inches high, and shot 100 foot rolls of film. Director Rich Correll, a friend during Lloyd's senior years, reports that this camera still works fine, and remains part of the Lloyd Estate. The circle above and to the right marks the Angels Flight observation tower.

Lloyd staged thrilling scenes for *Girl Shy* (B) and *For Heaven's Sake* (C) by careening NW down 3rd Street in a horse wagon and a runaway bus, respectively. The Angels Flight observation tower appears at the end of the street during both scenes. The prominent dome of the extant Million Dollar Theater building at 3rd and Broadway (*arrow, left*) also appears beyond the crest of the hill. Running above the Third Street Tunnel, this upper section of 3rd Street was a convenient place to stage city stunts. The street was less than two blocks long and had very little through traffic, so it could be shut down easily. The rooftop "B.P.O.E No. 99" sign refers to the Benevolent and Protective Order of Elks, whose Lodge 99 stood on Olive Street adjacent to the top of Angels Flight.

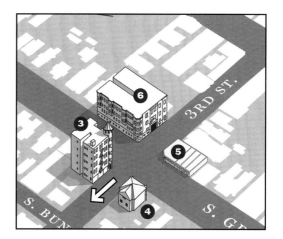

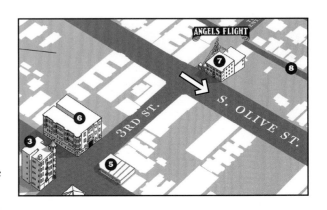

In *Hot Water*, Harold pushes his car away from a traffic jam in Santa Monica, to arrive next at the top of Bunker Hill above the Third Street Tunnel (*below*).

Harold stands at 3rd Street, beside the summit entrance to Angels Flight (7), as his family races down Olive Street. The shadow of the Angels Flight observation tower (*oval, bottom right*) appears in the foreground. For *Hot Water*, Lloyd also filmed a pickup shot of the cop directing the "Santa Monica" traffic jam in front of the Angels Flight Pharmacy (5), as discussed later. The arrow above and below marks the path of the car down Olive Street.

Col. J.W. Eddy built the Angels Flight funicular railway in 1901, adjacent to the Third Street Tunnel, running 315 feet up a 33 percent up-hill grade from Hill Street to Olive Street. Originally painted white, it was later painted its now iconic orange and black colors beginning in the 1930s. The two counter-balanced cars are named Olivet and Sinai, after mountains from the Bible. The railway adopted its name after a base arch entryway reading "Angels Flight" was installed in 1908. In June 1909, the letters "B.P.O.E." were added to the base archway to guide Elks attending a national convention to the Elks lodge atop the hill.

The railway operated continuously until 1969, when it was put in storage during the civic redevelopment that completely transformed Bunker Hill. The railway was reinstalled half a block SW from its original site in 1996, but following a fatal accident in 2001, was shut down for nine years until re-opening in 2010.

At left, the summit entrance at its new and former locations.

Corresponding views (*left and right*) looking SW down Olive Street from 3rd towards 4th. A modern park extends over Olive mid-way, and is the new site for the summit entrance of Angels Flight, relocated a half-block from the corner of 3rd, where it originally stood.

The car races SW down Olive Street from 3rd, past The Ems, towards the Olive Inn and the corner of 4th Street, beyond. The auto park billboard advertises *Thy Name Is Woman* (1924) starring Barbara LaMarr and Ramon Navarro.

At left, a frame of Harold passing the Olive Inn overlaps a similar vintage photo. Above, Harold races towards The Ems apartments.

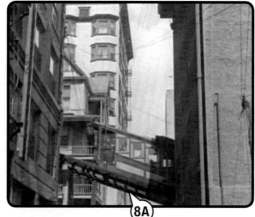

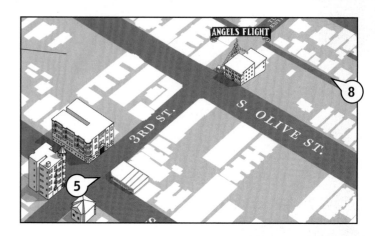

In *For Heaven's Sake*, a runaway bus drives NE along a narrow alley named Clay Street (8), which ran under the elevated tracks of the original Angels Flight, while crossing above the mouth of the Third Street Tunnel. The two views (*above left and far left*) are likely the same action filmed by different cameras from opposing points of view. Angels Flight has appeared in scores of motion pictures, including the noir drama *Act of Violence* (1948) (*below left*). Directly above is a shot of Angels Flight crossing over the alley (8A) from the Oliver Hardy short comedy *Hop to It!* (1925).

In order to drum up new patients for a struggling physician in *Never Weaken*, Harold pours soap powder before an oncoming water wagon (*middle right*) and passes out the doctor's business cards to the resulting victims. At the far right, from *Hot Water*, a traffic cop supposedly untangling a traffic jam in Santa Monica barks out an order. At the near right, Rita Moreno walks in front of the Hotel Nugent in the 1960 production *This Rebel Breed*. All three scenes show the Angels Flight Pharmacy (5) in the background.

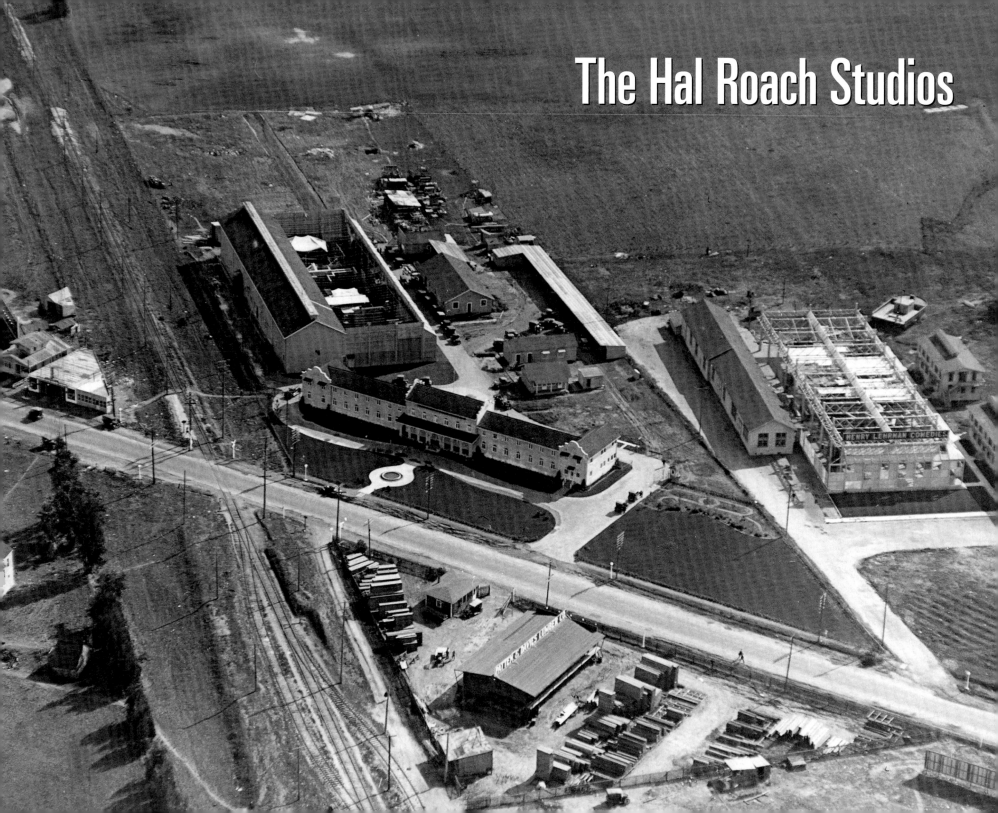

The Hal Roach Studios

Get Out and Get Under

(1920)

Released in 1920, much of *Get Out and Get Under* (GOGU) was filmed in Palms, along a block of Motor Avenue (*rectangle, right*), and at a five-way intersection-undercrossing (*square, right*) located just blocks from the Roach Studios in Culver City (*oval, right*). The plot mostly concerns Harold's auto problems and resulting trouble with the police.

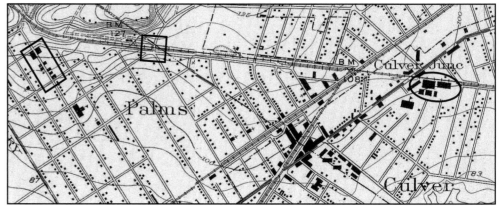

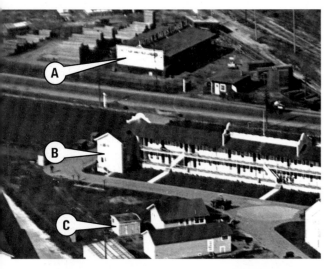

As Harold argues with a neighbor (*lower left*), we see a billboard for the Patten-Davies Lumber Co. (A) across the street and the left corner of the studio administration building (B). Lloyd filmed near (C), a fireproof cement vault where the highly flammable nitrate film stock was stored.

With growing success, Hal Roach was eager to expand the Rolin Company's output. Requiring much larger facilities than the cramped quarters at the Bradbury Mansion downtown, Roach purchased a tract of land in Culver City in November 1919, where his new studio, under the new name "Hal E. Roach Studios," quickly sprang up. The facilities were completed in April 1920. During this time of transition for Roach, Harold Lloyd was still recovering from his bomb accident the prior August. The early months at the new studio were not trouble-free. Due to a fee dispute with the city, the phone company placed a freeze on all new service to Culver City, leaving Roach without phone service except for sharing a single party line with local residents.

Scenes late in the film (*right*) take place in front of the Roach Studios fountain (*below*), a popular spot for Roach comedians to be dunked.

Overleaf: The Hal Roach Studios in 1921, at the junction of Washington Boulevard and the Pacific Electric rail line, future route of National Boulevard.

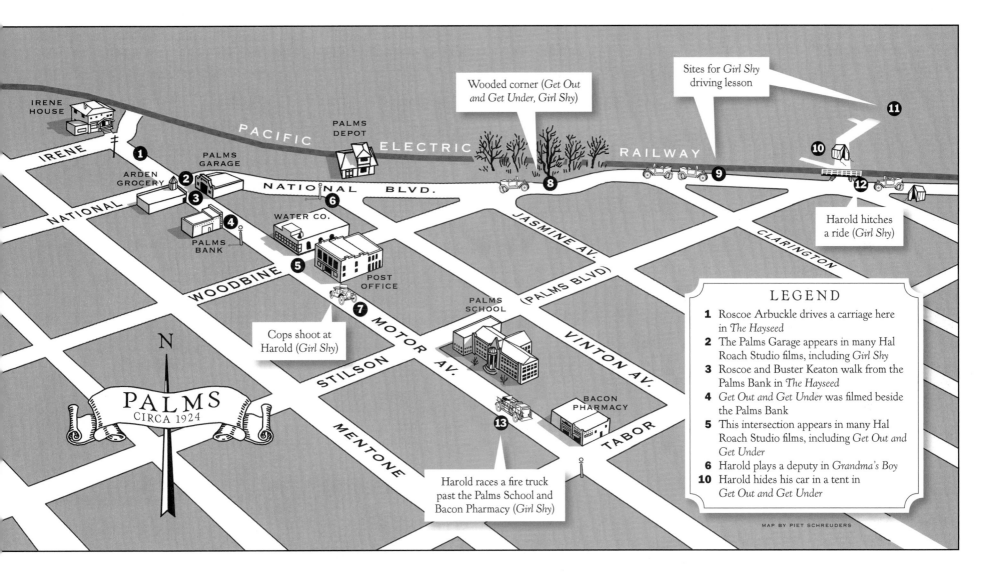

The quaint community of Palms, California, is the oldest suburb of Los Angeles, sitting midway between downtown and the beach. Founded in 1886, it was annexed into Los Angeles in 1915. Nearby Culver City, promoted by developer Harry Culver, where Hal Roach built his studio in 1920, was not incorporated until 1917. Palms was one of the Roach Studios' most popular places to film. Located just blocks from the Roach Studios, the stretch along Motor Avenue, pictured above, appears in dozens and dozens of Roach comedies. In particular, the nearby residential streets appear in many Our Gang comedies. Presumably the community's wide, lazy streets were ideal for controlling traffic and filming exterior shots with minimal disruption. The Palms Garage, Palms Bank, Peoples Water Company, and Bacon Pharmacy buildings (identified above) all remain standing.

Above, Roscoe Arbuckle and Buster Keaton stroll from the Palms Bank (4) towards the Arden Grocery (3), which served as the primary location during their 1919 comedy *The Hayseed*. The side window detail on the bank (*oval, above and left*) remains today.

Views of the Palms Bank in *GOGU* and in *Girl Shy* (*far right*).

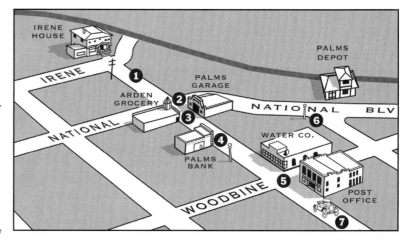

Harold's auto troubles begin (*top left*) in front of the former Palms Bank building, now a hair salon (4). Harold gallantly instructs the woman bystander to cover her ears before swearing at his car. During a break in production, the bank's door and woodwork were painted white, creating a slight continuity problem (*right*). At the far right (in a scene from *Girl Shy*), Harold drives past the Palms Bank as he discovers bottles of bootleg booze on the back seat of the car.

1A

1B

7

7

5

5A

5

At left (5), Harold eludes the police in *GOGU* by driving his car into the open back of a moving van parked in front of the Peoples Water Co. building.

5B

5

The "Irene" house at the end of Motor Avenue, now gone, appears frequently on film, including: the Our Gang comedy *Free Wheeling* (1932) (1A); Roscoe Arbuckle in *The Hayseed* (1B); and Harold in *GOGU* (7) running towards (5), with (1) at the end of the street. A modern view matching (7) appears to the left.

The intersection of Motor Avenue and Woodbine (5) was a very popular filming spot for Roach productions. At the far left (5A), Joe Cobb and Norman "Chubby" Chaney taunt each other in the Our Gang comedy *Boxing Gloves* (1929). At left (5B), Charley Chase in *Big Red Riding Hood* (1925).

The views (A) and (B) are from *GOGU*. To the upper left, Harold tinkers with his car while dealing with an inquisitive Ernie "Sunshine Sammy" Morrison. Captivated by the youth's charm and mega-watt smile, Hal Roach signed Ernie to a two-year contract in 1919, before he had turned seven, making him reportedly the first black performer awarded a long-term Hollywood contract. Ernie ap-

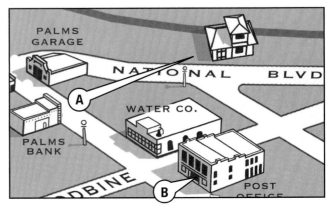

In (B) below, Ernie notices Harold working on his car and decides to check it out. A POST OFFICE sign appears to the right. The same window sign appears in *Girl Shy* (B1). The window also appears to the right of Allen "Farina" Hoskins (B2) in *Spook Spoofing* (1928). A broad view of the corner (B3) appears in *Dog Heaven* (1927).

peared in three Lloyd pictures and numerous other Roach productions before becoming the first cast member of the original Our Gang.

The frame blow-up points to the back of Palms Depot behind Harold and Ernie during filming. A closer view of the depot (A2) appears during the Our Gang comedy *Old Gray Hoss* (1928). Built in 1887, originally for the Southern Pacific Railroad, the Pacific Electric Railway Palms Depot, as seen from the front (A3), has been relocated to the Heritage Square Museum in Los Angeles.

Harold's adventures move far afield, as he encounters a political rally at the corner of Spring Street and Ord Street (D), north of the Plaza de Los Angeles, in an area that would later become the "new" Chinatown in the 1930s. The Lincoln Fireproof Storage Company (A) up Spring Street, appears later during *Speedy* (*upper left*). The two buildings on Ord Street, (B) and (C), are the locations where Charlie Chaplin filmed a scene in *Police* (1916) (*left*), and the home of Philippe's, a landmark Los Angeles eatery.

This view above looks up National Boulevard as it crosses beneath the Palms rail line and the Santa Monica Freeway. The old rail line will be revived as part of the light rail Phase II expansion of the Los Angeles Metro Expo Line from between downtown and Santa Monica.

Buster Keaton and Sybil Seely pass beneath the Palms rail line overpass (10A) in *The Scarecrow* (1920); Lupino Lane rides down Hughes Avenue away from the overpass (12B) in *Fool's Luck* (1926); and Harold tries to hitch a ride in *Girl Shy* in front of the overpass (12C). The two *GOGU* images below nearly form a panorama combining the tent's original position (T) with the corner leading to the overpass (12) to the right.

Returning to Palms, Harold attempts to elude the police by hiding his car within a picnicker's tent before fleeing up National Boulevard beneath the Pacific Electric tracks (and now, also, the Santa Monica Freeway).

Below, matching views looking down Palms Boulevard from the rail overpass. The top of the Palms Elementary School on Motor Avenue (see item 13 on the primary Palms map earlier in this chapter) appears in the distance (*oval below*). As later discussed, the school appears during *Girl Shy*.

I Do (1921)

Newly married Harold sports a baby carriage, using it to transport bootleg liquor instead of a bundle of joy. To the right, Harold strolls past a traffic cop standing in the intersection of Santa Monica Boulevard and Western Avenue. The same corner appears in Buster Keaton's 1921 short *The Goat* (*far right*). The Sam Selig grocery store on the right corner was recently remodeled (*modern view, bottom left*). The Selig grocery store chain would later become the Safeway chain in 1925. The bank on the left corner in the vintage photo below was built in 1923, after Harold and Buster filmed here in 1921. (An early scene from *I Do* also appears in the *Girl Shy* chapter.)

Above, the Larry Semon comedy *The Suitor* (1920).

Distracted, Lloyd leaves his carriage beside the Warren Drug Co. corner store, and walks off with a White Wings' rolling trash can instead (*above*). The building stands at 6075 Santa Monica Boulevard on the corner of Beachwood Drive (*right*). The same corner appears in the 1920 Larry Semon comedy *The Suitor*. The setting is across the street from the west end of the Hollywood Forever Memorial Park, where Lloyd's former leading lady Bebe Daniels is laid to rest, along with hundreds of Hollywood luminaries including Cecil B. DeMille, Douglas Fairbanks, and Rudolph Valentino.

Never Weaken

(1921)

Never Weaken was Lloyd's final short production. The sequence that strands Harold on a high-rise construction site appears in the *Visions of L.A.'s Historic Core* chapter, *infra*, while the scene where Harold trips people with soap appears in the *Visions of Bunker Hill* chapter, *supra*.

Harold's beloved Mildred will lose her job working for a physician unless business picks up, so Harold sets off to find the good doctor new patients. Harold's accomplice, an acrobat, pretends to take nasty falls on the sidewalk, attracting a crowd. Harold then jumps in to resuscitate him, using the doctor's methods. When the fully "recovered" acrobat walks away, Harold distributes the doctor's business cards to the impressed audience. The plan backfires when a suspicious cop scares the acrobat off, and Harold mistakes a true accident victim for his friend, resulting in Harold innocently manhandling the semi-conscious man.

At right, the acrobat takes a fall. The acrobat sidewalk scenes were filmed at 1266–1262 Lake Street, at the juncture of Hoover Street and Pico Boulevard (*right*), where Otto Andersen (*middle right*) had a tailor shop, and Dr. G. H. Reeves (*bottom right*) practiced dentistry on the corner.

The building on Lake Street (*right and below*) still stands, and still has an illuminated billboard on the roof.

The final scenes from the film, after Harold returns safely to earth, were filmed in back of a Roach Studios stage (*left*), built with distinctive large square bricks, visible here.

Ben Turpin and Madeline Hurlock also filmed scenes beside the Citizens Trust and Savings Bank in *The Prodigal Bridegroom* (1926) (*below, left*). The large curtained-window of the Hotel Christie appears behind them, below.

Stuck with a semi-conscious man on his hands, Harold tries to ditch the body while staying clear of the police. Above left, Harold steps into the doorway of Walter Dunn's Men's Shop at 6714 Hollywood Boulevard, east of the Citizens Trust and Savings Bank, at the east corner of the "T" intersection, where McCadden Place terminates at Hollywood Boulevard. Above, Harold shares awkward moments with a cop at the bank corner. The auto garage behind Harold in the center frame was demolished for the Hotel Christie site.

When Lloyd filmed at the Hollywood Branch of Citizens Bank in 1921 (*above*), none of its landmark Hollywood neighbors had been built. In 1922, Grauman's Egyptian Theater opened at 6712 Hollywood Boulevard next door to Dunn's Men's Shop, and the Hotel Christie—on the other corner of Hollywood and McCadden Place—opened in 1923. In 1927, the iconic Pig 'N Whistle restaurant opened next door to Grauman's on the site of the former Dunn's Men's Shop. The restaurant closed in 1953, but was renovated and re-opened in 2001.

This vintage view looking west down Hollywood Boulevard pre-dates the Pig 'N Whistle's 1927 opening. The Dunn's Men's Shop (D) and the Citizens Bank (B) appear between Grauman's Theater and the Hotel Christie. The train engines standing at the Grauman's entrance are there to promote the 1924 John Ford classic *The Iron Horse*.

Today, the hotel is one of the many Hollywood properties owned by the Church of Scientology (*below*). The former corner Citizens Bank (*behind the tree*) has been remodeled beyond recognition.

The Red Car Pacific Electric Railway (PERY) line cut diagonally across Sunset at Gardner, creating the distinctive triangle-shaped lot visible today (*right*), and behind Harold in *Never Weaken* (*left*). The sidewalk sign to the far left suggests the neighborhood was called Gardner Junction.

Above, Harold dispenses with the semi-conscious man by tethering him to a departing ice wagon, only to be confronted by a suspicious cop. The round arched entryway at 7507 Sunset Boulevard is marked with an arrow in several of the images on this page. To the left, Harold races east down Sunset past the same entryway in *Girl Shy*. Below, to the left, a panhandler bending to retrieve a coin tossed by Harold stuns the cop with his walking billboard.

One of the PERY lines traveled diagonally, northeast from Santa Monica Boulevard to Hollywood Boulevard, crossing Sunset Boulevard diagonally, as shown on the next page. Lloyd filmed many scenes around Gardner Junction.

These scenes, looking eastward from *Hot Water* (E), *Never Weaken* (C), and *Girl Shy* (W) (*lower left and below*), show the east end, center, and west end, respectively, of the block of Sunset Boulevard between Gardner Avenue and Sierra Bonita Avenue. In *Hot Water*, Harold climbs through a car stopped in traffic to reach a trolley car in the center of the street.

E   C   W

These scenes from other movies were filmed at the same setting looking west down Sunset Boulevard from the corner of Sierra Bonita Avenue. Above, (A) from *Girl Shy*, shows Harold's potential ride being towed away, and (B) from *Hot Water* shows Harold waiting to board a trolley with a live turkey. The corner of Sunset and Sierra Bonita (C) appears at the upper right in this modern view and in the vintage view below.

The block of Sunset between Sierra Bonita and Curson once marked the west end of the Sunset commercial district. Presumably there was less traffic to contend with here than in the center of Hollywood, making it easier to film.

This view (*below and right*) was taken from the extant Wattles Mansion, looking south. The orchard in the foreground is now part of the Wattles Garden Park.

 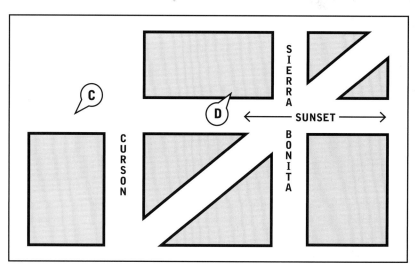

A Sailor-Made Man

(1921)

The opening "country club" scenes from both *A Sailor-Made Man* and *Why Worry?* (A) were filmed on the front gardens of the Beverly Hills Hotel, subsumed now by a parking lot. Developer Burton Green built the hotel on an isolated bean field in 1912, to draw people to his burgeoning housing developments nearby.

Lloyd plays a wealthy idler in *A Sailor-Made Man*. In order to earn Mildred's father's blessing of their planned engagement, Harold proves his worth by joining the Navy. This four-reel comedy is considered to be Lloyd's first feature-length film.

The hotel was an instant hit with the Hollywood elite, who could now choose to socialize either here or at the Hollywood Hotel. The Mission Revival style hotel was renovated in the 1940s, with a pink and green motif, earning it the moniker "The Pink Palace."

This view to the left looks up the hotel's entrance driveway. The lamp post (*circle*) is the same post appearing to the right with Mildred and her many suitors, and to the middle right, in Charlie Chaplin's 1921 film *The Idle Class*. The location of the lamp post is also circled on the aerial view below.

This aerial view shows the hotel grounds, and the triangular Sunset Park (now Will Rogers Memorial Park) that opened in 1915, across from the hotel, south of Sunset Boulevard running left to right across the center. The park steps (*star below*) likely appear in the background after Harold rescues Jobyna from a bigamist wedding in *Girl Shy* (lower right).

Mildred and her posse assemble on the steps at the southern tip of the park, watching with amazement as Harold and the other new recruits briskly march by. The oval in the vintage photo above marks the east side of the central fountain where Charlie Chaplin spent a few idle moments (*right*) in *The Idle Class*. Chaplin filmed many scenes here, running through the park. The concluding scenes from *A Sailor-Made Man* appear in the *Visions of the Coast* chapter.

Harold and his fellow recruits are likely marching up Cañon Drive (C), to the left, two blocks from the hotel (H). Gently curving Beverly (B) and Cañon Drives are lined with alternating Canary Island palms, and the taller Mexican fan (*Washingtonia robusta*) palms, many of which are now over 100 feet tall.

Grandma's Boy (1922)

Timid Harold captures a menacing tramp, and vanquishes the neighborhood bully, after his grandmother hands him a magic talisman that had given Harold's grandfather courage during the Civil War. When she later reveals the talisman is only an umbrella handle, Harold realizes his true courage comes from within, and wins the "girl" in the process.

Grandma's Boy was one of 1922's most popular and critically acclaimed films, and was among Lloyd's personal favorites. It was his first film to integrate dramatic elements with more naturalistic humor, a format Lloyd would repeat with great success in *The Freshman* and *The Kid Brother*.

This shot of Harold's grandfather (*left*) always gets a big laugh. To the right and below, newly deputized Harold strolls from the home at 3351 Vinton Avenue in Palms to the corner of National Boulevard (6), attempting to join up with a sheriff's posse. Visible down the street is the back of the extant Palms Garage building (2). The far left frame of the panorama to the right comes from the Charley Chase comedy *Jeffries Jr.* (1924). A full view of the home and corner appears (*above center*) in *Fire Fighters* (1922), the second Our Gang comedy ever made.

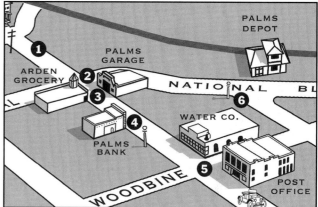

Below, Harold chases the tramp in a car before running him down. These scenes were filmed about 20 miles north of Culver City.

Above, Harold approaches the north corner of Haddon Avenue and Branford Street (originally named Sheldon) in San Fernando, looking towards the Pacoima Hills and the San Gabriel Mountains.

Above, Harold "borrows" a rancher's car to run down the vagrant. This was filmed at the same spot as the scene to the left. The ridge lines in the two movie frames align directly beneath the background hills.

Paul Ayers made all of the discoveries on this page. He began by noticing the tall mountains in the background, inferring they were likely filmed looking north at a traverse range such as the San Gabriel Mountains. He then leafed through Wayne Bonnett's book of 100-year-old Southern California photos, and found a matching view of the San Fernando Valley. Then, Paul "simply" studied vintage USGS maps, and drove around until he had discovered each Lloyd location.

12135 Branford Street, about one mile north of Haddon Avenue where Lloyd filmed, was a setting from *Pulp Fiction* (1994) (right). The International Auto Wrecking yard there today doubled as Monster Joe's Truck and Tow, the ultimate destination for Marvin the headless corpse from that film.

To the right is a modern view of the corner of Haddon Avenue and Branford Street, appearing in the movie above. The image above it shows Harold chasing the tramp up Branford Street, just a bit north from the "T" intersection with Haddon. The slight descent in Branford appears in the movie image, and in the modern view beneath. The tiny dark hill at the end of the road in the movie frame appears on the 1926 USGS maps, but was subsumed by the construction of Hansen Dam, completed in 1940.

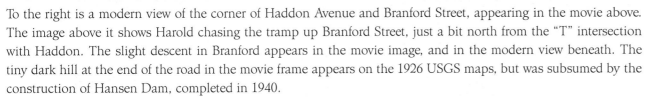

Back in Culver City, Harold chases the tramp off of Higuera Street (*far right*) near the Henry Lehrman (L-KO Kompany) and Hal Roach Studios, visible in the background. Harold crashed through the same fence, at nearly the same spot, in a scene from *Now or Never* (inset, middle right).

LEHRMAN

ROACH STUDIOS

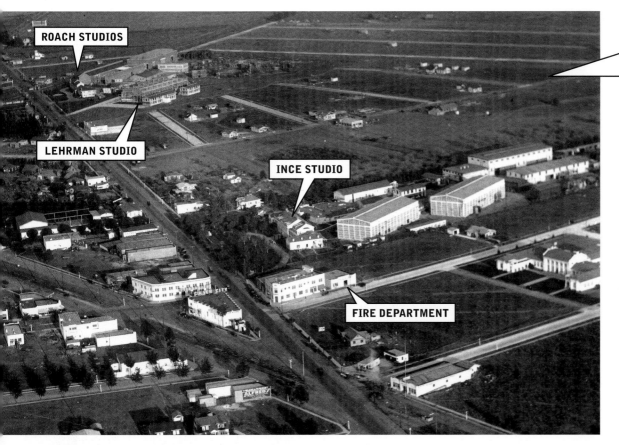

ROACH STUDIOS

LEHRMAN STUDIO

INCE STUDIO

FIRE DEPARTMENT

This 1924 view to the left shows in the foreground the prominent "X" intersection of Culver and Washington Boulevards in Culver City. The Ince Studio administration building to the left, patterned after George Washington's home Mt. Vernon, still stands as part of the Culver Studios below.

Left, Harold proudly displays the vanquished tramp to a terrified matron, who flees with babe in arms. Harold borrows her abandoned buggy to transport the tramp to jail. This scene was filmed at the Higuera Bridge over Ballona Creek, just a few blocks from the Roach Studios. By the time Our Gang filmed *Fish Hooky* at the same spot in 1933 (*lower left*), the adjacent Forty Acres parcel (discussed in the *Dr. Jack* chapter) was being used to film the Skull Island jungle gate scenes for *King Kong* (1933). This same bridge likely appears twice in *Among Those Present* (1921), right.

Dr. Jack's encounter with some road-hogging cows was filmed nearby on this private road.

BRIDGE

FUTURE SITE OF FORTY ACRES

BALLONA CREEK

ROACH STUDIOS

THOMAS INCE STUDIO

MAIN STREET CULVER CITY

PATTEN-DAVIES LUMBER CO.

A

Harold and Charles Stevenson battle atop a barn at the Roach Studios. The billboard for the Patten-Davies company appears across the street. The box above matches the box on the adjoining aerial photo of the studio, and (A) marks the west corner of the studio administration building in each image above.

PATTEN-DAVIES LUMBER CO.

A

SITE OF STUDIO BARN

At the far left, Harold prepares to give Charles another thrashing. Behind them, and to the immediate left, is the back of the Roach Studios administration building.

Dr. Jack (1922)

Although Lloyd presumably signs this prescription for laughter playing Dr. Jack, Lloyd's injury required a hand double for the shot. Buster Keaton, who lost the first joint of his right index finger by accident, also used hand doubles frequently when filming close-ups. The use of hand doubles is actually common, as it obviates the need for stars to spend time filming routine shots.

Lloyd plays a beloved young country doctor, whose fresh air and sunshine prescriptions cure almost any ailment. Mildred plays a "Sick Little Well Girl," the daughter of an overprotective millionaire unwilling to let her experience life outside of her shuttered room. After a chance encounter, Harold is hired to care for Mildred. With a little common sense, fun, and excitement, Dr. Jack soon restores Mildred's health and wins her heart. The girl's home portrayed in the film was the Milbank Mansion, located at 3344 Country Club Drive (right).

The Milbank Mansion also appeared in Laurel and Hardy's *Wrong Again* (1929) (*above*). The mansion's rear gardens appear in Lloyd's short comedy *Haunted Spooks* (1920).

The Culver City setting discussed on the next page also appears during scenes from Lloyd's short comedy *Now or Never* (1921) (*left*).

Harold is delayed from his rounds by a herd of cows. This view (*left*) looks south towards Higuera Street, running across the image, and the Baldwin Hills beyond. Ballona Creek lies out of view, below grade, behind the trees. The general area behind Harold, to the right and on the far side of Higuera, is where the exterior sets once stood for the town of Mayberry, appearing in the 1960s sitcom *The Andy Griffith Show*. The structure within the oval is a façade, and likely an early set. Harold's dirt road was situated on or near present-day Hayden Avenue (*above*).

By 1917, the H.J. Heinz Company had installed a giant cement "57" on a steep hillside that would become known as "Pickle Hill." Stunt drivers during the 1920s would pilot their cars on the surface of the "5," more than 100 feet long, over grades as steep as 60 percent. The ketchup maker placed similar hillside signs in San Francisco and across the country. Famed director Cecil B. DeMille acquired the Ince Studio in Culver City in 1924, and began using an adjacent 29-acre field as a movie set backlot in 1926. Known as "Forty Acres" (despite its true size), the triangular lot stood on the wedge of land between Higuera Street, Ballona Creek, and Lucerne Avenue. DeMille built sets there depicting Jerusalem, including a large temple for his 1927 production of *The King of Kings*. After acquiring the backlot in 1928, RKO incorporated elements of the temple set in the massive Skull Island gate set appearing in *King Kong* (1933). David Selznick acquired the property in 1937, and built the exterior sets here for *Gone with the Wind* (*GWTW*) (1939). The Skull Island gates, and remnants of other sets, were torched during the famous burning of Atlanta sequence in the movie. The small jungle and lake for the Tarzan movies stood across from Forty Acres, due south, wedged between Ballona Creek and the Baldwin Hills.

This 1920 photo (*left*) shows the future site of Forty Acres.

CAMP HENDERSON, *GOMER PYLE, U.S.M.C.*

STALAG 13 SETS FOR *HOGAN'S HEROES*

ATLANTA TRAIN DEPOT SET FOR *GONE WITH THE WIND*

MAYBERRY SETS FOR *THE ANDY GRIFFITH SHOW*

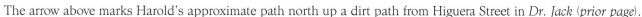

The arrow above marks Harold's approximate path north up a dirt path from Higuera Street in *Dr. Jack* (*prior page*).

The Tara mansion set from *GWTW* (*oval*) appears above, before it was replaced by Stalag 13 for the 1960s sitcom *Hogan's Heroes*. The bridge above was once the rustic bridge that appears in *Grandma's Boy* (*prior chapter*).

After appearing in dozens of movies over the years, the Forty Acres lot began to appear in early television shows, such as *The Adventures of Superman*. In 1957, Desilu Productions, owned by Lucille Ball and Desi Arnez, acquired the studio and backlot, and for the next 10 years the exterior sets built at Forty Acres appeared in some of television's most beloved shows, including *The Untouchables*, *Gomer Pyle, U.S.M.C.*, *Batman*, and most notably, *The Andy Griffith Show* (1960–1968), for which the *GWTW* street sets were transformed into the town of "Mayberry." The Stalag 13 prison camp set for *Hogan's Heroes* was built where the Tara mansion from *GWTW* once stood. When Lucille Ball sold Desilu to Paramount in 1967, it marked the end of an era. Forty Acres fell into disuse and disrepair, and by 1976, was bulldozed to make way for the industrial park that stands there today.

Why Worry? (1923)

Harold plays a hypochondriac millionaire who visits a South American banana republic for a bit of rest and relaxation, and unwittingly stumbles into the midst of a revolution. With the help of his loving nurse, Jobyna, and a gentle giant he rescues from prison, Harold quells the revolt. The movie closes with Harold and Jobyna, now married, celebrating the birth of their first child.

Above, Harold runs through traffic down Hollywood Boulevard to share the news of his baby boy with his friend the giant, now a traffic cop. In the background stands the same store that appeared nine years earlier in the Charlie Chaplin–Marie Dressler Keystone comedy *Tillie's Punctured Romance* (1914), credited as being the first feature length comedy. The arrow in each image on this page marks the same building, which still stands at 6410 Hollywood Boulevard. In 1913, it was the Hollywood Grocery Co., and was an F.W. Woolworth store in 1923.

The middle photo shows a large group of bystanders at the NW corner of Hollywood and Cahuenga watching Lloyd film the scene. The car (*circle*) in the far right photo matches the spot of the car (*circle*) to the near right from *Girl Shy*, when Jobyna visits Harold's publishing house.

Visions of the Coast

Number, Please?
(1920)

... also *An Eastern Westerner* (1920),
Why Pick on Me? (1918),
By the Sad Sea Waves (1917),
and *A Sailor-Made Man* (1921)

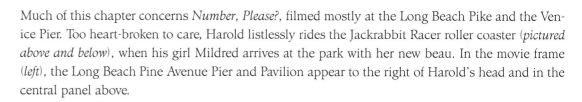

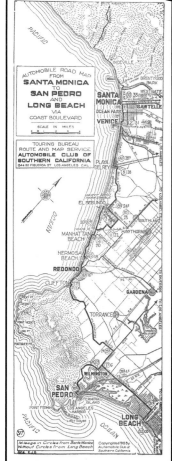

Much of this chapter concerns *Number, Please?*, filmed mostly at the Long Beach Pike and the Venice Pier. Too heart-broken to care, Harold listlessly rides the Jackrabbit Racer roller coaster (*pictured above and below*), when his girl Mildred arrives at the park with her new beau. In the movie frame (*left*), the Long Beach Pine Avenue Pier and Pavilion appear to the right of Harold's head and in the central panel above.

Dozens of silent comedies were filmed along the Southern California beaches. During the course of the five films reviewed here, Harold takes us from Long Beach to beyond Santa Monica, hitting most of the major beachfront amusement parks along the way.

To the right is an aerial view of the Silver Spray Pier, located at the Long Beach Pike. This photo was taken before the Jackrabbit Racer roller coaster was rebuilt with steeper hills in 1930.

As the wind and wild ride toss people's hats, scarves, and toupees into Harold's face (*above*), many Long Beach Pike landmarks appear in the background during the ride, including the tower to the Looff Hippodrome (the Pike carousel) (1), the face of the Majestic Ballroom (and skating rink) (2), and an eastern tower of the Long Beach Bath House (Plunge) (3).

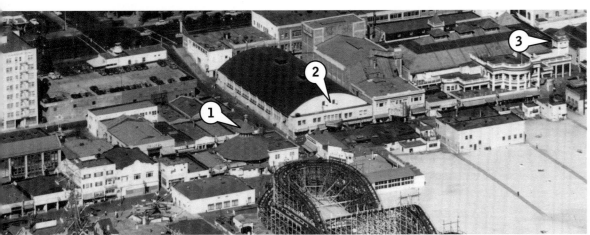

The Jackrabbit Racer, pictured here, was built in 1915. The racing roller coaster had dual tracks, allowing two trains to "race" each other. This coaster plays a major role in the Roscoe Arbuckle–Buster Keaton comedy *The Cook* (1918), as shown in these two frames to the right. When the ride was expanded and rebuilt in 1930, it was renamed The Cyclone. When it was demolished in 1968, The Cyclone was the last racing coaster in the country.

Above, a man loses his toupee while passing the Hotel Virginia in the background.

Harold chases after Mildred's runaway dog east from Cedar Avenue, down a street called The Pike (the "Walk of a Thousand Lights"), towards the Majestic Ballroom (A) and the Strand Theater (B). The former Jergins Trust Building (1916–1985), at the NE corner of Pine and Seaside Boulevard, runs across the back end of the walk. The corner of the Looff Hippodrome at Cedar Walk stands behind Harold, and casts its shadow in the foreground.

To the right, Harold and his rival, Roy Brooks, chase after Mildred's dog in front of a concession stand (C) beside the Long Beach Bath House, pictured below.

A similar view, circa 1932 (left), looking east down The Pike from the intersection with Cedar Walk. The Strand Theater is showing *This Reckless Age* (1932) and *Fanny Foley Herself* (1931). The extant Ocean Center Building (1929) along Pine Avenue, across the far background, now blocks the view of the Jergins Trust Building behind it.

At left, Harold watches Mildred's dog ride off on the Looff Hippodrome Carousel (*right*). Buster Keaton filmed here as well (*far left*) for an early scene in *The High Sign* (released in 1921). The carousel was created by master carver Charles Looff in 1911. Among his other creations are the carousels still in use at the Santa Monica Pier (discussed later) and the Santa Cruz Beach Boardwalk.

Unlike other local carousels that were either completely indoors, or only open on one side, the Looff Hippodrome (*above*) was open on three sides, providing sufficient light for filming. This likely explains why Keaton filmed his carousel joke at Long Beach, even while his movie was otherwise filmed entirely at the Abbot Kinney Pier in Venice. The Hippodrome was changed to a gaming hall in 1941, housing a Lite-A-Line (bingo/pinball) game, and the carousel was relocated and later burned down in 1943. When the Pike closed in 1979, the Lite-A-Line continued operating at the Hippodrome until at least 1985, and remains open at a different site today, although the Hippodrome was demolished in 2001. The site of the former Pike is now home to The Pike at Rainbow Harbor, below, a retail-entertainment complex.

Above, the Looff Hippodrome dome tower stands out, near the entrance to the Jackrabbit Racer to the far right. The Looff family lived in an apartment above the carousel. The Hippodrome dome was spared (*below*), and sits in a parking lot near Pine Avenue and Seaside Way. The east side of the Hippodrome building, along with the Jackrabbit Racer towards the back (*below, right*), appear in the Arbuckle–Keaton comedy *The Cook*, which takes place at the Pike.

The Pike at Rainbow Harbor (*above*) has a real Ferris wheel. What appears to be a roller coaster is public art along a pedestrian overpass.

An Eastern Westerner

(1920)

Leaving Long Beach, we travel north along the coast to Manhattan Beach, where Lloyd filmed railroad scenes for *An Eastern Westerner* (1920). In the movie, Lloyd plays a spoiled Ivy Leaguer sent west for his own good. Once west, Harold meets Mildred and ends up protecting her from a band of thugs. The arrow above shows where the former track (now parkway) curves inland to avoid the extant refinery.

Paul Ayers found this location after noticing the track in the film runs through sandy terrain, as near a beach. He then spotted the faint profile of the Palos Verdes Peninsula in the background of this railway shot (*below*) and a large oil tank (T) appearing beyond a curve in the tracks, behind Mildred and Harold (*above*). Vintage maps confirm the AT&SF tracks ran near the beach, before curving sharply inward to avoid the Standard Oil refinery. The former rail line is now the Veterans Parkway (Hermosa Valley Greenbelt). Lloyd filmed near where the tracks curved eastward, at around 16th Street.

A view south down the tree-lined pathway (*right*) matching the train shot above, and a corresponding view from the nearby beach, clear of the trees, looking south towards Palos Verdes (*far right*).

We now travel north, from Manhattan Beach to the Abbot Kinney Pier in Venice. Except where noted otherwise, the balance of this chapter examines scenes from *Number, Please?* The view above looks north, with the west coast on the right. The view below looks to the southeast, and was taken days before a fire destroyed the pier on December 20, 1920.

Harold and rival Roy Brooks each hope to join Mildred for a date aboard this balloon (*above*). This scene was filmed south of the Big Dipper roll-ercoaster on the Abbot Kinney Pier, which appears in the background. The roller coaster opened in May 1920, and was the only attraction to survive the December 1920 pier fire.

This establishing shot looks down the Venice Pier towards the shore from the Dancing Pavilion (near the fore-ground), to the bandstand tower on Ocean Front Walk. The callout above, and in the two aerial views, points from the tower to the Dancing Pavil-ion.

This view from Keaton's *The High Sign* (*right*) looks north up Ocean Front Walk towards the same bandstand tower (*circle*).

During the film, Harold happens upon Mildred's lost purse. He mistakenly thinks the purse is stolen, and attempts to get rid of the incriminating evidence in order stay out of trouble with the police. Harold attempts to throw the purse away, but a considerate dog continues to return it to him, during this sequence filmed on Ocean Front Walk near the Venice Pier. Above, Harold shows his frustration. Behind him is the north end of the Venice Fire Department No. 1, Engine Company No. 63 station, once located at 1713 Speedway, just south of the pier. The helpful dog appears in the middle shot above, and the station stands in the photo to the far right.

At right, this view looking north up Speedway, towards the Venice fire station (*box*), appears in this scene from Buster Keaton's *The High Sign*.

To the right, the Venice Fire Station stands adjacent to the Seaward Apartments (*oval*). At the far right, Buster Keaton passes the Seaward Apartments in this shot from *The High Sign*.

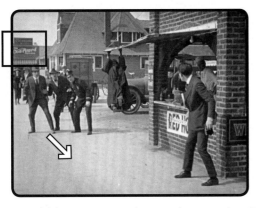  

Harold hopes to sneak past the cops by disguising his height, aided by Ernie Morrison perched atop his shoulders, but Ernie gets stuck on a hot dog stand at the corner of Ocean Front Walk and Wavecrest Avenue in Venice (*upper left*). The center view above looks south down Ocean Front Walk toward the Waldorf Hotel, at the corner of Westminster Avenue. The Waldorf Hotel (*upper right*) was built in 1913, and still exudes a stately beachside presence.

To the left, this view of Ocean Front Walk, north of the Venice Pier, was taken after the tiny corner hot dog stand was demolished, and the vacant lots were all developed. The left box matches the retail building to the upper left, the left oval matches the BATH HOUSE sign (*oval, above*), and the square matches the corner of the Waldorf Hotel, pictured above.

This aerial view below actually shows the tiny hot dog stand at the corner of Ocean Front Walk and Wavecrest.

To the right, Harold dashes across the outer end of the pier beside a brightly colored Sunkist orange juice stand (S), and toward the tower of the Captive Aeroplane ride. The railing in the background is near where Charlie Chaplin stood when he dumped Eric Campbell into the water (*movie frame, lower right*).

The arrow in this aerial view (*right*) corresponds to the arrow in the middle frame below. The (S) marks the Sunkist stand shown above, and the oval marks the "MUIRAUQA" AQUARIUM sign discussed at the lower right.

This view above looks east down the pier towards the shore, from the Ferris wheel towards the Ship Café, a landmark restaurant popular with the Hollywood crowd, constructed in the shape of a large sailing ship. Before the 1920 fire, the Ship Café ran parallel to the pier along the south side. After the fire, the Ship Café was rebuilt perpendicular to the pier to face parallel to the shore.

From left to right (*above*) appears the Ship Café, the Ferris wheel, and the Captive Aeroplane tower. If you were to stroll down the pier past the Ferris wheel, you would pass a large skating rink on the left, then the Venice Auditorium on the right, and finally the Venice Aquarium further down on the right. At the end of the pier was an amusement ride called Over the Falls.

During *The Adventurer* (1917), above, Charlie Chaplin spills Eric Campbell into the water beside the Captive Aeroplane ride on the Venice Pier. The Venice Auditorium fills most of the background. The "MUIRAUQA" sign (*oval*) is the same AQUARIUM sign in the Harold frame to the left.

To the left, Harold and Roy take turns hiding the supposedly stolen purse, while a suspicious cop searches them. In the background is a sign (*oval*) for the "Venice Racing Derby 10¢," marked with a (D) in these aerial photos.

The original derby was destroyed in the 1920 fire, but was rebuilt, appearing here (*left*), in the Thelma Todd–ZaSu Pitts Hal Roach comedy *On The Loose* (1931). The Venice Pier succumbed to mounting costs and dwindling attendance over the years, and closed forever in 1947, shortly before it was destroyed by yet another fire.

Harold, Mildred, and Roy are standing beside the entrance to the Ship Café (S). Harold finally learns that the purse he has been trying to ditch actually belongs to Mildred, but a goat eats it from his hands before he can return it to her.

Believe it or not, renting goat carts to travel around amusement piers was once a popular attraction. In this scene from *The Cook*, to the right, Buster assists Alice Lake from his cart beside the Goatland attraction on the Long Beach Silver Spray Pier.

The Venice Miniature Railway appears above in this scene from *Number, Please?*, and to the right in this shot of Harold and one-time leading lady Bebe Daniels riding along in *By the Sad Sea Waves* (1917).

Abbot Kinney installed the Venice Miniature Railway in 1905, as both a tourist attraction and as a means to escort potential home builders and buyers to look at the subdivided parcels he was promoting. The train was very popular for its time, but it did interfere with traffic, and merchants along the route began to complain. It was shut down in 1925, when Venice was incorporated into Los Angeles.

These similar views both look west down Windward Avenue to the ocean. Developer Abbot Kinney built his ambitious project with Venetian style architecture situated around a network of canals.

Number, Please? closes with Harold sadly riding off into the sunset, without Mildred, on the Venice Miniature Railway (*above*), beside the entrance to the Race Thru The Clouds rollercoaster (*upper right*). The narrow gauge train tracks (T) appear in both images.

The Race Thru the Clouds roller coaster (1911–1924), was the first twin-track racing roller coaster built on the West Coast. Each track was nearly 4,000 feet long. The coaster sat beside a man-made lagoon situated at the end of Windward Avenue, due east of the Abbot Kinney Pier in Venice (*right*). Notice the Venetian gondola in the above photo.

Why Pick On Me?

(1918)

The scenes on this page are from *Why Pick On Me?*, and were all filmed near the Venice Lagoon. Below, from left to right: Harold and Bebe Daniels stand near the lagoon (A), with the Antler Hotel in the background; Harold crosses the Coral Canal Bridge (B); Harold jumps off of the Coral Canal Bridge (C), with the Antler Hotel behind him; and Harold rows towards the Lion Canal Bridge (D). The large canals north of the pier and the lagoon (seen here) were drained and paved over once Venice was annexed as part of Los Angeles in 1925. The series of smaller canals south of the lagoon still remain as one of the most distinctive neighborhoods in all of Los Angeles.

ANTLER HOTEL

We now move further north, away from the Abbot Kinney Pier, towards the community of Ocean Park situated between Venice and Santa Monica. The Pickering Pier (P) appears in the background in each view above. The middle frame above is from *Number, Please?*, and the other three frames on this page are from *Why Pick On Me?*

This view below looks south from the Pickering Pier in Ocean Park toward the full length of the Abbot Kinney Pier in Venice. These two scenes from *Why Pick On Me?* (*left and right*) match the photo below.

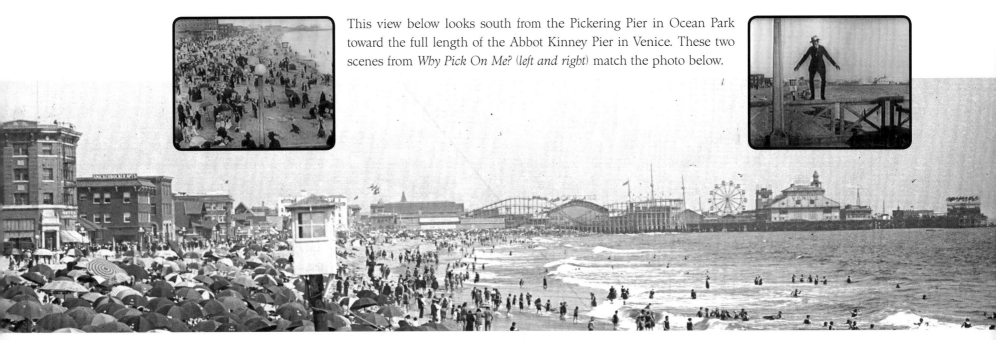

In *Number, Please?* (*left*), Harold and Sunshine Sammy stroll past cops in front of the Denver Hotel (DH) on the corner of Ozone Avenue at 201 Ocean Front Walk. The hotel building was remodeled, apparently in 1930, but is still standing.

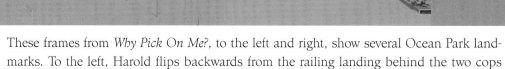

These frames from *Why Pick On Me?*, to the left and right, show several Ocean Park landmarks. To the left, Harold flips backwards from the railing landing behind the two cops rushing at him. The long-since demolished Ocean Park Bath House, built in 1905, appears behind, as well as the extant Denver Hotel (DH) on the corner of Ozone, and the extant Ocean View Hotel (OV) on the corner of Rose Avenue. To the right, Harold leapfrogs over a tourist blocking his path. Behind them stands the extant Cadillac Hotel (CH) on Dudley Avenue. These structures appear in the modern aerial view above, and in the vintage and modern views below.

We travel further north from Ocean Park to the Looff Amusement Pier in Santa Monica, built in 1916 by Charles Looff, the man who built the Pike Hippodrome in Long Beach. To the right, Harold poses as a lifeguard in *By the Sad Sea Waves* (1917). The distinctive Looff Carousel and Hippodrome behind Harold still stands today, and is Santa Monica's first National Historic Landmark.

Above is a view of the Looff Amusement Pier. The bowling and billiard parlor to the right of the Hippodrome opened in 1917. Further to the right stands the Blue Streak Racer, another dual track racing rollercoaster. The Hippodrome and carousel served as an important location for the 1973 production *The Sting*.

The prominent Looff Hippodrome still stands today (*far left, above*). In the far background lies the Palos Verdes Peninsula, visible in *An Eastern Westerner*. In the foreground, a modern circus has temporarily set up tents in the beach parking lot.

To the right, in *Why Pick On Me?*, Harold frolics with some bathing beauties on the beach north of the Hippodrome and billiard parlor on the Looff Pier.

During *Why Pick On Me?* (*far right*), Harold and Snub Pollard get into a fight over ice cream. Behind them (*circle*) is the triangle-shaped parapet of the building located at 1611 The Promenade in Santa Monica, just south of the pier.

The triangle-shaped parapet at 1611 The Promenade still stands today (*circle, right*). This view looks south from the pier.

To the left are vintage (*above*) and modern (*below*) views of the Looff Hippodrome in Santa Monica.

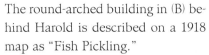

The round-arched building in (B) behind Harold is described on a 1918 map as "Fish Pickling."

Several more scenes from *Why Pick On Me?* were filmed among this group of buildings just north of the Santa Monica Pier. This scene of Harold leaping over a bicyclist from *Number, Please?* (A) repeats a similar stunt from *Why Pick On Me?* (B).

This panorama (C) stitched from the Billy Bevan comedy *Be Reasonable* (1921) provides a wide view of the beachfront area. Today, the site is a parking lot.

A modern view of Palisades Park in Santa Monica, overlooking the pier and Santa Monica Bay (*right*).

Harold meets up with the police at Palisades Park in Santa Monica in *Why Pick On Me?* (*above left*), and assesses an artist's handiwork (*above right*) in his 1921 production *A Sailor-Made Man*.

 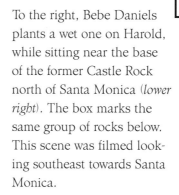  

To the right, Bebe Daniels plants a wet one on Harold, while sitting near the base of the former Castle Rock north of Santa Monica (*lower right*). The box marks the same group of rocks below. This scene was filmed looking southeast towards Santa Monica.

Charlie Chaplin flirts with Edna Purviance in *By the Sea* (1915) beside a bench located in Palisades Park (*above left*). Buster Keaton used the same setting to film this dramatic interlude for the opening of his 1923 short, *The Love Nest* (*above right*).

In his 1917 comedy *The Adventurer* (*below left*), Charlie Chaplin filmed at the base of Castle Rock (*below center and right*), a former beach landmark north of Santa Monica and about half a mile east from the mouth of Topanga Canyon Boulevard.

A Sailor-Made Man

(1921)

TOPANGA BEACH

BIG ROCK

BIG ROCK (IN BACK)

TOPANGA BEACH

CASTLE ROCK

Concluding our coast tour, this scene from *A Sailor-Made Man* (1921) was staged at the north end of Santa Monica Bay, at the west end of Topanga Beach. The hill profile in the upper left photo is the eastern ridgeline of Piedra Gorda Canyon, which meets the ocean at Big Rock. The vintage photo above was taken about a mile further east, looking west towards Topanga Beach. Although homes along the once barren coast block the view today, the aerial view to the far left clearly shows Harold's filming site relative to the visible landmarks. Castle Rock (*above*) appeared frequently in early films, but was deemed a traffic hazard and leveled in 1945.

BIG ROCK

TOPANGA BEACH

Before 1929, traveling along the coast beyond Santa Monica was a real adventure. The public road terminated at Las Flores Canyon, and through traffic ran only as far as Topanga Canyon Boulevard before turning inland to the San Fernando Valley. The remaining coastline from Malibu north to Ventura was then privately owned. May Rindge, widow of wealthy ranch owner Frederick Rindge, fought tenaciously for decades, following his death in 1905, to keep their massive Malibu land holdings private. She built locked gates and hired armed guards to keep out trespassers, and even built a private rail line to preempt Southern Pacific from claiming legal rights to lay tracks across her land. After years of legal battles, the U.S. Supreme Court affirmed California's eminent domain rights in 1923, leading to the construction of the Roosevelt Highway (today the Pacific Coast Highway), which opened in June 1929.

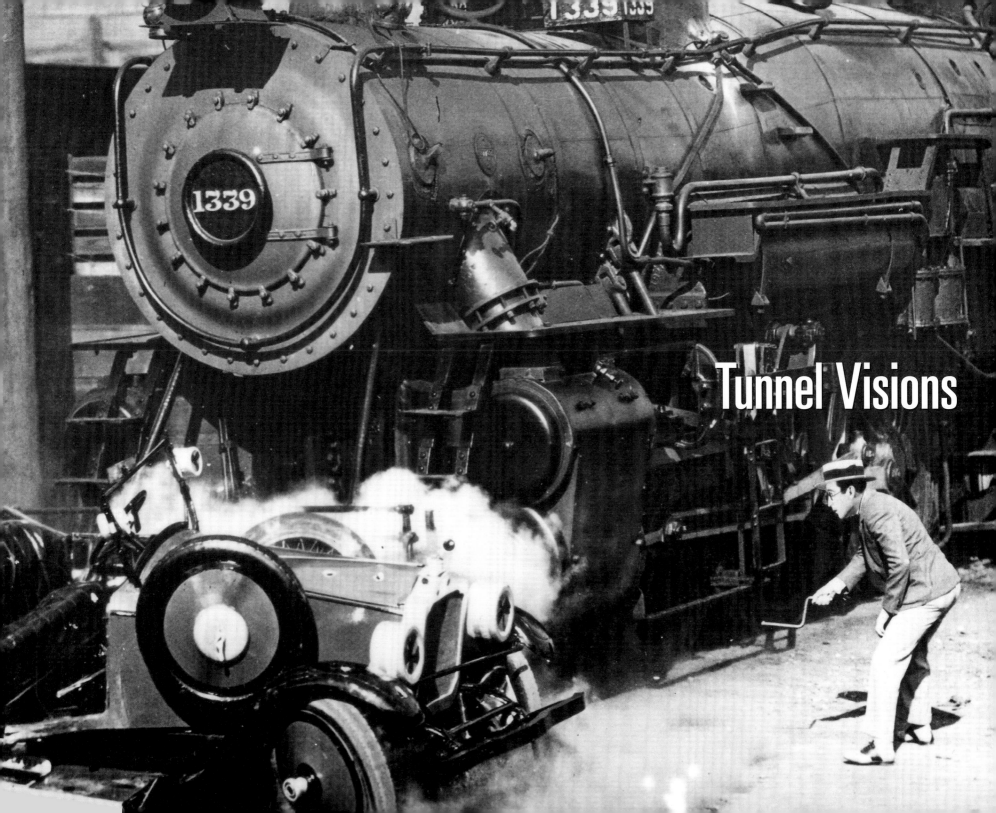

Tunnel Visions

Now or Never (1921)

Like many silent-era comedians, Lloyd frequently used tunnels, train stations, and locomotives for gags and plot developments in his movies. This chapter discusses many train elements that appear in Lloyd's work. The *Girl Shy* and *Movie Crazy* chapters also discuss train elements.

In *Now or Never* (1921) (A), Harold is trapped on top of a train, and suddenly realizes he is fast approaching a low tunnel. This scene was filmed looking due north up the tracks from near the Chatsworth Southern Pacific station. The triangles in the views to the right mark the same peaks, with Oat Mountain the uppermost. The water tank (*circle*) that appears in the vintage view of the Chatsworth station to the right is the same tank (as discovered by Paul Ayers) that Buster Keaton used for a stunt in his 1924 feature *Sherlock Jr.* (B). It stood west of the tracks just south of Devonshire Street.

As shown on the map below, Chatsworth lies 25 miles northwest of Hollywood. The rail line runs east from Simi Valley, through Santa Susana Pass, to Chatsworth, through a series of three tunnels closely spaced together. Of the three tunnels, numbered 26, 27, and 28, the westernmost tunnel, Tunnel 26, runs 7,367 feet, and is the longest tunnel on the West Coast.

Right: Buster Keaton in *Sherlock Jr.* by the Chatsworth water tank.

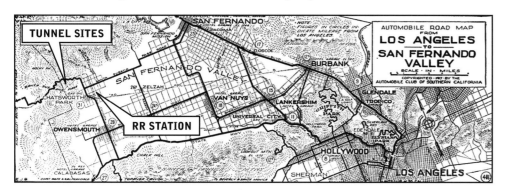

Overleaf: Harold loses his second car of the day in *For Heaven's Sake*.

Below, this view from an early scene in *Girl Shy* shows a sharp curve in the tracks NW of Chatsworth, as the rail line runs along Santa Susana Pass Road west of Stony Point Park (see map, next page).

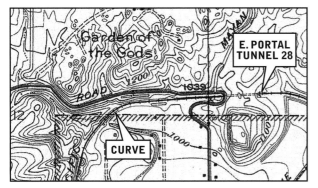

E28a

A

Harold approaches Tunnel 28's east portal (E28b) in *Now or Never* (B). The prominent rocks above the tunnel (E28a) confirm the setting. The movie captures the original cross-timber portal before it was replaced with a cement arch in 1921. The dirt hillside (once flush with the portal) has eroded, exposing the right corner (A, *square*), and has been stabilized with shotcrete. A terrible head-on collision occurred here in 2008, moments after the engineer had been texting with a teenage train enthusiast, when he failed to see a red warning light.

Harold's train in *Girl Shy* (*below*) enters and exits a tunnel from the same portal, the "new" east portal of Tunnel 28, built in 1921. The matching bush and rock pattern (*circles, below*) in (E28c) and (E28d) confirm these settings are the same. The wire fence along (E28d) (*rectangle*) is another unique feature, visible in (E28b) (*rectangle*). The same Tunnel 28 (E28e) also appears in the suggestive climax to the 1959 Alfred Hitchcock classic, *North by Northwest*, where the action cuts from lovers reclining in a train sleeping car to this shot (E) of a train surging into a tunnel. Hitchcock is quoted as saying it was "probably one of the most impudent shots I ever made."

In *Welcome Danger*, Harold passes into the west portal of Tunnel 26 (W26), the portal closest to the Santa Susana train station from which Lloyd is filmed departing prior to this scene. The sloped right corner (*square*, C *and* D) makes W26 unique among the six portals of the three tunnels. This portal also appears in James Cagney's *White Heat* (1949).

E28b

B

C

W26

E28c   E28d

My friend E.J. Stephens took detailed photos for me of the six tunnel portals in the area, confirming that each portal has unique proportions and characteristics. By 1959, the dirt standing flush against the right corner in (E28c) and (E28d) above had eroded, revealing a unique cut-in to the cement (*square*, E *and* A) that pairs (E28e) with (E28a). The portals were created by pouring successive loads of cement into wooden forms. The resulting strata in the hardened cement, although difficult to see here, further confirms that *Now or Never*, *Girl Shy*, and *North by Northwest* were all filmed at the same east portal to Tunnel 28 in Chatsworth.

D

W26

E28e

E

THE END

NORTH BY NORTHWEST

The particularly low tunnel entrance (*below*) in *Now or Never* was a piece of canvas painted to look like cement. It can be seen moving in the wind as Lloyd's stunt double races atop the train.

E28f

The dome of the Santa Fe depot built in 1893 (*left*).

Four stations appear on this page. Both the Chatsworth train station (*top left*), the Moorish dome of the Santa Fe station in downtown Los Angeles (*top center*), and the back of the Santa Fe station (*above center*), appear during scenes from *Now or Never*. The Santa Fe station also appears in the *Girl Shy* and *Movie Crazy* chapters. The waiting room and exterior of the Southern Pacific station (*right and lower right*) appear in *Just Neighbors*, and will appear again briefly in the *Girl Shy* chapter.

The Southern Pacific station appearing in *Just Neighbors*, above and below.

Paul Ayers discovered that the small station appearing in *An Eastern Westerner* (1920) (*left*) was the station at Tropico, a small town south of Glendale that appears on the map two pages back. Tropico was annexed to Glendale in 1918, which explains why "DALE" now appears on what was once the "TROPICO" station sign.

An Eastern Westerner, below.

Welcome Danger

(1929)

Lloyd produced *Welcome Danger* as a silent film, but decided to make it a talkie shortly before its planned release. Lloyd kept some footage, filmed more, and released the film as his first talking picture. The novelty of Lloyd speaking made this uneven film his highest grossing picture.

The movie begins as Lloyd and new leading lady Barbara Kent almost meet at the former Santa Fe station in Pasadena. To the left, Harold is too smitten with Barbara's photo to notice she is right beside him (A). The same setting appears in Buster Keaton's 1921 short *The Goat* (A1). To the far right, Harold stands near the north end of the station (B), which appears in Charlie Chaplin's *The Idle Class* (1921) (B1), and in Buster Keaton's *Go West* (1925) (B2). Though the original 1887 station is gone, the tower (*oval above and right*) of the Moorish-Spanish style Castle Green Hotel, built in 1897, remains in place. The landmark hotel is a popular filming location.

To the near left, Harold and Barbara race towards the Southern Pacific Santa Susana train station. The station (*far left*) has been relocated to 6503 Katherine Road in Simi Valley, and is home to the Rancho Simi Foundation and the Santa Susana Pacific Model Railroad Club. To the right, humorist Will Rogers runs towards the same station in the Hal Roach comedy *Jus' Passin' Through* (1923).

Visions of L.A.'s Historic Core
The Lloyd "Thrill" Picture

Among his many accolades, Lloyd was acclaimed the "King of Daredevil Comedy," a sobriquet he downplayed but likely relished. Besides staging numerous pulse-pounding chase sequences in his films, Lloyd today is best remembered for his self-described "thrill" pictures, such as *Safety Last!* (*overleaf*), in which he performs comedic stunts at great heights. The evolution of Lloyd's many thrill sequences and the corresponding commercial development of downtown Los Angeles are so integrated that this chapter examines them together. Lloyd filmed throughout what is called the Los Angeles "Historic Core," from the Broadway theater district (*lower left*) to the Civic Center (*lower right*). Many historic buildings appearing in Lloyd's films still stand today.

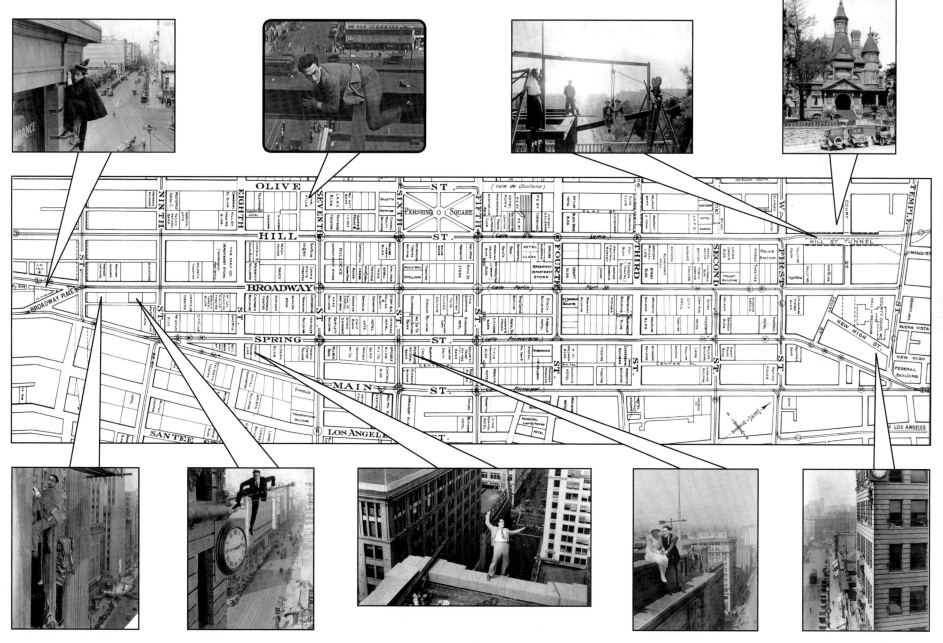

Prologue—Ask Father

(1919)

The roots for Lloyd's thrill pictures are evident in two early comedies he filmed nearly in succession during the summer of 1918: *Ask Father* and *Look Out Below*. In the former title, Harold seeks a harried executive's permission to marry his daughter. After being repeatedly ejected from the man's office, Harold climbs the exterior of the office building to enter from the window. To the lower left, Harold has unknowingly captured a couple of crooks.

Lloyd filmed his climb at the International Bank Building (later the Bank of Italy), at the corner of New High and Temple. The bank would later play the "real" building during long shots of Harold's famous climb in *Safety Last!* The rectangle (*below*) marks the future location of the current Los Angeles City Hall. The still extant Hall of Justice (1925) (J) is nearing completion on the left. Other prominent buildings, now lost, include the Post Office (P), next to the bank, the County Courthouse (C), and the Hall of Records (H), next to the court.

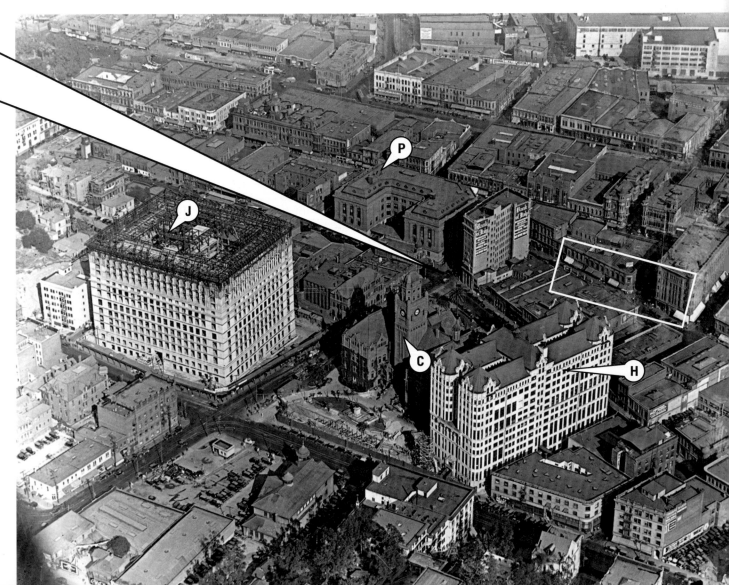

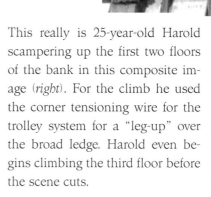

This really is 25-year-old Harold scampering up the first two floors of the bank in this composite image (*right*). For the climb he used the corner tensioning wire for the trolley system for a "leg-up" over the broad ledge. Harold even begins climbing the third floor before the scene cuts.

Arguably, Lloyd began his thrill picture career with this initial step filmed during August 1918, at the corner of Temple and New High. The ellipses (*right and above*) shows the sign for the Oak Bar, a tavern with stained glass windows and fancy appointments, where great men of the day would socialize after conducting business on the upper floors.

The building's facile climbing surface was used to good effect in other films, such as comedienne Dorothy Devore's *Hold Your Breath* (1924). The edge of the former post office appears at the bottom right of the image above.

991 – Hall of Records and County Court House, Los Angeles, California.

Buster Keaton filmed this scene from *Cops* (1922) on New High Street, at the back of the court, near the corner from where Harold filmed his climb.

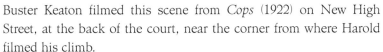

The SW corner of Temple (*left*) and Broadway (*right*), circa 1928, showing the front of the court. When Lloyd filmed at this spot in 1919, City Hall, to the far left, had not yet been built.

Built in the 1880s, the Clifton House, at 231 S. Broadway (*rectangle*), appears in the background as Harold stands on the Temple Street sidewalk next to the court. Perhaps to avoid drawing attention away from the stars, neither *Cops* nor *Ask Father* actually shows the towering court house building.

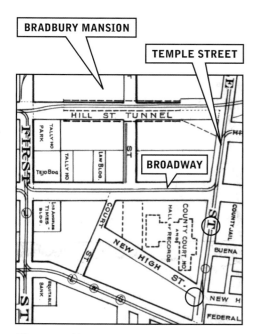

The two filming locations (*circles*) were just a stone's throw away from the Rolin Studio at the Bradbury Mansion atop Court Hill.

This composite view, with *Ask Father* shots at each end, looks west down New High from the corner of Temple. Nothing of this view remains today. The Criminal Courts Building (1966) (*right*), venue for the O.J. Simpson murder trial, stands in place of the former court house (1891–1935), which was condemned following the 1933 Long Beach earthquake. Echoes of the sidewalk retaining walls are present in the new structure. The Hall of Records (1911–1973), with its wild variety of window shapes and sizes, served as the seat of the county government until 1960. It was here from his big front office on the 11th floor that District Attorney Thomas Lee Woolwine questioned Mabel Normand during the William Desmond Taylor murder investigation in 1922. Although the Hall held on until the 1970s, the idiosyncratic landmark did not blend with its modern, box-like counterparts, and was demolished.

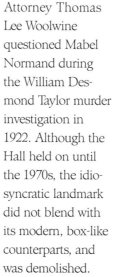

Phase 1—Look Out Below (1919)

Lloyd filmed his initial thrill picture during September 1918. As demonstrated on the following page, the movie resulted from a chance occurrence, a clever idea, and L.A.'s unusual topography.

Hill Street originally had no tunnel at all. The left bore opened in 1909, to accommodate trolleys from Hollywood. The right bore, for automobiles, opened soon after. The tunnels were demolished in 1955, to make way for the rapidly expanding Civic Center.

Court Hill and its distinctive twin bore tunnels appear behind Bobby Dunn dancing on a rooftop in *Hot Foot* (1924).

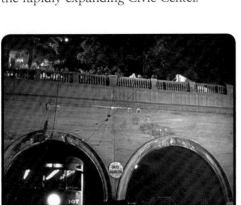

The tunnel made a perfect film noir setting for the Robert Wise boxing drama *The Set-Up* (1949).

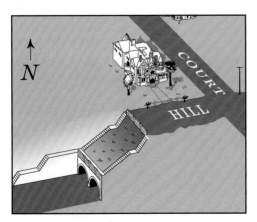

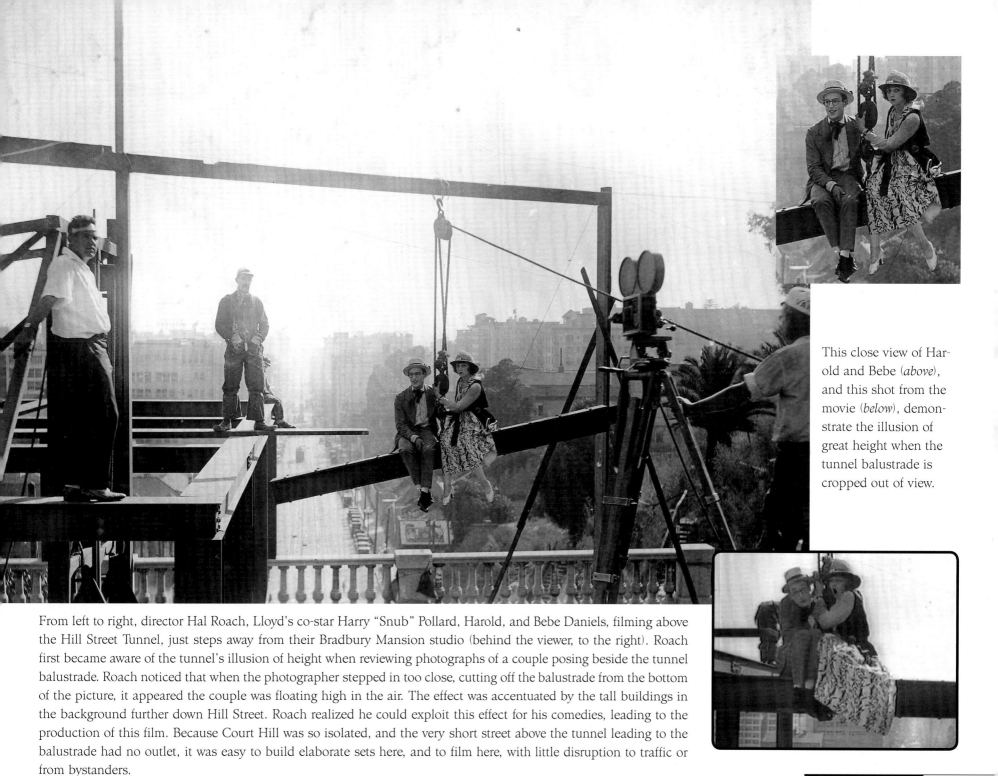

This close view of Harold and Bebe (*above*), and this shot from the movie (*below*), demonstrate the illusion of great height when the tunnel balustrade is cropped out of view.

From left to right, director Hal Roach, Lloyd's co-star Harry "Snub" Pollard, Harold, and Bebe Daniels, filming above the Hill Street Tunnel, just steps away from their Bradbury Mansion studio (behind the viewer, to the right). Roach first became aware of the tunnel's illusion of height when reviewing photographs of a couple posing beside the tunnel balustrade. Roach noticed that when the photographer stepped in too close, cutting off the balustrade from the bottom of the picture, it appeared the couple was floating high in the air. The effect was accentuated by the tall buildings in the background further down Hill Street. Roach realized he could exploit this effect for his comedies, leading to the production of this film. Because Court Hill was so isolated, and the very short street above the tunnel leading to the balustrade had no outlet, it was easy to build elaborate sets here, and to film here, with little disruption to traffic or from bystanders.

Phase 2—High and Dizzy (1919)

For his next thrill picture, Lloyd expands on the idea by constructing a much more elaborate set above the Hill Street Tunnel, matching exactly the details of the Citizens National Bank Building it is supposed to represent. Harold plays a doctor, and Mildred is his sleepwalking patient. During the film, both Mildred, in a trance, and Harold, "accidentally" inebriated, face many perils on the skyscraper ledge.

This production still from the 1921 Universal serial *The Terror Trail* (*below*), reveals how Lloyd's set was similarly situated. The Hotel La Crosse, a conspicuous landmark located at 122 S. Hill Street, appears in each image (*circle*).

Many comedians of the era filmed atop the Hill Street Tunnel, including Buster Keaton for this stunt (*right*) from *Three Ages* (1923) and Charlie Chaplin longing for home in this shot (*below right*) from *Shoulder Arms* (1918).

To the far right, a stunt double for Mildred Davis sleepwalks along the 11th floor window ledge of the extant Citizens National Bank building, across 5th Street from the extant Alexandria Hotel. The view looks west down 5th Street from Spring. These buildings also appear in the immediate background of this still from *Safety Last!* (*below*). The unique trolley track intersection (four-way with a right-hand turn) in the background (*far right*) ultimately led to this discovery. Lloyd's set (*near right*) was an exact replica of the bank building façade. The elegant ornamentation detailing the upper floors of the bank building (*lower right*) have been stripped away.

This vertigo-inducing insert shot from *Never Weaken* (*left*) shows the iconic corner clock of the Security Trust and Saving Bank at the corner of 5th and Spring. It was filmed from the 12th floor fire escape of the Citizens Bank building (*above*), also standing on 5th and Spring, on the opposing corner from the Security Bank.

Phase 3—Never Weaken

(1921)

For the first time, Lloyd expands his production to include two sets, built to represent different levels of height. The lower elevation set was built once again above the Hill Street Tunnel, and a second set was built higher up on the roof of a nearby building. The plot involves Harold's efforts to commit suicide after mistaking Mildred's brother for a rival suitor.

High-rise construction site scenes from Clyde Cook's *Should Sailors Marry?* (1925) (*below left*), a Roach Studios production, and from *Never Weaken* (*below center*), display in the background the iconic crenellated tower and dome of the adjacent Los Angeles Times Building located at 1st and Broadway

Relative to the photo at left, Lloyd's set was about here.

This view shows the position of Lloyd's tunnel set (*right*) relative to the first two blocks of S. Broadway. The left rectangle marks the former City Hall (*foreground*) and the Million Dollar Theater (with dome), appearing behind it, both located on Broadway. The small white square marks the Hotel La Crosse, at 122 S. Hill Street. The L.A. Times dome and tower appear in the right foreground.

Harold swings away, hanging on to a girder (*below, left*). Each image marks the corner of the former Central Police Station on 1st Street between Hill and Broadway. The station opened in 1897 to great fanfare, when Chief Glass commanded 93 officers and one matron, for a town of about 87,000 people. Patrol wagons would unload at a narrow dead-end alley in back, and swing around on a turntable in order to exit. The station's four horses were stabled in the basement. Although declared unfit for habitation many times, the station remained in use until 1954, and was finally demolished in 1956.

This composite view shows that during filming Harold was still relatively high from the ground. The rectangles above and below mark the distinctive Hotel La Crosse, evident in every movie filmed from above the tunnel.

The Million Dollar Theater appears in *Safety Last!*

Mistaking the sound of a breaking light bulb for a fatal gunshot, blindfolded Harold fails to notice that an errant girder from the high-rise construction site across the street has lodged under his chair, lifting him out through his office window. Upon hearing a music studio's harp recital, Harold loosens his blindfold to be greeted by a heavenly figure that is actually part of the office building's ornamentation. Harold's reverie abruptly ends, however, when the sounds from a nearby rooftop jazz party makes him question whether he has gone to "the other place," and he nearly swoons from his chair.

The jazz party (*below center*) was held on the roof of Hamburger's Department Store (1906) (later May Company, and still standing), that appears prominently during scenes in *Safety Last!* Behind the band, across the street in the background, is the Charles C. Chapman Building (1912) located at 756 S. Broadway, now converted into lofts. At the lower left is a 1930s view from the Hamburger's roof, looking up Broadway, towards the Chapman Building. At the lower right is a current street-level view of the Chapman, with the Tower Theater clock tower in the foreground.

The thrills now move to a higher level, from the Hill Street Tunnel, to a set constructed on the roof of the Ville de Paris Department Store (1916) at 7th and Olive. The movie took advantage of the extant Loews State Theater Building (1921) at 7th and Broadway that was under construction during filming. This establishing shot (*composite, far right*) taken from the Loews construction site, looks west up 7th Street, towards the dome of the extant Pantages Theater (1920) at 7th and Hill, and behind it the extant Los Angles Athletic Club (LACC) (1912) at 7th and Olive. Built by Marcus Loew, co-founder of MGM, the State Theater was the largest downtown movie palace, with 2,450 seats. The arrow runs east down 7th from Olive, corresponding with the easterly pointing arrow in this circa 1922 photo (*below*) and movie frame (*near right*). The photo below was taken after the State Theater, and the extant Sun Drug Co. Building (1922), both standing between the Ville de Paris and the State Theater, had completed construction. The Ville de Paris was owned by Bernal Dyas, a close friend of Hal Roach. Its interiors were used to film the department store scenes in *Safety Last!*

The arrow points east down 7th Street from Olive Street. The elegantly domed Warner Building–Pantages Theater stands at the corner of Hill Street.

In *City Lights* (1931), Charlie Chaplin and his drunk millionaire companion round the corner from east on 7th to south on Olive, past the corner of Coulter's Dry Goods in the foreground, and the Ville de Paris at back.

This composite panorama was created from a woozy point of view shot as Harold nearly swoons from the building.

The 10-story addition to the Bullock's Department Store at 7th and Hill (*dotted lines, below*) was completed in 1928. The original seven-story Bullock's at 7th and Broadway (*white arrow in each image*) opened in 1907. Bullock's was owned by Arthur Letts, whose Hollywood mansion appears at the conclusion of Lloyd's feature *Girl Shy* (1924).

The black arrow (*above and lower left*) points to the three-tiered roof of the Bartlett (Union Oil) Building at 7th and Spring, that also appears in *Safety Last!* and *Feet First*.

A modern view looking west up 7th at the Pantages Theater (dome) and the L.A. Athletic Club behind it.

Harold ponders his next step, oblivious to the girder passing overhead. The callout shows the Pantages Theater sign, now advertising "Diamonds."

The LACC appears behind Harold in this gag shot.

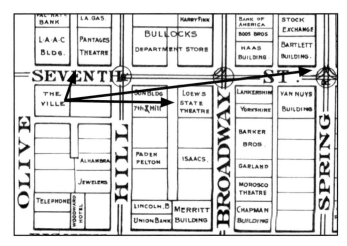

The arrows show the filming angles from atop the Ville de Paris. The Sun Building was not yet built. Today the Pantages, the Sun Building, the Ville de Paris (*below*), the Bullock's expansion, and other surrounding buildings are home to various jewelry marts, part of downtown's "Diamond District."

Established in 1880 as the first private club in L.A., the Los Angeles Athletic Club moved into these quarters at 7th and Olive in 1912. The LACC was the first building in Southern California to have an indoor swimming pool on an upper floor, the sixth floor, in fact. (The pool's atrium roof appears above.) Today, the LACC remains a posh club and boutique hotel. Valuing the club's privacy, Charlie Chaplin lived here during his formative years, and Lloyd and Douglas Fairbanks were also early members. Over the years, the club has served as the training grounds for scores of Olympians.

The Ville de Paris is now the L.A. Jewelry Mart.

Phase 4—Safety Last! (1923)

Lloyd's thrill-making format reached its zenith with his masterpiece *Safety Last!* For the first time, Lloyd abandons the familiar Hill Street Tunnel, and expands the production to include sets built atop three increasingly taller buildings.

Eager to earn money to send for his girl back home, Harold and his construction worker roommate (real-life "human fly" Bill Strother) concoct a plan to capitalize on Bill's ability to climb tall buildings. To collect a large publicity stunt fee, Bill, publicized as an incognito "mystery man," will climb the store where Harold works as a salesclerk. Set to begin the climb, Bill runs inside when he spots a cop he had previously angered. Improvising, Harold announces he is the "mystery man" and begins the climb, hoping Bill will switch places with him one story up after ditching the cop. Despite Bill's floor-by-floor pleas for Harold to climb "just one more floor," Bill can't shake the cop, and the promised transfer never takes place. The resulting climb, as Harold scales the entire height of the skyscraper, is one of the most exciting and meticulously crafted comedy sequences in film history.

Looking north up Broadway from 10th (now Olympic) (2009).

The prominent Blackstone's sign appears during all scenes comprising the first stage of the climb.

A bag of popcorn, carelessly spilled atop Harold's head, attracts a flock of pigeons, one of the many comic obstacles he must overcome on his way to the top. Notice the distinctive "Y" split in the trolley lines as Broadway splits from itself into Broadway Place to the right. The Blackstone Building (1917) (*top right photo*) still stands at 901 S. Broadway. The first climbing set (*right*) was built on the two-story rooftop (*box*) shown in the foreground of this circa 1922 photo, looking north up Broadway from 10th Street (*left*).

Looking south down Broadway at the now demolished Los Angeles Investment Co. Building where Harold filmed (left), and the extant multi-domed Herald Examiner Building further down the street.

ROOFTOP

ROOFTOP

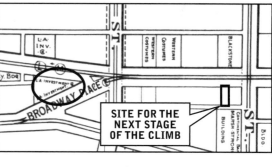

SITE FOR THE NEXT STAGE OF THE CLIMB

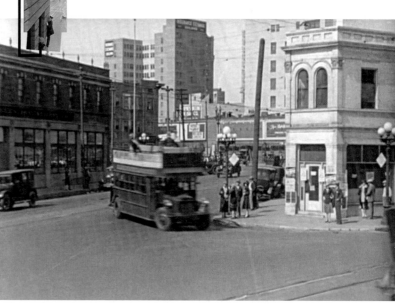

Lloyd filmed the first stage of the climb atop the triangle-shaped Los Angeles Investment Co. Building, where Broadway Place splits off from Broadway at 10th Street (renamed "Olympic" for the 1932 L.A. Olympic Games). Lloyd must have built the climbing set here with interchangeable façades, as the two-tier set appearing in some scenes had a plain façade (*above, left*), while in other scenes the set had a pair of ledges (*above, right*). Lloyd could have built a single four-tier set to accommodate the different scenes, but such a dangerously tall set would have defeated the purpose of providing Lloyd with a relatively safe place to film. Moreover, all of Lloyd's other climbing sets were built to be only two-tiers in height. The movie frame of Oliver Hardy from *Liberty* (1929) (*above, right*) shows the top of the building (*oval*) where Lloyd filmed. The map shows the filming location, while the bold rectangle marks where the next stage of the climb was filmed further up Broadway. This movie frame from *For Heaven's Sake* (*right*) shows the side of the triangle building (*left edge*), with a representation of how the rooftop set might have looked from the street.

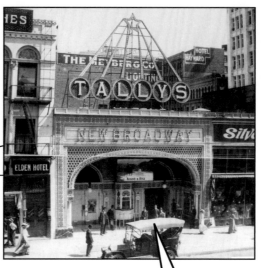

The next stage of the climb was filmed atop the Western Costume Company Building (1914) at 908 S. Broadway. Many memorable scenes featured this clock set (*left*).

Three prominent Broadway landmarks appear in the background during filming: the Majestic Theater (1908–1933), Tally's Theater, and Hamburger's Department Store (1906) (later the May Company).

Tally's Theater (1910–1929) was demolished to make room for a 10-story addition (*dotted lines, below*) to the May Company (formerly Hamburger's) Building (*below*). Tally's was originally one of downtown's finest movie palaces, with the then-remarkable capacity of 900 seats.

The Western Costume Company Building at 908 S. Broadway (*above, left*). In the photo above, center (from left to right) is sound-man Eric Brazier, cameraman Frank Haysom, and award-winning directors and film historians Kevin Brownlow and David Gill, visiting the rooftop site to film part of their 1989 Emmy-nominated documentary *Harold Lloyd: The Third Genius*. The box above David's head marks the original Hamburger's Building that appears prominently in the background of the scenes filmed from this setting. The full extent of the clock set built here is visible in this composite image (*above, right*) created from a vertical panning shot from the movie.

Although news of Lloyd's devastating hand injury in 1919 was publicized at the time, audiences most likely failed to appreciate that Lloyd performed all of his subsequent stunt work missing the thumb and index finger of his right

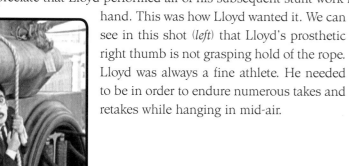

hand. This was how Lloyd wanted it. We can see in this shot (*left*) that Lloyd's prosthetic right thumb is not grasping hold of the rope. Lloyd was always a fine athlete. He needed to be in order to endure numerous takes and retakes while hanging in mid-air.

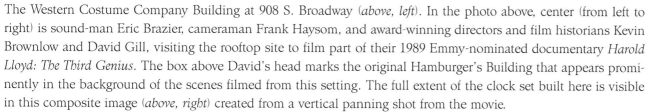

David Gill recreates a famous Lloyd pose (*middle right*). Brownlow, Gill, and Haysom (*near right*).

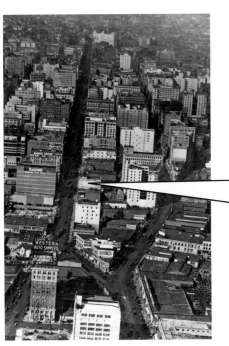 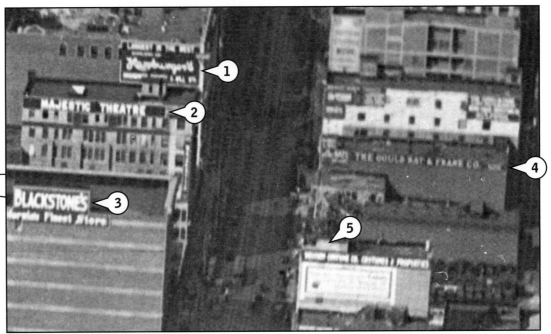

The clock set was built atop the Western Costume Co. building (5) at 908 S. Broadway (1914), which still stands just south of 9th Street. In the background are signs identifying Hamburger's Department Store (1) "Largest in the West" (1906), still standing; the former Majestic Theatre (2); Blackstone's "California's Finest Store" (3) (1917), still standing; and the former Gould Hat & Frame Co. (4). An annex tower to the Hamburger Building replaced Tally's in 1929. The Majestic Theatre was razed in 1933, for what is now the site of a two-story parking garage. The buildings at the NE corner of Broadway and 9th were replaced by the Orpheum Theater (1926), and the Art Deco Ninth and Broadway Building (1929), both appearing in *Feet First*.

Leaving Harold's climb for a moment, this earlier scene of Bill Strother at work (man looking to the left) was filmed in front of the former Alhambra Building at 5th and Broadway, from a department store under construction during the time of filming across the street. The vertical marquee for the extant Title Guarantee Building (1912), now Jewelry Trades Building, appears at the far right (*ellipse*). Beneath Bill you can see

the trolley tracks curving south from Broadway, joining the tracks going east on 5th.

The former Alhambra Building at the NE corner Broadway (*left*) and 5th (*right*) was demolished to make way for the Chester Williams Building (1926). One banner reads "Closing Out Sale–Building Coming Down March 31st." The tall building at back with the many windows is the rear of the extant Citizens Bank, discussed elsewhere in this chapter.

A vintage shot looking east down 5th (*to the left*) and south down Broadway (*to the right*). The corner of the Alhambra Building (*box*) appears at the far left. The ellipse matches the ellipse on the vertical marquee above.

Looking east down 5th from Broadway today, the Chester Williams Building at the left, and the Title Guarantee Building on the right. The marquee is still in place.

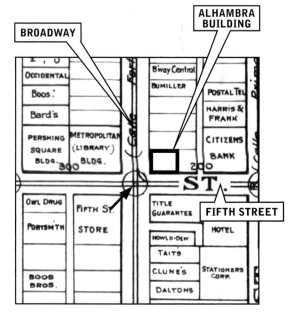

Million Dollar Theater
307 S. Broadway (1917)

Second City Hall
226-240 S. Broadway (1888–1928)

On September 7, 1922, human fly Bill Strother climbed to the top of the International Bank Building, as four movie cameras captured his climb. The resulting footage was used for long shots of "Harold" on the building. This view looks down Main Street, five years before the neighboring City Hall began construction in 1927. Strother began his career in 1914, and climbed buildings across the country, raising funds for the Great War Liberty Loan Drive. He was especially acclaimed for scaling the 57-story Woolworth Building in New York. After witnessing an earlier Strother climb in person, Lloyd had felt so anxious, and yet so irresistibly compelled to watch, that he immediately decided to incorporate Bill into his next production. *Safety Last!* was Bill's only screen appearance. A minor accident prior to filming had injured Bill's leg, leading to his character being named "Limpy Bill." Aside from climbing the International Bank Building, Bill also climbed the Lane Mortgage Company Building and the Biltmore Hotel in Los Angeles during 1923. Bill got out of the business in the 1930s, and lived until age 61, when he died in a car accident.

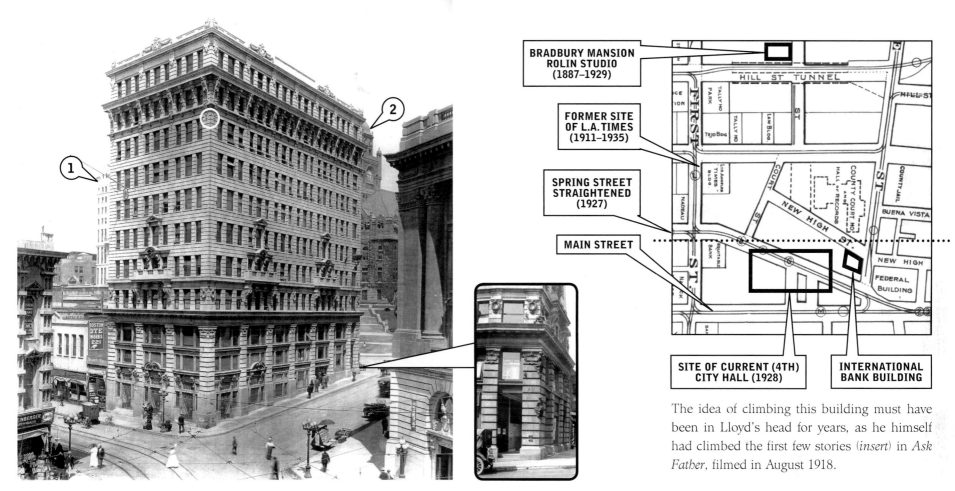

The idea of climbing this building must have been in Lloyd's head for years, as he himself had climbed the first few stories (*insert*) in *Ask Father*, filmed in August 1918.

Above, the Hall of Records (1) and County Courthouse (2) peek out from behind the International Savings and Exchange Bank Building (1907-1954) at 116 Temple Street. The former Post Office/Federal Building stood across Temple Street, at the far right edge of the photo. None of the buildings pictured here remain. The circle marks where Lloyd's crew constructed a fake clock on the bank building for stuntman Bill Strother's climb.

The Bank of Italy (later Bank of America) acquired the building in 1917, staying there until the city purchased it in 1926, with plans to demolish it for the grounds surrounding the new City Hall (1928). The bank was spared the immediate wrecking ball when, in 1927, the city managers decided it could house all of the city Health Department's scattered offices there on a temporary basis, until a permanent, central home for the department was constructed. The sub-basement bank vaults were used to store records, and city clerks dealt with the public through the former tellers' cages. Although a bond measure funding construction of a new Health Department building eventually passed in 1947, it was not built until 1954. The bank was demolished shortly after the Health Department vacated its 27 year-long "temporary" occupancy. At the time, one Bank of America vice-president who had worked there was glad to see the "horrible eyesore" go. A columnist in 1940 once described it as an archaic, architectural menace, and a breeding space for bad smells. (Nostalgic for the 72-hour, seven-day work week, the same columnist also complained that the county workers would soon be switching to a 40-hour, five-day work schedule!) While there is no accounting for taste, admittedly the stately building's wiring and plumbing were ill-functioning and outdated, and the bank was never outfitted with fire escapes. Nonetheless, one can only imagine its once magnificent high-vaulted marble lobby, and the opulent upper-floor offices occupied by the city's early movers and shakers.

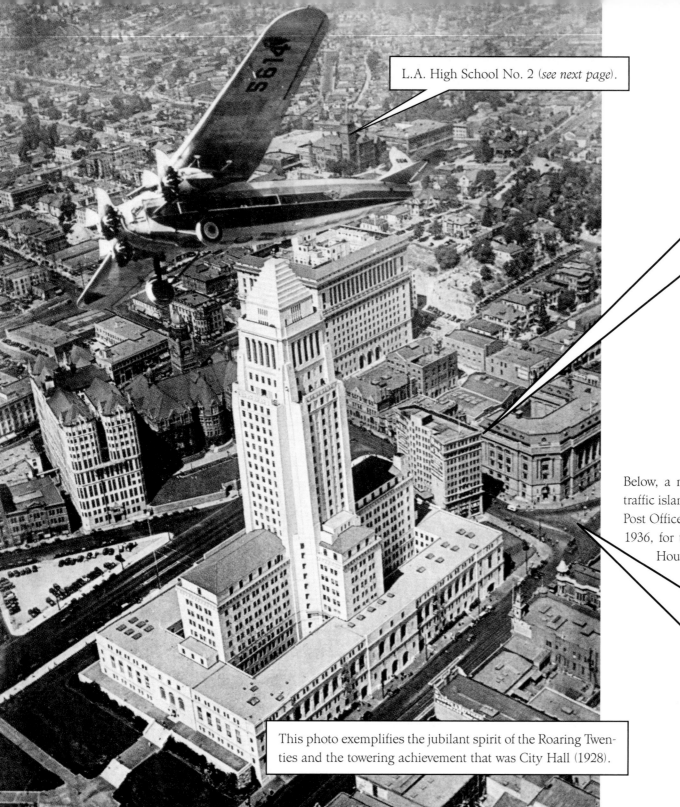

L.A. High School No. 2 (*see next page*).

This photo exemplifies the jubilant spirit of the Roaring Twenties and the towering achievement that was City Hall (1928).

Below, a mesmerized crowd watches Bill Strother from a traffic island formed by three rail lines in front of the stately Post Office and Federal Building, which was demolished in 1936, for the current Post Office and U.S. District Court House.

Harold and Mildred filmed this scene (*right*) atop the Washington Building (5), with the Million Dollar Theater (1) in the background. The tower (2) is part of the Rolin Studio at the Bradbury Mansion, and (4) marks the L.A. Times Building tower, both previously discussed. The middle tower (3) belongs to the Los Angeles High School No. 2 (1891) high atop Fort Moore Hill (3a), now long lost to history. The current L.A.

High School No. 9, in nearly the same location as the original (3b), projects a rather different sensibility.

To the left, three prominent, extant buildings appear immediately behind Harold. The Alexandria Hotel (1906) (A) stands at the corner of 501 S. Spring. Citizens National Bank (1914) (B) stands across the street at 453 S. Spring, and appears briefly in *High and Dizzy*, discussed earlier. Reflecting the hotel's original success, a taller annex (C) was built in 1910. Until the Biltmore Hotel opened nearby in 1923, the Alex was L.A.'s premiere hotel, well-known for the U.S. presidents, silent film stars, and historical figures who stayed there. Its lavish Palm Room, now a designated landmark, hosted the city's most prestigious social events for years. The Alex was recently renovated and converted into low-income apartments.

Lloyd atop the final climbing set built on the roof of the National Merchants Bank Building, 548 S. Spring Street. The revolving wind gauge later stuns Harold, leading to the climax of the film.

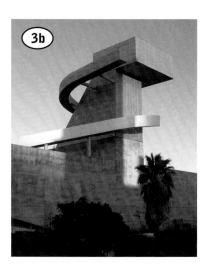

Although the danger was minimized, Lloyd was just as high in the air as he appeared to be during these scenes. Wishing secrecy, Lloyd did not photograph the climbing sets built for *Safety Last!*, and in later years was coy about how it was filmed. But at least one newspaper revealed the secret in 1923, although the graphic above depicts Harold on a set nearly four stories tall! As shown, Lloyd built a façade on the roof of a tall building, placing a tall camera tower nearby. The camera looked down on the set from the tower, while keeping the real building's roof outside of the movie frame. Because the camera recorded exactly what was there to be seen, these scenes crackle with authenticity that blue-screen computer effects fail to replicate. While the pilot episode of the 1980s hit television series *Moonlighting* used this technique to pay homage to Harold's work (*below*), it puzzles me that this ingenious effect is not employed more often.

The Alexandria Annex sign (*ellipse, above left*) appears behind Harold. Above is a view of the Alexandria Annex, the shorter Alexandria Hotel, and the Citizens Bank (*arrow, above and above left*). Sadly, the upper floors of the bank building have been stripped of all ornamentation.

Old school stunt-work from the *Moonlighting* (1985) pilot episode.

The final stage of the climb was filmed atop the Merchants National Bank building at 548 S. Spring Street (*above*), which now houses private lofts.

Dazed by a wildly spinning wind gauge, Harold slips off the roof, only to be saved by a stray rope caught around his ankle. (Lloyd recalled to Kevin Brownlow that a circus acrobat performed this stunt.) This view looks down Spring Street towards several landmarks, all still standing: the Van Nuys Building (1913) (1)—prominent in *Feet First*—at the corner of 7th and Spring, the Bartlett Building (1911) (2), with its

distinctive three-tier top, occupied at the time by the Union Oil Company; and the seventh home of the L.A. Stock Exchange (1918) (3), all still standing. The climbing set, which normally faced away from Spring Street, must have been rotated counter-clockwise 90 degrees to achieve this shot. I assume the set was rotated as the window signs and random brick details pictured here are identical to the shots of the set when it was facing away from the street.

Safe *at last*, Harold clutches Mildred for the happy ending. This very brief closing sequence was filmed atop three different buildings. Mildred greets Harold atop the Merchant's National Bank Building (1), where the final segment of the climb was filmed. In this view, the original Rosslyn Hotel (1913), still standing at the NW corner of 5th and Main, appears in the background, its giant iconic sign, also still extant, towers above Mildred's head. The Rosslyn sign faces east, away from downtown, towards the city train stations. A hotel annex of similar design, also extant, was later built across 5th Street at the SW corner of Main. Now converted into lofts, the two Beaux-Arts style hotels were connected by a marble subway, and together offered 1,100 rooms in what was once touted as the largest hotel on the Pacific Coast.

Looking west, Angels Flight and the Third Street Tunnel appear in the background.

In the closing scene (2), Harold and Mildred laugh in relief as they watch the resolute policeman continue to chase Bill Strother across another rooftop off camera below. This single insert shot was filmed atop the 13-story Washington Building (1912) at the NW corner of 3rd and Spring. Behind them stands a prominent landmark, the extant Million Dollar Theater (1917) (*above*) at 3rd and Broadway, built by showman Sid Grauman, the later impresario of the Egyptian and Chinese Theaters in Hollywood. The building's dome (D) remains a prominent downtown landmark.

Standing between these two buildings, out of view, is the Bradbury Building (1893), the oldest extant downtown commercial building. Its plain façade belies its internal five-story high glass-roofed atrium, intricate detailing and railings, and birdcage elevators. A popular filming location, the Bradbury Building has appeared in *D.O.A.* (1949), *Blade Runner* (1982), and *(500) Days of Summer* (2009). It was built by Leland Bradbury, owner of the Bradbury Mansion nearby, the original home to Lloyd's Rolin Studio.

Looking east down 3rd Street from Grand, the dome of the Million Dollar Theater (D) appears in this view from *Girl Shy*.

J. EPSTEIN
HIGH GRADE
LADIES TAILOR
SIXTH FLOOR

A year later, comedienne Dorothy Devore filmed a similar scene atop the same building in *Hold Your Breath* (1924). Note that for her scenes the stunt set faced towards the street.

As the closing scene continues, Harold and Mildred embrace (3), this time back atop the Western Costume Building where the clock set was built. The building signs appearing behind them match the signs evident during the clock stunt sequence.

Author and Mack Sennett expert Brent Walker pointed out that, nearly 90 years later, one can still discern "HIGH GRADE LADIES TAILOR SIXTH FLOOR" on the wall of the F.W. Braun Building, 820 S. Broadway.

The film fades out with a final joke (4) back atop the Western Costume Building. Harold is so relieved and love-struck that he fails to notice the loss of both his shoes and then his socks as he walks across a sticky tar patch. The clock set was built in front of where Harold is standing. Visible across the street (oval) is the corner of the Blackstone Building at 9th and Broadway. Harold and Mildred were married in real life on February 10, 1923, a few weeks before the film's April 1, 1923 premiere.

The stars above and below mark where Lloyd expert and author Annette D'Agostino Lloyd (above, right) stood during her video tour from the Harold Lloyd Comedy Collection. She is pointing at the Hamburger Building up the street. In a scene from the *Moonlighting* pilot episode, Bruce Willis sits high above the buildings used for Harold's stunts.

FEET FIRST
SECOND SET

SAFETY LAST!
CLOCK SET

BLACKSTONE
BUILDING

This photo (*right*) reveals the stunt set built atop the Western Costume Building employed by Dorothy Devore in *Hold Your Breath*, as depicted on the prior page. (Her set faces the street below.)

Harold's *Safety Last!* clock set was built in a similar fashion, atop the same building, only with the facade of Harold's set facing *away* from the street.

Phase 5—Feet First (1930)

Lloyd's previous feature, *Welcome Danger* (1929), began production as a silent film, but after much re-working was released as Lloyd's first movie with a soundtrack. Still uncertain of how to best transition to sound, for his next feature Lloyd returned to familiar territory, creating his final thrill picture, *Feet First*. As before, Lloyd filmed atop three increasingly taller rooftops for his climb, even filming the first sequence atop the same triangular building as its *Safety Last!* counterpart.

In *Feet First*, to avoid being captured as a ship's stowaway, Harold hides in a large canvas airmail bag and is flown to shore. Once in the city, the bag is left momentarily unattended upon a painter's scaffold lying on the sidewalk. Harold's adventures begin once the painter hoists the scaffold high in the air.

Although *Feet First* was filmed just eight years after *Safety Last!*, the two films bookend the decade of the Roaring Twenties, revealing the tremendous change and growth that took place during that remarkable time. One obvious difference is that instead of scaling a stately building from a bygone era, Harold clings for life from a streamlined Art Deco façade, fashioned after the Ninth and Broadway Building that had opened earlier that same year.

The opening scenes were filmed looking north up Broadway from atop the two-story Los Angeles Investment Company building (now demolished), the same setting used for the initial climb sequences in *Safety Last!* Notice the distinctive split of the trolley tracks in the background. The rooftop of the Southern California Gas Company Building (1913) (*rectangle, below*) was the setting for filming the second stage of the *Feet First* climb.

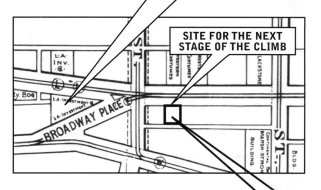

SITE FOR THE NEXT STAGE OF THE CLIMB

Three similar views up Broadway from 10th (now Olympic). Four major new buildings appear in the *Feet First* frame (*left*), two standing in front of, and two standing behind, the Blackstone's Building by Harold's head in *Safety Last!* (*below*).

The Majestic Theater (*rectangle*), so prominent during corresponding scenes from *Safety Last!*, stands barely visible sandwiched between its two new neighbors, the May Company annex (1929) at 833 S. Broadway, which replaced Tally's Theater, and the corner Eastern Columbia Building (1930) at 849 S. Broadway. Four other prominent buildings appear in *Feet First* that were nonexistent in 1922, during the filming of *Safety Last!*; the 11-story Western Costume Building (1923) 939 S. Broadway, the United Artists Theater (1927) 933 S. Broadway, the Ninth and Broadway Building (1930) 850 S. Broadway, and the Orpheum Theater (1926) 842 S. Broadway.

The set and filming tower used during the second stage of the climb were built atop the extant Southern California Gas Company Building at 950 S. Broadway. As before, the camera looked down on the set from a tower, while excluding the rooftop from the bottom of the frame. The tower platforms allowed the cameraman to create different illusions of height by changing the vantage point. Notice the split trolley lines (*right*). The *Safety Last!* clock set stood atop the Western Costume building up the street.

Although no similar shots are known to exist for *Safety Last!*, this time the studio kept photographic records of some of the stunt sets built for the film (*upper right*). The face of this set appears on the next page.

The set replicates the decorative elements of the Ninth and Broadway Building (*right*) almost exactly. Comedian Willie Best and stuntman Harvey Parry smile from the open window (*left*) as Harold looks on from below. The skimpy mattresses don't look reassuring.

This composite image below shows the full height of the climbing set, and the prominent Eastern Columbia Building (1930) in the background. For reasons to be explained later, the top third-most section of the building is a hollow shell.

EASTERN COLUMBIA   NINTH AND BROADWAY BUILDING

This photo of Brownlow and Gill atop the *Safety Last!* filming site shows two prominent Art Deco buildings constructed in 1930, at the NW and NE corners of 9th and Broadway, which both appear in *Feet First*. The Ninth and Broadway Building stood in for the "real" building during the climb, its 9th Street side facing us in the above left photo. In a scene filmed from the Eastern Columbia Building (*middle frame*), stuntman Harvey Parry tangles with the scaffold on the Broadway side of the corner building, with a view east down 9th Street to the right. The Marsh-Strong Building (1913), which Charlie Chaplin used for a scene in *The New Janitor* (1914) (*right*), appears to the right of the central image above. A modern view of the middle frame appears to the upper right.

Boldly clad in turquoise and gold terracotta, the Zigzag Moderne Eastern Columbia Building became an instant classic. It originally housed two clothing companies under common management, the Eastern Outfitting Company and the Columbia Outfitting Company. Columbia had previously operated from a one-floor corner building at the same site, adjacent to the Majestic Theater. The Eastern has now been converted into lofts, with a swimming pool installed on its roof. Its clock tower remains one of downtown's great architectural icons.

Chaplin, in *The New Janitor*, poking out from the Marsh-Strong Building, with 9th Street in the background.

At left, Bruce Willis stands before the Eastern Columbia Building clock tower during the *Moonlighting* pilot episode. Behind him stand the Ninth and Broadway Building (*arrow*), and the Western Costume Building, used for the clock set from *Safety Last!*

SAFETY LAST! CLOCK BUILDING

This striking photo was taken sometime after City Hall was completed in 1928, but before the two corner Art Deco buildings, prominent in *Feet First*, were built in 1930. The Ninth and Broadway Building now completely obscures the painted Orpheum Theater sign. The clock set from *Safety Last!* and the intermediate climbing set from *Feet First* were built atop the respectively identified buildings. On second glance you might notice something odd about this cityscape. Except for the four items identified above, nothing else extends above the horizon. For more than 50 years, Los Angeles enforced a building height limit of 150 feet (13 stories), resulting in a remarkably flat sky-

UNITED ARTISTS
THEATER TOWER

CITY HALL

ORPHEUM
THEATER SIGN

GAS PLANT
STORAGE TENTS

line. Prior to 1957, the lone exception was granted to City Hall (1928), towering at 454 feet (28 stories). The gas processing plants adjacent to Chinatown were not subject to the law, and the tallest of the massive gas storage tanks stood at 378 feet. For decades, then, in most cityscape photos, only City Hall and the gas tanks rise above the crowd. City planners extolled the height limit, noting that lower density construction reduced congestion and transportation demands, while allowing more parcels to share in rising land values. Starting in 1927 or so, a growing trend developed. Under city plans, it was permissible to construct above the height limit so long as the portion exceeding 150 feet was not habitable. Thus, the eye-grabbing tower for the United Artists Theater, pictured here, is a visibly hollow shell. The beautiful Spanish Gothic theater was financed by United Artists, the studio corporation founded by director D.W. Griffith, and stars Charlie Chaplin, Douglas Fairbanks, and Mary Pickford. The faces of these three stars adorn murals inside the main lobby.

The final phase of the *Feet First* climb was staged atop the Great Republic Life Insurance Building (1923) at 756 Spring Street, at the SE corner of 8th. This beautiful building was one of the many financial institutions along Spring Street that earned it the moniker "the Wall Street of the West." Today, the Great Republic is beautifully appointed with modern lofts.

Looking upward at this precarious filming set (*below middle*) is daunting, to say the least. While Lloyd's crew took every precaution—well, almost every precaution (*see caption at right*)—you have to admire Lloyd's work ethic. Lloyd was a young, carefree bachelor when shooting *Safety Last!*, but by the time he filmed *Feet First*, he was 37 years old, and an extremely wealthy family man. At a time when he could have easily "cheated" by using rear-projection effects, or simply rested on his laurels, Lloyd's dedication to the public and to his craft pushed him to endure yet another rigorous shoot in order to produce another first-rate motion picture.

This back platform, cushioned for a possible fall with thin mattresses (*ellipses above*), did not have *any safety railing* between it and the edge of the building! Given the tight camera angles, a railing would have appeared in the movie frame.

To the left, looking north up Spring Street from the Great Republic Building.

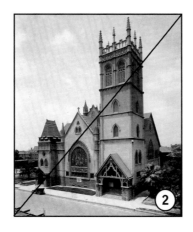

Of the four landmarks visible behind the rooftop painters, only the Trinity Auditorium (1) at 851 S. Grand, shown as it appears in *Bumping Into Broadway* (1919) (*left*), remains standing. The First Congregational Church (2) on Hope Street between 8th and 9th, the domed Hill Street RKO Theater (3) at 8th and Hill, and the Methodist Episcopal Church (4) at 8th and Hope, are all lost. Famed Hal Roach Studios character actor James Finlayson (sans trademark moustache) plays the painter to the far left.

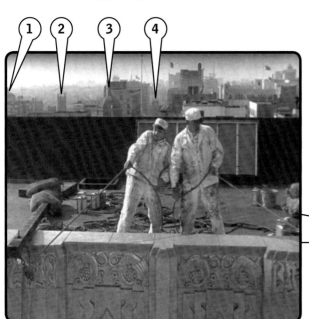

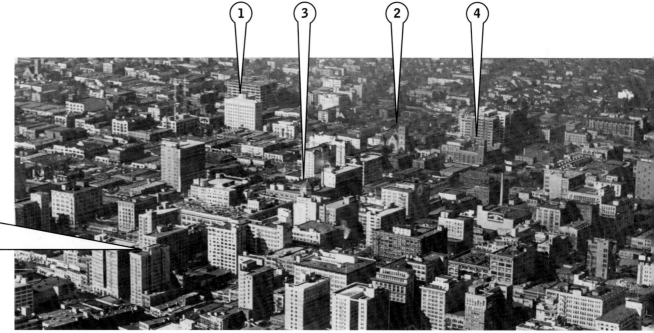

Harold struggles during the final stage of the climb. Behind him, looking north on Spring Street, stand the Van Nuys Building, the Bartlett Building with its three-tier top, and the seventh home to the L.A. Stock Exchange (*ellipse*), and the same three buildings, in reverse order, as they appear in this shot looking south on Spring Street (*insert*) from *Safety Last!* Built in 1959, the protruding 25-story United California Bank Building (now SB Tower Lofts) blocking the view of City Hall (*upper right*), is one of the few buildings built on Spring Street after the 150-foot height restriction (*dashed line*) was lifted. It stands on the SE corner of 6th Street, across the street from the Merchants National Bank, used for the final stage of the *Safety Last!* climb. The modern giant skyscrapers are all built west of the Historic Core.

Harold briefly reaches the rooftop before the effects from a spilled bottle of ether sends him tumbling back over the edge. Behind his head stands a nearly 400 foot tall gas storage tank located near Chinatown. Immediately beside him, to the left, stands the multi-windowed Board of Trade Building (1926), and the Hotel Cecil (1924) at 640 S. Main is to the right. The L.A. Furniture Manufacturing Association was proud to boast that the Cecil, with 700 rooms, was the first major downtown hostelry to be appointed exclusively with locally made furniture, over 4,000 pieces, delivered in over 100 truckloads.

The final set for the climb had not only a façade, but for the first time also had a false rooftop and an interior windowed wall. As Harold pulls himself up along a rapidly unspooling fire house (*right*), we can see the clock tower of the Tower Theater at 8th and Broadway in the background (*top left and middle right*). The tower served as one perch for the battling robots in *Transformers* (2007). Immediately behind the tower is the Hamburger's (May Co.) Building, previously discussed. Though built on only a 50-foot-wide lot, the Tower Theater (*lower right*) was cleverly configured to seat 1,000 people. The Chapman Building stands at the right edge of the two left photos.

Eastern Columbia Tower rises above the 150-foot height limit (*dashed line*).

Beginning at noon on July 26, 1923, Harold's human fly pal Bill Strother climbed the Lane Mortgage Building, pictured at the far left, before a reported crowd of thousands. Strother told the *L.A. Times* he had climbed buildings throughout the U.S. and Canada, but that the conditions for this climb were the most difficult he had ever faced, as the window ledges slant towards the street. Strother's hands were cut and bleeding following the ordeal.

Los Angeles in 2007 (*left*) and circa 1920 (*below*). Over the years, development has migrated west of Olive Street (*dotted line*), away from the Historic Core that centered around Broadway and Spring Street, leaving many core buildings intact. The Los Angeles Athletic Club (1912) at 7th and Olive (*circle*) and the Blackstone Department Store (1917) at 9th and Broadway (*rectangle*) are marked for comparison.

The conclusions to the *Safety Last!* and *Feet First* thrill sequences almost reflect a sign of the times. *Safety Last!* ends satisfyingly, with Harold safely aboard the rooftop in the arms of his love, building conquered, fame assured. Despite the movie's overall happy ending, the *Feet First* sequence ends with a funny but anticlimactic joke. Eyes clenched in fear, Harold clings desperately to a metal window grille, unaware he is only inches off of the ground. Revived by the laughter of passersby, down-to-earth Harold sheepishly retreats, his anonymous ordeal unheralded, the devilish building unconquered.

Though both films were meticulously crafted, the most obvious dissimilarity between *Feet First* and its predecessor was that, for the first time, Harold made a thrill picture using sound, unintentionally causing an entirely different effect. Silent film creates an alternative reality for viewers, both seemingly real, and yet separate and apart, insulated by the silence. Harold's grunts and cries for help during the climb broke this silent spell, making the sequence too uncomfortably real to be seen simply as funny. Reportedly, some theater projectionists actually turned off the sound during the climb in order to compensate.

Feet First received universally good reviews, but for Lloyd it marked the end of an era. Lloyd would make four more feature films during the 1930s, but his can-do, All-American Boy persona became more difficult to play as he approached 40, and was seen as increasingly out of sync by a nation struggling against the Great Depression.

Los Angeles, circa 1922, after the Loews State Theater Building was completed in 1921, but before the Hall of Justice (1925) and City Hall (1928) were constructed. The dotted line marks Olive Street.

Los Angeles, 2008. The dotted line marks Olive Street. The Bradbury Mansion, Hill Street Tunnel, and International Bank Building (*upper left*) are all long gone, but remarkably all of the other buildings used by Lloyd (pictured here) remain.

Epilogue—Safety Last!

Early in *Safety Last!* Harold becomes locked in a laundry truck, prompting his heroic efforts to return to work on time before being fired. At right, a driver gives Harold a lift on Cahuenga Boulevard. The two stores behind Harold, a furniture store and a tire store at 1614 and 1612 Cahuenga, respectively, both appear in Buster Keaton's feature *The Cameraman* (1928) (*middle, right*), as Buster rides a fire engine north up Cahuenga and turns into the fire station across the street.

There is a decent chance this building (scaled by Bill Strother early in the picture) is still standing. Despite numerous clues, the mystery of this most elusive Lloyd location remains unsolved.

Harold is released from the laundry truck beside the same two stores shown above.

1614 and 1612 Cahuenga appear to the left of the vertical lines in every image on this page (arrow). The former furniture store and tire store are now a tattoo parlor and the Velvet Margarita Cantina. The large two-story building on the corner to the right was built in 1926, between the times Lloyd and Keaton filmed here.

As Harold's driver is ticketed above, Harold hastily excuses himself and continues on his mad dash to work. This scene was also filmed on Cahuenga, a bit further north towards the Hollywood Boulevard intersection. The Kwik Lunch at 1626 Cahuenga (to the right of the cop's head) appears above Buster Keaton's head (*above, left*) during a scene from his 1925 feature *Go West*. Buster's cow, Brown Eyes, stands in front of 1628 Cahuenga, the same LINOLEUM store appearing to the left of the cop. The same row of buildings pictured in these two movie frames stand between the vertical lines (*above*) to the far right. The fire hydrant near the cop stood in front of the former joint fire-and-police station on Cahuenga Boulevard.

During *Hot Water*, below, Harold and family race south down Cahuenga past the fire station, and the same fire hydrant (*oval*) that appears in the *Safety Last!* frame above. The fire station and the alley to the south of it appear in several Buster Keaton films.

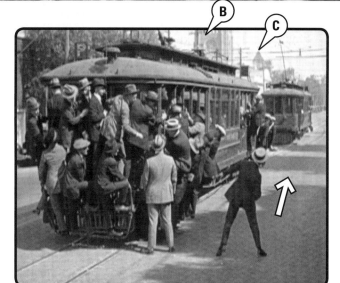

The trolley car appearing here, and during the Larchmont trolley scenes in *For Heaven's Sake*, both have a "P" designation, which stood for the unrelated Pico Boulevard Line. Perhaps in both cases a spare "P" car was made available for Harold to use.

The empty trolley is not running, so Harold attempts to squeeze aboard a trolley on University Avenue (*right*) to return to work. The dome of what was originally called the Los Angeles County Historical Art Museum (later the Museum of Natural History) (A) appears in the background to the left. The circa 1925 aerial view above shows Harold's position on University Avenue (*arrow*) and the museum dome (A).

The USC Bovard Administration Building (B) was dedicated in June 1921. Prior to its addition, the now sprawling USC campus comprised of but a single block, bounded by Watt Way (Hoover), Hellman Way (W. 35th), Trousdale Parkway (University Avenue), and W. 34th Street. The Exposition Park–USC neighborhood was a popular place to film. The near right frame is from the Bobby Dunn short *Hot Foot* (1924), and the middle frame is from Buster Keaton's feature *Seven Chances* (1925). At the far right, the statue of USC mascot Tommy Trojan now stands before the Bovard Building.

Looking north up University Avenue, one can see the USC Bovard (B) and Old Campus (C) buildings.

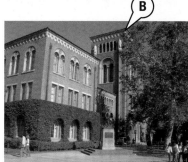

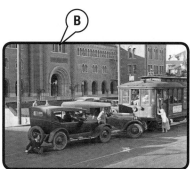

The "new" Shrine Auditorium was dedicated in 1926, the same year Lloyd was initiated into the Shriners' Los Angeles Al Malaikah Temple. The auditorium seats 6,300 people and contains the largest proscenium stage in North America. Lloyd was an active Shriner most of his life, and in 1949, was elected to the Shriners' highest national office, Imperial Potentate.

The frame above looks east down Jefferson Boulevard towards the Marin Apartments (M) located across the street from the original Shrine Auditorium, which burned to the ground on January 12, 1920. The above aerial photo shows the historic fire, the Marin Apartments, a box marking the same build-

BOVARD FIELD

ing as in the movie frame, the trolley corner (*arrow*), the Old Campus Building (C) discussed on the prior page, and Bovard Field, where the football practice scenes from *The Freshman* were filmed.

Harold pretends to faint beside an idle ambulance. After the ambulance scoops him up and races towards the hospital, Harold "recovers" and directs the driver to drop him off at work instead. Below, the ambulance races north up Broadway at 7th Street, identifiable by the unique trolley track intersection. The prominent Hass Building at the corner still stands, but is barely recognizable after a 1970s modernization.

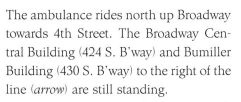

The ambulance rides north up Broadway towards 4th Street. The Broadway Central Building (424 S. B'way) and Bumiller Building (430 S. B'way) to the right of the line (*arrow*) are still standing.

The Bob Hope movie *Never Say Die*, visible on the marquee to the right, premiered in 1939.

Lloyd's Hollywood Studio

Above, left, the studio in Harold's day. The studio remains in use today (*above, center*) under the name Hollywood Center Studios.

This scene from *For Heaven's Sake*, where Harold meets Jobyna Ralston at the rescue mission, was filmed on the Lloyd backlot. Notice the women doing laundry in the background. The tall set behind Harold appears in this aerial view (*below*).

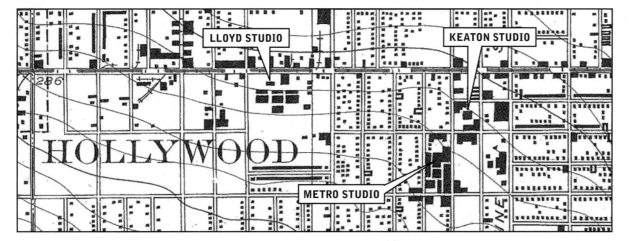

Above, the Lloyd and Keaton studios were located just a few blocks apart. The arrow (C) in front of the Lloyd Studio (*overleaf*) marks where Buster Keaton pulled himself onto the back of a "San Francisco" cable car in *Daydreams* (1922) (*right*).

Overleaf: The Hollywood Metropolitan Studios, along Santa Monica Boulevard near Las Palmas, circa 1923. Lloyd would take over the studio the following year. The Metro Studio appears in the upper-left corner, the Keaton Studio stands off camera to the far left.

Girl Shy (1924)

Released in 1924, *Girl Shy* was Lloyd's first independent production following his amicable departure from the Hal Roach Studios. Harold plays a shy tailor who dreams that his earnest (but unintentionally hilarious) guidebook to attracting women will make him a famous author. Harold befriends a young woman (Jobyna Ralston) on his train ride to meet with publishers. When his book is first rejected, Harold deems himself unworthy of pursuing Jobyna, who reluctantly agrees to marry another man instead. After receiving a generous advance for selling his manuscript as a comic novel, Harold learns Jobyna's fiancé is already married, which sets in motion Harold's breathless race to the church to stop the wedding.

Harold filmed his train arriving at the Santa Fe Depot (*right*), the same station appearing in *Now or Never* (see *Tunnel Visions* chapter). The station was a popular filming location, which Lloyd revisited for his talkie *Movie Crazy* (see later chapter). The towering gas storage tanks looming in the background remained a Los Angeles landmark until they were demolished in 1973. Lloyd filmed near the left tower in *For Heaven's Sake*.

Above is a front view of the Santa Fe Depot. It was built in 1893, and demolished after being damaged from the 1933 Long Beach earthquake. At the top is a view of the site today.

Harold's fictional account, *The Secret of Making Love*, describes his methods for seducing various female prototypes, such as the "Pollyanna" (cut from the film), and the "Vamp." In the fantasy scene to the left, Harold checks off a vanquished "Flapper" from his list.

As shown on the next page, although Harold and Jobyna arrive at the Santa Fe Depot, she surprises him with a goodbye kiss (*near right*), in front of the Southern Pacific Depot a few blocks away! The two depots are identified on the map to the far right.

Other scenes filmed at the Southern Pacific Depot include Stan Laurel's 1923 solo comedy *Mother's Joy* (left), and Douglas Fairbanks's climbing stunt from *When the Clouds Roll By* (1919) (far left, center).

The broad, stately columns of the Southern Pacific Depot on Central Avenue appear behind Harold as he recovers from Jobyna's surprise kiss (right). Below, Harold rushes from the station after Jobyna's departing taxi heading west down 5th Street towards downtown. The extant Rosslyn Hotel (1913) at 5th and Main (R), appears in the background during the scene below. The US Bank Tower, the tallest building on the West Coast, dominates the modern skyline (lower left). At 1,018 feet, the building stands nearly seven times as tall as the 150-foot height limit imposed in L.A. for many decades. I don't think anyone involved with filming this scene could have imagined that the downtown skyline would someday appear this way.

Above, the spot where Harold watches Jobyna drive away, matches the oval to the upper left.

At the upper left, Jobyna arrives in front of the publisher's office (*star*) to wait for news from Harold. The building used is the extant Security Bank building at the NE corner of Hollywood Boulevard and Cahuenga. The (A) in each image marks an alley off of Cahuenga down the street. The alley was employed in Buster Keaton's iconic short comedy *Cops* (1922) (*upper right*), for an amazing stunt where he grabs hold of a passing car with one hand that whisks him out of view. The real estate office of S. Clark Patchin, next to the alley at 1640 Cahuenga (*circle*, *bottom right*) appears behind Mildred Davis and Roy Brooks (*lower left*) during Lloyd's 1921 short comedy *Never Weaken*.

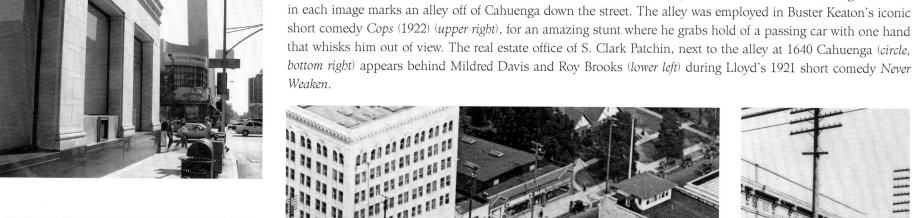

Dejected over the initial rejection of his book, and thinking himself unworthy, Harold decides to break up with Jobyna to spare her the shame. He does so by pretending to be a cad, flirting with a strange woman in Jobyna's presence. This sequence was filmed in Hollenbeck Park, a long narrow park in Boyle Heights east of downtown Los Angeles. Harold first meets the "other woman" (*upper left*) at the north end of Hollenbeck Lake, looking south towards its unique arched bridge. The same bridge was used for Harold's second attempted suicide in *Haunted Spooks* (*left*), and appears prominently during Laurel and Hardy's 1929 talkie short *Men O' War*. The panorama below was made with frames from both movies. The 6th Street Bridge across the park (*right*) appears behind Harold (*rectangle below*). Matching views looking south down the lake appear above at the middle and at the right.

The 6th Street Bridge (*above*) and the arched bridge (*left*) no longer exist.

Standing in the breezeway leading to the small boathouse pavilion (*square left, lower left, and below*), Harold sends the other woman on her way (*upper right*). The stars above and below correspond to the same spot.

This vintage aerial view looks north (N) along the length of Hollenbeck Park, located about two miles east of downtown L.A. The two bridges are now gone, and the dotted lines represent the path of the Golden State Freeway across one corner of the park. At left, a modern view north of the park.

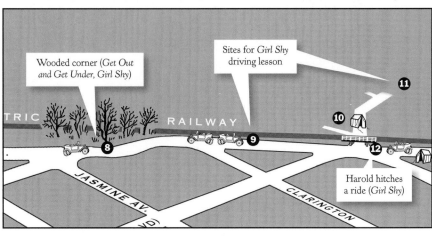

Harold desperately tries to hitch a ride (*left*) so that he can prevent Jobyna's bigamous wedding. All of the shots from this sequence were filmed on or near National Boulevard in Palms.

The dotted lines below mark the elevated road bed of the Pacific Electric tracks running parallel to National/Exposition Boulevard.

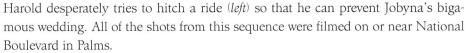

The trees identified above are identical. Both scenes depict a car heading south down National Boulevard, rounding the curve past Jasmine Avenue. (8A) shows Harold passing a motorcycle cop in *Get Out and Get Under*, and (8) shows a student driver in *Girl Shy*.

The subdivision signs in the background (11) (*below*) refer to Castle Avenue, later Castle Heights Avenue, off of National Boulevard east of the Pacific Electric tracks.

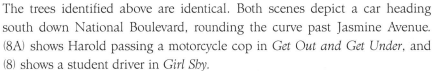

The fits and starts of an oblivious student driver (8), (9), and (11), frustrate Harold, who mistakenly thinks the student is slowing down to give him a ride.

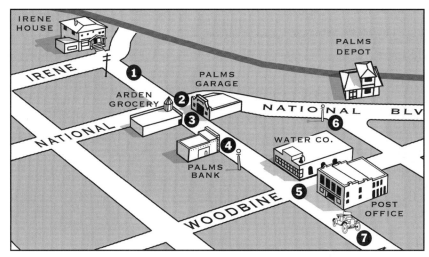

For his race to the altar, Harold unknowingly commandeers a convertible full of bootleg liquor, attracting the attention of a pair of cops. The "Revenuers" chase Harold in Palms, along National Boulevard, running past the Palms Garage on Motor Avenue (2) (*above, left*). Completing the collage is a scene of Harold's former partner Snub Pollard riding a runaway grand piano on wheels (2A) past the garage in *Sold at Auction* (1923). Snub later rides past the Peoples Water Company (5A), the same corner passed by the cops chasing Harold at (5) and (7) (*below, right*), and that also appears, as mentioned previously, in such Hal Roach comedies as *Boxing Gloves* (1929), and *Big Red Riding Hood* (1925).

The Palms Garage appears in Stan Laurel's *Hustling for Health* (1919) (2B) (*left*), in Roscoe Arbuckle's *The Hayseed* (1919) (2C) (*lower left*), and in dozens of Hal Roach Studios comedies. The back of the Palms Garage appears during scenes from *Grandma's Boy*. Stan is running past the Arden Grocery (3).

Though "modernized," the corner Palms Garage building still stands today.

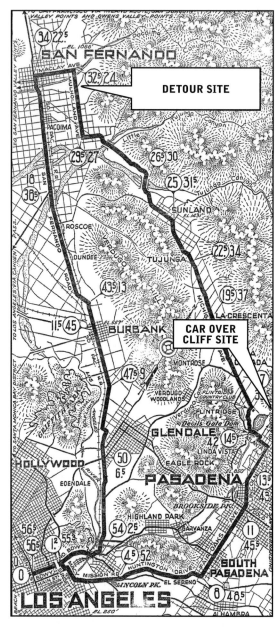

Temporarily evading the Revenuers, Harold confronts a road block that sends him on a detour across a bumpy dirt road (*upper left*). This setting, located by Paul Ayers, is in San Fernando, where Harold drives northwest along paved Foothill Boulevard (formerly Mulholland Avenue) before turning at a road block onto Arroyo Street, at the time a dirt road. The modern view above shows that the crest near Vaughn Street has been graded flat to accommodate construction. Harold's detour site appears on the 1922 Auto Club map (*right*), while the scene where the car tumbles over an embankment (discussed on the next page) appears to the right.

1922 Automobile Club of Southern California map.

Harold leaves Mulholland for the dirt road that would become Arroyo Street. The extant Southern California Edison twin power lines running parallel to Mulholland appear prominently in all of the shots. The 1927 USGS topologic map for Pacoima (not shown) confirms the location of the dirt road and the route of the power lines.

These scenes were filmed about two miles north of the Pasadena Rose Bowl, beside the Arroyo Seco (*circle, right*) north of the Devil's Gate Dam, and across the arroyo from the former Flintridge County Club.

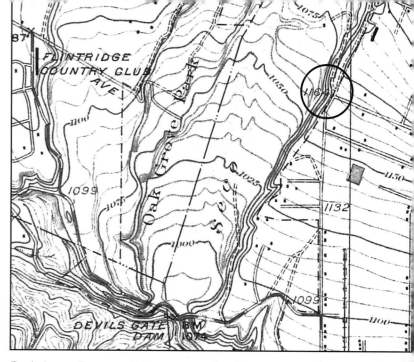

Paul Ayers discovered these scenes by first noticing what turned out to be the back of the Devil's Gate Dam in the distance as Harold's car plummets over an embankment (*rectangle, below*). The steep dirt road climbing out of the arroyo (*upper left*) is now called Explorer Road. As Harold labors to restart the car (*lower left*), we can see the bed of the arroyo behind him, and the site where today stands the California Institute of Technology Jet Propulsion Laboratory (*lower middle*). At the left, Harold chases after a car at a four-way intersection beside the arroyo. (A) points south down Windsor Avenue, (B) points east on Ventura Street, (C) points north up Explorer Road, and (D) points north up Arroyo Boulevard.

Stealing a horse, Harold gallops up Main Street from the corner of Culver Boulevard (B), before falling off beside a vacant lot (A). This single block of Main Street, located steps away from the Roach Studios, appears in dozens of Roach comedies, including this early appearance of Oliver Hardy and Stan Laurel in the 1927 two-reeler *Duck Soup* (B1). A modern view of the corner appears above.

Losing the horse, Harold next grabs a ride aboard a Culver City fire truck (*right*) (D). The town's original movie theater (C1) was replaced by the landmark six-story Culver Building (C) in 1924, shortly after Harold filmed here. The fire department building on Van Buren Place (D) is still standing. To the upper right, middle, Laurel and Hardy (*oval*) walk towards the fire station in *We Faw Down* (1928).

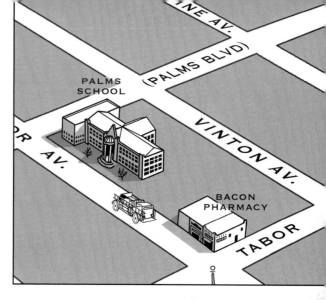

A view of the Palms School (*above*) from the Our Gang comedy *Old Gray Hoss* (1928).

While Harold struggles to climb aboard, the fire truck races up Motor Avenue in Palms, past the Bacon Pharmacy at the corner of Tabor Street (with stunt double) (*below center, right, and modern view, lower right*), and the Palms Elementary School (*above*). A November 1923 news account reports that Lloyd was injured during filming when the fire-hose nozzle slipped from his hands and hit him between the eyes. The original Palms Elementary School was remodeled during the 1930s, but sits at the same site.

The front of the Palms School auditorium (*oval, lower left*) appears in this shot of Wheezer, from the Our Gang comedy *Bouncing Babies* (1929), returning home from the hospital after asking the nurses there to send his annoying baby brother back to heaven. Wheezer crosses the busy street by breaking a light bulb, tricking drivers into stopping to check their tires long enough for him to cross.

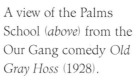

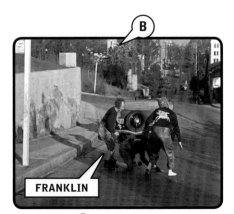

The tower to Castle Glengarry (B) (*above*), appears in this view looking east down Franklin towards Vine, taken from the Three Stooges comedy *Three Little Pigskins* (1934).

Physician and financier Dr. A.G.R. Schloesser built two fabulous estates on Argyle Avenue: Castle Glengarry (B) in 1908, and Castle Sans Souci (A) in 1914. The doctor later sold Glengarry to silent film actor Sessue Hayakawa. Sans Souci appears during several scenes in the Charlie Chaplin–Marie Dressler film *Tillie's Punctured Romance* (1914) (*above*). The two castles are lost to history.

The oval in the *Girl Shy* frame below, and in the photo above, marks the same pillar standing at the NW corner of Argyle and Franklin. (C) points south down Argyle in each image.

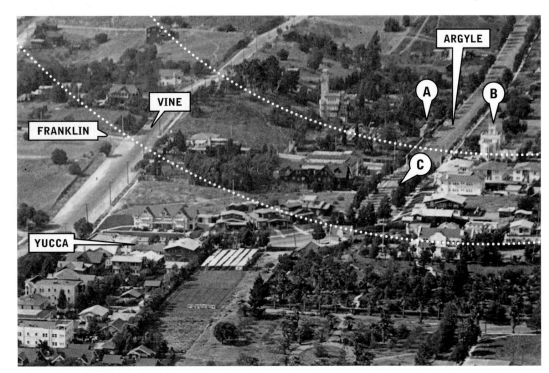

This 1920 aerial view shows the intersection of Vine Street and Franklin Avenue, and the route of the Pacific Electric Railway running from Vine to Franklin along the curved block of Yucca Street/Argyle Avenue. Harold filmed the scenes on the next page, from many different angles, along this curved block connecting Vine and Franklin. Today, the Hollywood Freeway (*dotted line*) cuts a wide swath across the way.

Harold's adventure on a runaway trolley car was filmed from every possible vantage point as the car travelled from Franklin to Vine along the curved stretch of Yucca/Argyle. A few of the different viewpoints from the movie are shown here.

Above, the tracks curve south, then west, as Argyle merges into Yucca.

Above, Harold rides south down Vine after turning from the SE corner of Yucca and Vine.

Above, this view looks east down Yucca as Argyle merges into Yucca from the left.

Today, the SE corner of Yucca and Vine is home to the Capitol Record Building, built in 1956. The building is 150 feet tall, to comply with the Los Angeles height restrictions, then in effect. At night the tower lights atop the building blink out "Hollywood" in Morse code. The arrow above corresponds to the arrow on the left movie frame.

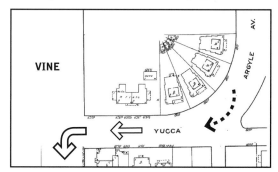

This view looks due east down Yucca as Harold falls through the soft convertible roof of a passing car.

Below, the arrows on this map correspond to the Lloyd movie frames on this page.

After dropping inside a hapless man's convertible, Harold carjacks the vehicle by pressing the man's foot down on the gas pedal. This view above looks west down Sunset Boulevard. The oval at the back marks a "Y" split in the trolley tracks at Sunset and Gardner, discussed further on. The Sunset Building, at 7441 Sunset Boulevard (*box, above*), still stands (*above, right*), near Gardner Street. Harold later races by the Sunset Building on a motorbike (*box, above center*). Its arched doorway (D) is marked in each image above.

The oval (*left and right*) marks the same corner of the Johnny Grant Building.

Above, the car drives east down Hollywood Boulevard past Orange Drive. The palm trees on the left corner stand in the front of the home of Mary Moll, an early Hollywood commercial developer and subdivider, who donated a strip of land across her property that became Highland Avenue. Her home, the first large residence built on the street, was later demolished as the site for the landmark Roosevelt Hotel (*right*), which opened in 1927, and hosted the inaugural 1929 Academy Awards ceremony. Grauman's Chinese Theater, opening in 1927, now stands to the right of Harold's car. The oval above marks the east corner of what is now called the Johnny Grant Building (discussed further), which still stands today (*oval, right middle*). The trees to the far right stand before the Garden Court Apartments (discussed further).

The Garden Court Apartments, at 7021 Hollywood Boulevard (*left*), opened in 1919. The opulent residential hotel was reportedly the home of many stars, including John Gilbert, Rudolph Valentino, and Lillian Gish, and in later years Marilyn Monroe. The property fell on hard times and was shut down in 1980. Transients and squatters vandalized the vacant place, earning it the nickname "Hotel Hell." Despite protests from preservationists, it was demolished in 1984. The short-lived Hollywood Entertainment Museum built on the site is now a gym.

"H.P. REHBEIN" SIGN IS ON THIS COVERED WALL

Harold's car was heading east in the prior shot, yet here (*above*), it is heading west when the cop comes over to chat. The trees on the left, in the background, stand before the Garden Court Apartments. In the background to the right, the H. P. Rehbein Richfield gas station stands on the SW corner of Sycamore and Hollywood Boulevard. The distinctive white service station sign (HP) appears in each image on this page. A five-story office building replaced the corner gas station in 1925, and three additional stories were added in 1929. The oval at the back marks the east corner of the extant Johnny Grant Building.

The Rehbein gas station (*box*) also appears in this concluding shot from *Why Worry?* (*left*), and down the street as Buster Keaton exits his bank vault front door in *Sherlock Jr.* (*right*) (compare *box* to photo *above*).

Above, as the cop tickets the driver for speeding, Harold sneaks off on the cop's motorcycle. The car is once more facing east! This frame and the modern view above both look east down Hollywood Boulevard from Sycamore Avenue. The palm trees in the movie frame (P) stand in the front of the Mary Moll residence, now the site of the Roosevelt Hotel. The ovals mark the extant east corner of the Johnny Grant Building (discussed below). The Christie Hotel building (C), now a Scientology center, stands in the distance.

At the beginning of his short comedy *I Do* (*far right*), Harold crosses Hollywood Boulevard from in front of the Garden Court Apartments heading towards the Garden Court Garage building. The structure was two separate buildings configured with a common façade featuring nine similar arches. The surviving retail building to the left, now called the Johnny Grant Building, has five arches in the front. The other four arches shown here (*far right*) comprise the front of the garage, which was demolished to build a larger garage. This modern view and the movie frame to the right recreate the original nine-arch façade.

The nine arches of the Johnny Grant Building/Garden Court Garage appear to the left of the man in this shot from the Carter DeHaven comedy *Christmastime* (1922) (*left*), and in the composite view below.

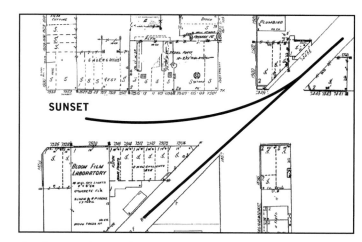

Rewinding a moment, this earlier movie frame above shows another view of Harold racing in the car, this time west down Sunset Boulevard towards Sierra Bonita Avenue. The (A) above and below marks the same Van de Kamp's Dutch Bakery, a chain of bakeries identified with blue rooftop windmills. The box above and below marks the same group of buildings.

As discussed more fully in the *Never Weaken* chapter, Lloyd filmed frequently along the block of Sunset between Sierra Bonita and Gardner, pictured above. The trolley line along west Sunset ran for only a few blocks before merging at Gardner, with the main line running diagonally up to Hollywood Boulevard.

Below, Harold speeds east by motorcycle down Sunset Boulevard past Gardner Street, and a distinctive "Y" trolley track intersection. The arch doorway at 7507 Sunset appears below (*oval*), and in *Never Weaken* (*left*) and still stands today (*lower right*).

Harold avoids blocked traffic at the Ca-huenga Public Market, on the SW corner of Selma (*right*), by riding across the sidewalk. Although it has been heavily remodeled, I believe the same building still stands at the corner (*far right*). The market also appears to the rear during a scene from *Hot Water* (*below*).

SEE BUNKER HILL CHAPTER FOR THESE SCENES

Harold crashes the motorbike, then commandeers a horse-drawn wagon. Many wagon scenes were filmed downtown atop Bunker Hill at Third and Grand, as discussed in the *Bunker Hill* chapter. After leaving Bunker Hill, Harold magically appears on Main Street in Culver City, terrorizing this poor cyclist (*middle, below*). The arrows below all point in the same relative direction. Harold's wagon rides past where Harold fell off of a different horse earlier in the chase (*lower left*).

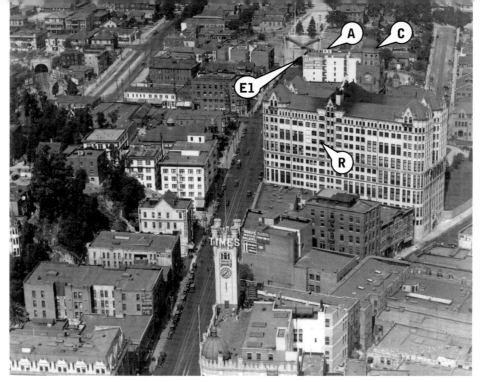

Back from Culver City, Harold chases the cyclist through the south entrance of the Broadway Tunnel (E) (*above*). The aerial photo (*near right*) portrays how Broadway looked at the time of filming. In 1923, the six-story Alhambra Hotel (A) was moved 120 feet closer to the tunnel entrance (E1) to make way for the Hall of Justice (J) (*far right*), completed in 1925, at the corner of Temple and Broadway. Given the timing and setting, the men pictured in the foreground of (E) could be real workers involved with either moving the hotel (A) or constructing the hall (J). During the early 1920s, the Hall of Records (R), the County Court House (C), and the Hall of Justice (J) comprised the Civic Center core before the new City Hall opened in 1928. Photo (E2) (*far right*) provides a direct view of the tunnel. The Hall of Justice remains standing, but has been vacant since the 1994 Northridge earthquake. The tunnel (E2), the hotel (A), and even the hill were all lost to make way for the Hollywood (101) Freeway. The top five floors of the hall (J) comprised the county jail, while the lower floors held court rooms and offices for the county sheriff, district attorney, and coroner. Mobster Bugsy Siegel served time here, as did Robert Mitchum in 1947 for marijuana possession. The 1944 Chaplin paternity suit, and the Charles Manson and Sirhan Sirhan murder trials were held here, while Marilyn Monroe and Robert Kennedy were autopsied in the basement morgue.

Harold and the cyclist exit (X) from the other end of the Broadway Tunnel (*right*).

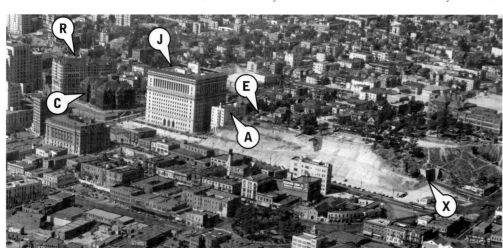

The length of the Broadway Tunnel, (E) to (X), appears in this 1930s aerial photo to the left. The view to the right shows a wider view of the tunnel's north end. The County Court House (C) to the left is being demolished, as the clock tower has already been removed. The Hall of Records (R) came down in 1973.

To the left, Harold races south down Broadway from 8th Street. Behind him to the left is the Hamburger's Department Store, and beside him two vertical signs read "Talley's" and "Theater," both visible in the background during his *Safety Last!* climb (*below left*). To the right, a modern view north up Broadway looking toward 8th Street.

For *Heaven's Sake* (*near left*) and *Girl Shy* (*below*) contain numerous scenes filmed on Broadway near the "Y" intersection at 10th Street, also appearing in *Safety Last!* (*bottom left*). A few examples appear here, with the low rise Western Costume Co. Property Department building (WC) identified in each image below. The dome tower of the Examiner Building appears directly below.

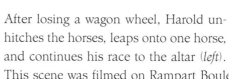

Harold continues to race south down Broadway, past 10th Street, and beside the Los Angeles Examiner Building on the SW corner of Broadway and 11th Street (*top left and center*). The Blackstone's sign so prominent in *Safety Last!* appears in the far background (*oval*).

This frame to the right was also filmed beside the Examiner Building, but with a different view that shows the extant Los Angeles Railway Building, on the NE corner of 10th and Broadway, directly behind Harold's head.

After losing a wagon wheel, Harold unhitches the horses, leaps onto one horse, and continues his race to the altar (*left*).

This scene was filmed on Rampart Boulevard by the NW corner of Third Street. The bungalow one up from the corner still stands (*below*). It also appears in the background of scenes from *For Heaven's Sake*, which were filmed going up and down Rampart. In the upper left corner of the left-hand movie frame (*box*) stands the formal stone fence

Left, the front of the McKinley Mansion.

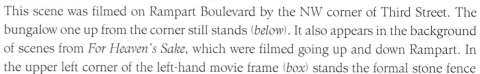

and back corner wing of the stately McKinley Mansion that once stood on the SE corner of Third and Lafayette Park Place. The mansion appears in further detail in the *Hot Water* chapter.

A Hollywood Home PhotoBeam

The mansion depicted in the movie as the Buckingham Estate (*above left*) was known in real life as the Holmby House. The estate belonged to retail magnate Arthur Letts, owner of Bullock's Department Store. The elaborate front gardens (*below*) appear as Harold runs off carrying Jobyna over his shoulder. The Letts Estate also appears in the 1926 Harry Langdon comedy *Soldier Man* (*above right*).

At left, Harold halts the wedding in the nick of time. The possibly apocryphal story goes that this ending inspired the finale of *The Graduate* (1967).

To the right, Harold sets Jobyna down so that he may propose marriage, leading to a happy fadeout. Given the unique landscaping depicted, I'm convinced this scene was filmed looking south down Beverly Drive in Beverly Hills, from near the corner of Sunset. In the background (*oval*) lie the steps leading down the east side of Will Rogers Memorial Park onto Beverly Drive. Lloyd also filmed *A Sailor-Made Man* at this park.

Hot Water (1924)

Hot Water is best known for its famous set pieces, including Harold's attempt to ride a crowded street car while carrying armloads of groceries and a live turkey, and Harold's disastrous inaugural outing in his new car, with his pesky in-laws in tow. The film opens with bachelor Harold vowing to his friend that he'll never fall for "a pair of soft-boiled eyes." No sooner said than done, Harold trips over Jobyna and succumbs completely to her ocular charms. Their encounter takes place in front of the Kaniwald Apartments, located at 1214 S. Lake Street.

Harold and Jobyna meet beside the Kaniwald Apartments.

Is it me, or does the groom in the opening scene look like Stephen Colbert's grandfather? This was filmed along Lafayette Park Place, discussed later.

A year after meeting, Harold and Jobyna are now newlyweds. When asked to pick up "a few" things on the way home, Harold ends up winning a live turkey at the market. With his arms full of packages and the turkey, Harold's ride home on the crowded trolley is an epic sequence of discomfort and embarrassment.

Harold takes Jobyna and his unwelcome in-laws out for a maiden voyage in his new car. The misadventures begin when Harold asks Jobyna to fix his bowtie for him. Her loving gaze distracts Harold from the road.

Above, Harry Langdon in *Saturday Afternoon*.

Above, the sign reading "Next Sunday is Mother's Day."

To the right, Harold plows through the intersection towards the extant Fountain Apartments building at 4914 Fountain Avenue.

Above, traveling west down Fountain Avenue, the car approaches the former University Baptist Church at the NW corner of Edgemont (now Hope International Bible Fellowship). When the church was built in 1921, the corner lot was vacant, as seen here. The church was remodeled in 1930, and an addition was built on the corner lot. The same church appears (*left*) during early scenes of Harry Langdon's Mack Sennett production *Saturday Afternoon* (1926). The drug store building on the opposite corner still stands. The church corner billboard (*below left*) proclaims "Next Sunday is Mother's Day [May 11, 1924]," meaning this sequence was filmed sometime during the work week of April 28–May 2, 1924.

The odd panorama above joins Larry Fine of the Three Stooges from *Pop Goes the Easel* (1935) with Harold and crew in 1924, showing the former Richfield gas station at the NE corner of Larchmont Boulevard and W. 1st Street. The Stooges' film contains many scenes filmed in Larchmont Village. The gas station site, a longtime fixture on Larchmont, is now a branch of the Bank of America. To the immediate right is another panorama of the corner, this time from the 1928 Weiss Brothers production of Hairbreadth Harry in *Rudolph's Revenge*. To the far right, Harry Langdon poses at the same corner in *His Marriage Wow* (1925). The house in the background at 101 N. Gower Street (H) still stands.

As the policeman instructs Harold how to make a proper left turn, the extant home at 108 S. Larchmont Boulevard appears in the background.

Situated at the SE corner of 3rd Street  and S. Lafayette Park Place (LPP), this 1915 French-Renaissance style home was later known as the McKinley Mansion, for the family that lived there from 1945 to 1986. Declared a historic monument, the green tile-roofed mansion survived an illegally attempted demolition on New Year's Eve in 1988. After ambitious plans to relocate the mansion fell through, the boarded-up home burned down in 1994, killing two transients within. The corner site is now home to a pre-school. Above, the mansion appears behind Poodles Hanneford in *Help Wanted* (1928).

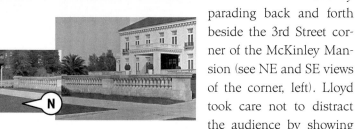

Lloyd filmed much of the drive with his in-laws by parading back and forth beside the 3rd Street corner of the McKinley Mansion (see NE and SE views of the corner, left). Lloyd took care not to distract the audience by showing too much of the mansion.

Above, the 3rd Street corner of the McKinley in Harry Langdon's *The First 100 Years* (1924).

Above, Lloyd chases a motorcycle cop north (N) towards the McKinley Mansion corner.

This aerial view (*right*) looks north (N) up tree-lined LPP to the left, once lined with stately homes, narrow Benton Place in the middle, and Rampart Boulevard (the filming site later used in *For Heaven's Sake*) to the right. The black box (L) marks a vacant lot explained on the next page. Once quite irregular, and unlike this photo, 3rd Street did not traverse the west side of LPP when Lloyd filmed here. Now completely crammed with apartment blocks, LPP is an unusually wide street that is just two blocks long. With "T" intersections at each end, the short street discouraged through traffic when filming, while the extra street width made it easy to film traveling shots alongside an actor's moving car. As such, LPP was a convenient and popular place to film.

Aerial detail of Lloyd's filming area *(arrow, below)*. At the time 3rd Street was disjointed, and did not cross the west side of LPP.

Directly across the street from the McKinley Mansion, from 323 to 267 Lafayette Park Place (LPP) *(represented by arrows)*, Lloyd filmed the following scenes: the groom running to church *(right and bottom)*; Harold unaware of

an oncoming laundry truck *(lower left)*; the truck spilling laundry on Harold's mother-in-law *(upper right)*; and the family playing chase with a motorcycle *(upper left)*. The two boxes below both mark common features of the 323 and 315 homes appearing in two different scenes. The view east across the then-vacant lot (L) *(bottom, middle)* reveals the back of the extant apartment at 349 Rampart, and the front *(oval)* of the extant duplex at 358-360 Benton Place *(lower right)*. Oil derricks once populated the area; some stood just two blocks east on S. Coronado Street. Above, the mansion appears behind Poodles Hanneford in *Help Wanted* (1928).

McKINLEY, AT SE CORNER OF 3RD AND LPP

FRONT OF 349 RAMPART

BACK OF 349 RAMPART   OIL DERRICKS

358–360 BENTON PLACE

Harold's woes continue when his car is struck, causing a traffic jam at 3rd Street and Utah Avenue (now Broadway Street) in Santa Monica. The corner building (*above*) is known as the Keller Block, constructed in 1893, which sits at the south end of what is now the Third Street Promenade, a pedestrian mall. The view below shows the Utah (Broadway) side of the building, including the circular arches and marquee for the Santa Monica Hotel.

Looking northeast, the circa 1920 aerial view of Santa Monica to the left shows the intersection of 3rd and Utah as detailed above. The G.G. Bundy Garage and Studebaker dealership at the SE corner appears above. The prominent tree-line road running across the aerial view is Wilshire Boulevard, north of which is scarcely developed.

Corresponding views up 3rd Street and up the Third Street Promenade (*above*).

SEE *BUNKER HILL* CHAPTER FOR THIS SCENE

Harold pushes the car from the Santa Monica intersection, only to lose it down a hill. This sequence is discussed in the chapter on *Bunker Hill*.

 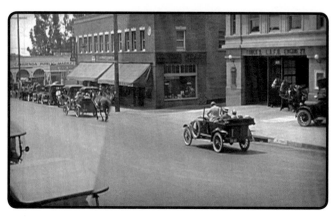 

Jumping from Bunker Hill to Hollywood, in the center frame above, Harold and family race past the L.A.F.D. Engine Company No. 27 and L.A.P.D. Police Station No. 6, located at 1629 N. Cahuenga Boulevard, towards the Cahuenga Public Market (appearing in *Girl Shy*). Buster Keaton filmed in front of this fire station for his initial comedy feature *Three Ages* (1923) (*above, left*). A modern view appears above (*right*).

The station appearing in the film (*above*) closed in 1930, and was later demolished. A replacement station, which is now a museum, opened in 1930 at 1355 N. Cahuenga.

This circa 1923 view (*left*) looks south down Cahuenga from Hollywood Boulevard. Buster Keaton filmed scenes here for seven different films. The oval at the far back marks the enclosed film stage for the Buster Keaton Studio at Lillian Way and Eleanor. The center rectangle marks the Metro Studio across the street from Keaton. The far right rectangle marks the greenhouse-style stages of the Hollywood General Studios, where Lloyd filmed and produced his independent feature films, including *Hot Water*.

The Freshman

(1925)

Harold plays a naïve college freshman who yearns to become popular by mimicking the hokey mannerisms of fictitious movie star Lester Laurel. While thinking himself admired for spouting phrases like "I'm just a regular fellow," Harold becomes a laughing stock instead, secretly ridiculed by everyone on campus. Only the "girl," played by Jobyna Ralston, sees Harold's true character. Jobyna encourages Harold to just be himself, and inspired by her love, he proves his mettle by winning the big football game.

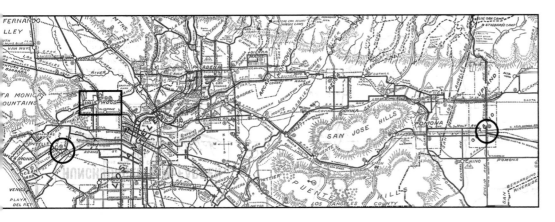

Harold looks on enviously from the Ontario Southern Pacific train station, just east of Euclid, at the jubilant reception for a college "hero." The *Los Angeles Times* erroneously reported on November 14, 1924, that Lloyd was filming a hair-raising railroad sequence in the Ontario area. The rail line is still active, but the station no longer exists.

Below, a similar view today looking west down the tracks at Ontario.

Paul Ayers discovered that most, but not all, of the train arrival scenes early in the picture were staged at the Southern Pacific depot in Ontario, California (*right circle above*), over 40 miles east of Hollywood (*rectangle above*). But as we will see, Paul also discovered a few other train arrival scenes were filmed near Hollywood, in Culver City (*left circle above*).

"I'm just a regular fellow ~ step right up and call me 'Speedy'"

Above, one of Harold's catch phrases.

Lloyd apparently decided he needed more reaction shots taken of the disapproving dean beside the train station. But Lloyd did not return to Ontario for the additional scenes, filming beside the Pacific Electric station in nearby Culver City instead. The station stood at Venice Boulevard (*oval, below*), immediately around the corner from Main Street, which Harold traversed on horseback during the climactic race in *Girl Shy*. Only confusing matters, by 1950 the Culver station was relocated a block further east (without its front arcade) to Culver Junction (*star, below*), where Venice meets Culver Boulevard. The nomadic Culver station no longer exists.

The Culver City station appears within the oval (*left*) and below. The station was later relocated to the star (*left*).

The dean (*top left*) arrives at the Ontario Southern Pacific station. Above, the same scowling dean appears in front of the Culver City station.

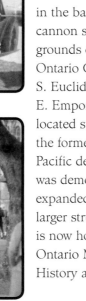

During these two scenes filmed in Ontario (*left*), you can see a civil war cannon in the background. The cannon stood on the grounds of the original Ontario City Hall, on S. Euclid Avenue at E. Emporia Street, located steps away from the former Southern Pacific depot. City Hall was demolished and expanded into a much larger structure that is now home to the Ontario Museum of History and Art.

The aerial photo at the lower left shows the cannon site (*oval*) between the former City Hall to the right, and the small former Chamber of Commerce building standing on an island in the middle of Euclid Street (*square*). The train station lies just off camera to the right of the aerial view.

The Chamber of Commerce building appears behind Harold in this scene filmed at the station below (the cannon appears as well [*oval*]), and on the postcard to the bottom right, which also shows City Hall. The Chamber of Commerce building was erected in 1910, and demolished in 1967.

Exposition Park and the original wing of the museum, both formally opened to the public on November 6, 1913, the day after William Mulholland opened the Owens River aqueduct.

A hungry mob sets out for the soda fountain, at Harold's involuntary treat. The group is walking along the west end of the sunken rose garden in Exposition Park, towards the entrance steps of the Los Angeles County Natural History Museum (*upper left*). The matching aerial view (*above, right*) shows ongoing construction of the new wing to the museum that opened in late 1925. These scenes were filmed within the shadow of the Los Angeles Memorial Coliseum, which opened in 1923.

Spotting Harold as an easy mark, the college cad abuses Harold's goodwill by inviting an increasingly larger crowd of students to join them for free sundaes, Harold's treat. The crowd accumulates alongside the former State Exposition Building (Bowen Hall) at Exposition Park, now the site of the modernistic Museum of Science and Industry, situated due north of the Los Angeles Memorial Coliseum.

Eager to make the team, Harold stands in for a broken tackling dummy, receiving hundreds of blows during practice (*left*). His fortitude eventually impresses the coach (*bottom center*). To the rear stands the entrance to Trojan Hall.

USC track and field coach Dean Cromwell, the "maker of champions," poses here in 1925 with an intercollegiate track trophy in front of Trojan Hall (*near left*). Lloyd replaced the word "Trojans" with "Tate" during filming.

The training sessions were filmed on the University of Southern California campus, at the former Bovard Athletic Field, at the SW corner of W. 34th Street and University Avenue (now Trousdale Parkway). The field honored the Rev. George Finley Bovard, elected USC's fourth president in 1913. The tower of the adjacent Old College Building, now demolished, is identified with an oval in each image. House (A) stood at 829 W. 34th and is now the site of the United University Church. The house to the left of (A) (not pictured) still stands, as do the fourth and fifth houses to the right of (A).

Harold kicks a football backwards over his head, at the corner of the locker room (*upper right*). Buster Keaton used the same setting for sports scenes in his feature films *Three Ages* (1923) and *College* (1927), pictured above.

The tower of the former USC Old College Building appears below.

The Harold Lloyd Motion Picture Sound Stage, part of the USC School of Cinematic Arts, now stands on W. 34th along the former west border of Bovard Field.

THE MEMORIAL STADIUM, UNIVERSITY OF CALIFORNIA, BERKELEY, CALIF.   206

© STANLEY A. PILTZ   5A-H936

Scenes for *The Freshman* were filmed on November 22, 1924, at California Memorial Stadium in Berkeley during the annual "Big Game" between the University of California and Stanford University. The 1924 Big Game, which ended in a 20-20 tie, was only the second Big Game held at the new stadium, which opened in 1923, in time to host the 1923 Big Game. Following the 1924 season, the odd-year games have been played at Stanford and the even-year games have been played at Cal. The trees in the near foreground have grown so thick that it is no longer possible to replicate the view. Berkeley's landmark Campanile clock tower overlooks the stadium in each view.

The Lloyd Studio had to act quickly to film crucial scenes during the brief halftime during the Big Game. The remaining football scenes were filmed using extras at the Rose Bowl in Pasadena.

Harold rests during a break while filming at the Rose Bowl (*right*).

Above, Cal Stadium as it appeared before its 2011 renovation.

The Cal Bears rooting section appears here behind Harold in 1924 (*right*), and during a contemporary game (*far right*).

For Heaven's Sake (1926)

"A man with a mansion—a miss with a mission." This opening title card pretty much tells the story. Harold plays an oblivious millionaire who turns philanthropic after meeting Jobyna, a missionary who works in the Bowery with her father. Harold devises a clever scheme to bring the local thugs to church. He runs through the tenderloin, taunting and kicking the locals. Enraged, they chase him straight back to the mission. The church thrives, and Harold and Jobyna are set to be married, selecting five former derelicts as groomsmen. Harold's wealthy friends kidnap him on his wedding day to prevent him from "making a mistake." As a result, the groomsmen believe Harold has abandoned them, and drown their sorrows in booze. Harold escapes and in a rousing sequence filmed aboard a double-decker bus, shepherds the drunken quintet to the church on time.

Charlie Chaplin filmed the rooftop chase from *The Kid* (1921) along Ducommun Street, with the Amelia Street School (A) in the background. Production stills suggest Lloyd filmed a deleted scene of him being mugged on Jackson Street, a block south of Ducommun. The gas storage tank behind Chaplin appears in Harold's photo behind the two new tanks in the foreground. The oval marks part of the tank on Jackson Street discussed on the next page.

Early in the movie, Harold's limousine is destroyed in an accident. Barely lifting an eyebrow, Lloyd leaves the wreck behind, strolls into a fancy auto dealership, and pays cash for a new car that he drives right out of the shop. Above, this shot prior to the accident shows Harold's car turning east from Rampart Boulevard onto 4th Street. The tall Villa d'Este Apartments, at 401 Rampart, stand in the background.

No sooner does Harold drive off with his new car than the police commandeer it to chase criminals. The car stalls near a gas storage tank (B) and is demolished by an oncoming train. The crash site (A) was at the east end of Commercial Street.

The Bradbury Mansion (C), home to the Rolin Studio, was located only a few blocks from the crash site (A) and the gas storage tank (B).

Harold's car stalls on Jackson Street, east of Center Street ((B) *upper right*). The side of the gas storage tank identified on the prior page appears down the street (*oval*). The building housed a compression plant for the natural gas stored in the tank. Charlie Chaplin used this same block of Jackson Street (B1) to film the early factory exteriors for *Modern Times* (1936). The plant was rebuilt in the 1950s, and appears somewhat different in this modern view (B2).

After a small accident, Harold thoughtlessly hands Jobyna's father a large check, thinking nothing further of the event. Jobyna and her dad use the money to establish a permanent mission, named in Harold's honor. Harold and his wealthy chum discover Harold's unintentional philanthropy while reading the morning headlines. Harold buys and trashes all the newspapers at hand, and storms off to confront the missionaries.

Above, Harold buys a newspaper in front of the Modena Apartments, located at 661 Shatto Place, south of Wilshire Boulevard. The semi-legible apartment name on the wall was enough of a clue.

To the right, Harold and his friend learn that Harold is the unintentional benefactor of a mission named in his honor. The corner behind them (*box*) is the same corner in the images to the upper left and below. The house behind Harold at the end of the street still stands at 4030 W. 7th Street (*right*).

To the left, Harold trashes the embarrassing news. Behind him stands 673 Shatto Place. Today, the brick detail on the front of the apartment has been stuccoed over.

Harold returned to New High Street, where he filmed *From Hand to Mouth*, to film two different sequences in the movie. (The (N) on each image points north.) At right, an angry mob chases an innocent man, confusing him for Harold. Harold leaps from a taxi cab in front of the mob, so they will chase him instead back to the church. The innocent man is turning the corner west onto Ord Street. The Lipton Tea sign across the street (*oval*) appears in a later scene as Harold's "friend" taunts him (*oval, top center*).

The same viewpoint of this movie frame (*above*) was captured in this vintage photo looking south down New High Street towards the corner of Ord Street.

Later on, Harold races by horse wagon south down New High Street past the same corner of Ord Street (*right*). A modern view of the extant corner building appears to the far right.

To the middle right, Harold runs south down New High Street to catch up with the mob, past the same corner of Ord Street pictured above. Later in the movie (*right*), Harold races a wagon north up New High past the same corner of Ord. A modern view appears to the far right. The box highlights a matching detail in the two movie frames.

Harold begins rounding up his five drunken groomsmen inside the Biltmore Hotel. His first challenge is to send them through the revolving door (*above*). Because the joke required viewers to focus on the actors and the spinning door, nothing more of the hotel exterior appears in the movie. This production shot (*right*) shows the Olive Street entrance of the hotel facing Pershing Square. (Two cameramen are filming side-by-side, a common practice used to create two original negatives. The second negative would be sent abroad to print copies for foreign distribution.) The Biltmore was the largest hotel west of Chicago when it opened in 1923, and has played host to celebrities, presidents, and royalty ever since. It was here that John Kennedy was nominated at the 1960 Democratic National Convention. The adjoining 1,700-seat Biltmore Theater (discussed later), opened in 1924 at the corner of 5th and Grand. For a time it was the premiere venue in town for live theater. The modern Millennium Tower annex now stands on the site of the former theater, which closed in 1967. The hotel's lavish Moorish Revival interiors, and stately exteriors, have made the Biltmore an extremely popular filming location, appearing in dozens of productions over the decades.

The Biltmore (*near right*), viewed from 5th and Olive. The tall tower, second from right in this photo, is the annex that replaced the Biltmore Theater.

To the left, Harold rushes into the street to rescue one of the fallen drunks. In the background to the left stands the Strand Apartments, located at 729 S. Union Avenue, a few blocks east of MacArthur Park. The two homes behind Harold, next door to the Strand Apartments, are lost to a parking lot, but the apartment, now called The Charleston, still stands.

Harold rallies the bums one by one into a waiting taxi cab, too distracted to notice they all exit one by one from the other side (*left*). This scene was filmed alongside the Strand Apartments looking north up Union Avenue (*far left*).

To the lower left, Harold discovers the potential accident victim is only a department store mannequin. Behind Harold we see the basement windows (W) of what is now the Stuart Hotel at 718 S. Union Avenue (*below*).

To the left, one of the bums runs south down Hudson Avenue towards Hollywood Boulevard and an unsuspecting woman, with a modern view beneath. To the far right, Harold wrestles with the mannequin at the NE corner of Hudson and Hollywood, with the extant Hillview Apartments in the background (*right*).

This marvelous photo (*right*) looks west down Hollywood Boulevard, and depicts the filming of the scene to the upper right. Harold is standing by the "Hollywood Branch" of the Cawston Ostrich Farm. Ostrich farms were popular Los Angeles amusements during the early 20th century, when ostrich feathers were a common fashion accessory.

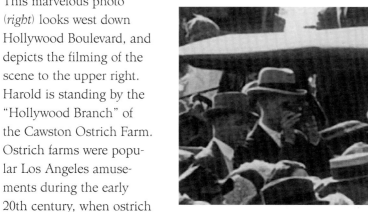

The tall man at the back appears to be taking Harold's picture.

With the gang momentarily reunited, Harold puts them aboard the Los Angeles Railway (Yellow Car) line that ran from the Southern Pacific Depot in downtown (discussed in *Girl Shy*) to Larchmont Boulevard in Hancock Park. The gang boards the trolley in front of what is now a Coldwell Banker office at 119 N. Larchmont Boulevard. The curve of the arched entryway of the building appears to the left of the woman passenger wearing a white hat. The transition between the building and its southerly neighbor at 113 Larchmont is marked with a (T), and discussed on the next page.

The Larchmont Village business district has always been a popular place to film. The large, seemingly dangerous trolley poles that once stood in the center of the street inspired many a silent-movie gag. The distinctive forward-pitched roof of 232-230 N. Larchmont, south from the corner of Beverly, appears above Harold's left hand (*right*). It also appears above a man's top hat in the Three Stooges comedy *Hoi Polloi* (1935) (*lower right*), above Snub Pollard's head (*right center*) in his short comedy *The Big Shot* (1928), and above the trees in the modern view to the far right.

Aside from *The Big Shot* (*above*), many other late-era silent films found in the Weiss-o-Rama Comedy Collection DVDs (produced by Kit Parker Films and compiled by Richard M. Roberts), were filmed on Larchmont, including *The Bum's Rush* (1927), *Better Behave*, *Fare Enough*, *Rudolph's Revenge*, and *Movie Mania* (all 1928).

To the right, Harold pauses at the SE corner of Larchmont and Beverly Boulevard, with a modern view at the center right. This corner appears in many silent comedies. A matching view (*far right*) appears in Buster Keaton's *Sherlock Jr.* (1924).

To the right, Harold loads up the gang on a double-decker bus and climbs aboard. The vertical marquees for a hardware store and drug store mark what is now home to Landis General Store (L), 140-138 N. Larchmont, a Larchmont Village institution since 1933 (*bottom*). This same stretch of Larchmont appears in the 1935 Three Stooges comedy *Hoi Polloi* (*below*).

Another local institution, Chevalier's Books (C) at 126 N. Larchmont, to the right of the tree (*upper right*), was once a barbershop as it appears during the movie above. Other views of Larchmont can be seen during *For Heaven's Sake* as well.

To the far right, Harold notices the bus taking off without him or the driver! The transition between the buildings (T) discussed on the prior page appears in both images looking north up the street. The real estate office (*rectangle*) marked in Harold's movie frame is the setting for a hopscotch game for the Three Stooges (*near right*) in *Pop Goes the Easel* (1935).

The action returns to Rampart Boulevard, where Harold wrecked his first car at the beginning of the film. Harold finds himself stuck on the roof of the double-decker, while one of the drunken groomsmen is at the wheel. Although some vintage buildings on the east side of Rampart have been replaced, the entire length of the west side of the street, from between 6th Street to 3rd Street, has hardly changed at all. Most of the apartments along this stretch of Rampart were built in 1922–1924, and thus, were fairly new at the time of filming. Lloyd filmed many scenes here for the movie, some of which appear in these pages. If you like using Google Street View, or Bing Maps Bird's Eye View, this section of Rampart is a particularly easy street to explore for locations.

Above, Harold notices his taxi is devoid of passengers driving south past 528 S. Rampart.

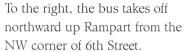

To the right, the bus takes off northward up Rampart from the NW corner of 6th Street.

To the left, Noah Young grips another bum hanging off the bus as he attempts to grab a banana from a passing fruit wagon. The apartments at 329 and 327 Rampart (*near left*) appear in the background.

Harold and crew race north up Rampart past the 44-unit Villa d'Este Apartments, across from 4th Street, the same five-story apartment identified at the beginning of this chapter.

The Lloyd crew also filmed looking north up Rampart. In this view (*above, left*), we see the NW corner of Rampart and W. 3rd Street in the distance to the left. The bungalow standing one lot north of the NW corner, at 267 Rampart (*above, middle right, and right*), was built in 1911 and stands today. The same bungalow appears during the conclusion of the *Girl Shy* race to the altar (*above, far right*).

Although it is difficult to see through the trees, this row of seven apartments has not changed except for one building, 512 Rampart (R), which was remodeled in 1956. The same section of tile roof (T), at 446 S. Rampart, appears in both images for comparison.

The apartments at 447, 441, and 431 Rampart Boulevard, respectively, appear in this movie frame (*above left*) and corresponding modern view.

Above, actor Noah Young staggers past 349 Rampart Boulevard.

Lloyd filmed along the entire length of Rampart, from 6th Street to 3rd Street, capturing nearly every building there in one shot or another. The apartments were all built between 1922 and 1924.

The apartment at 523 Rampart Boulevard (*box, above and to the left*) is the only building along the west side of Rampart that is no longer standing. It was replaced in 2000 with a larger apartment block.

TERMINUS OF WILSHIRE BOULEVARD

The aerial view of Rampart Boulevard (*box, right*) was likely taken in 1924, after the completion of the Elks Club Building (*right, center*) standing prominently at the NW corner of Westlake (now MacArthur) Park. At the time, Wilshire Boulevard terminated at Westlake Park and did not extend to downtown until a causeway across the lake was completed in late 1934. Lloyd filmed many scenes from *Hot Water* one block west of Rampart on Lafayette Park Place. As mentioned in that chapter, oil derricks (*ovals, above*) once stood on S. Coronado Street.

The drunken bus chases a cop (*above, right*) at the crest of Bunker Hill on Grand Avenue, between 3rd and 4th Streets. The fire escape in the center is part of the former Zelda Apartments (*below, right*) on the NE corner of 4th Street and Grand.

This photo (*above*) looks south down Grand Avenue towards 5th Street in the foreground. It was taken before construction of the Biltmore addition began in July 1927. (The original 1923 Biltmore Hotel (B) fronted Olive Street, but did not extend to Grand until late 1928.) The former lawn of the Los Angeles Central Public Library (L) is clearly visible. The distinct roofline of the extant Pacific Mutual Building (P) and the lost Biltmore Garage (G) are clearly visible in the movie frames above. Today (*right*), the same Pacific Mutual corner (P) barely peeks out from among the other buildings.

Together in *Duck Soup* (1927), but prior to officially appearing as a team, Stan Laurel and Oliver Hardy ride a bicycle down Grand (*below*), away from the same white garage building appearing beside the drunken bus above.

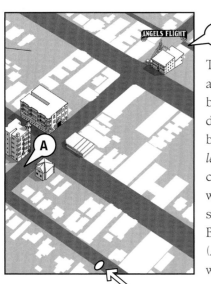

The garage appearing beside the drunken bus (*oval, left*) was close to where other scenes on Bunker Hill, (A) and (B), were filmed.

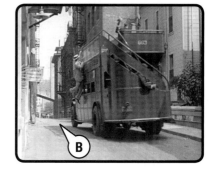

SEE BUNKER HILL CHAPTER FOR THESE SCENES

The teetering bus drives along many other street locations, most likely on S. Broadway, far south of downtown, that are not covered in this book. To the left, this view shows a ditch dug in Melrose Avenue, looking west to the corner of Larchmont.

To the left, the bus chases some poor soul into the Melrose ditch. In the background we see the corner of Larchmont (L) to the left, and to the right signs for a bakery and Melrose Hardware. To the lower left, we see the front of this bakery and hardware store appearing in the Three Stooges 1936 comedy *False Alarms*, and a corresponding modern view.

These views to the left show the "T" intersection of Larchmont meeting Melrose, the end of the "3" trolley line. Notice the small Safeway store next to the bakery in the movie frame.

The Kid Brother (1927)

Lloyd filmed most of *The Kid Brother* at the Lasky Ranch bordering Griffith Park near Burbank, the future site of the Forest Lawn Hollywood Hills Memorial Park, which opened in 1952. This test footage of the ranch (*right*) shows the Civil War battlefield from the D.W. Griffith 1915 epic *The Birth of a Nation*. The setting lies within the angle shown on the aerial photo (*below right*). Originally part of the Spanish-era Rancho Providencia, the Lasky Ranch was used for more than three decades as the filming location for scores of Hollywood productions.

Looking east, this circa 1922 photo (*right*) shows the former Lasky Ranch at the upper right. The future sites of the Walt Disney Studios (WD), the NBC Studios, and the eastern end of the First National–Warner Bros. Studios (WB) are also identified. The circle to the right marks the setting (*left*) where Harold knocks out the villain (actor Constantine Romanoff) against a tree branch (see also next page). The star at right is discussed on the next two pages.

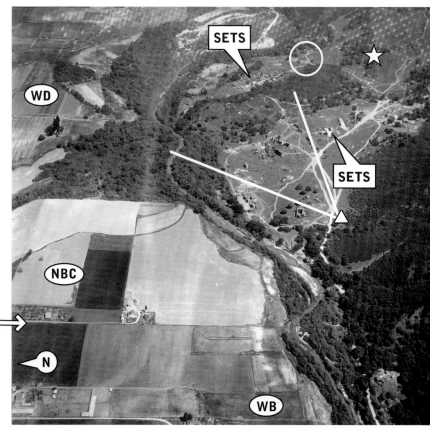

Charlie Chaplin (*left*) filmed scenes for *Sunnyside* (1919) in Burbank, looking south down California Street from Alameda. The arrow here (*left*) and on the aerial photo (*right*), both point south down California (Charlie's filming spot is out of frame on the aerial photo). The Lasky Ranch site appears on the Chaplin photo to the left of his shoulder.

This 1949 view looks south across the Lasky Ranch towards Mt. Lee. The twisting Mt. Hollywood Drive appears at the upper left. (N) points north.

The Kid Brother is widely regarded as Lloyd's masterpiece—a perfect blend of engaging story, incredible gags, and high production values. Harold plays the runt of the litter in a motherless family of mountain-men. Harold's father, the town sheriff, is entrusted with civic funds collected to build a new dam. When the strongman from a traveling medicine show steals the money, Harold captures the thief and returns the loot before a lynch mob attacks his father. In her final Lloyd collaboration, Jobyna Ralston plays an innocent dancer traveling with the show. While a puff piece in the *Los Angeles Times* reported the Lloyd Studio was busy scouting mountain top locales for this project near the Feather River in Northern California, *The Kid Brother* could not have been filmed any closer to home. The bucolic Lasky Ranch sat just a stone's throw away from Warner Brothers, and barely five miles from the Lloyd Studio. By contrast, most Lloyd filming spots, such as downtown L.A., USC, or Venice, were actually located much farther away. Paul Ayers first traveled to Forest Lawn to confirm these ridge lines.

Harold races his horse-cart beneath a low branch to knock out the villain. The same hills appear below in this publicity shot for *Four Horsemen of the Apocalypse* (1921), also filmed at the ranch.

This detailed view (*right*) from the upper left photo shows the path of Harold's wagon (*arrow*), and other landmarks appearing during the scene. The star marks the elevator tree scene discussed on the next page.

This 1922 view (*above, detail below*) shows a row of sets built at the Lasky Ranch behind the ridge that appears as the backdrop for the battle scenes from *The Birth of a Nation*. The circle marks the area on the prior page where Harold knocks out the villain.

This wedge-shaped partial bullfight stadium set was built for Rudolph Valentino's 1922 feature *Blood and Sand*.

During a charming scene, Harold climbs higher and higher up a tree in order to keep departing Jobyna in view as she recedes beyond the crest of a steep hill. This vertical tracking shot was filmed from an elevator platform that kept pace with Harold's climb. The scene looks slightly northwest towards the Verdugo Mountains, visible in the distance, while sets on the Lasky Ranch appear in the mid-background. My theory places the future site of the Disney Studios to the left of Harold's head.

The peak identified with a star (*upper left*) is the only likely filming spot. Other landmarks confirm the general area, and this peak is the only steep slope facing north near the ranch sets. Today, the few small peaks at the ranch have been severely graded to accommodate the memorial parks.

The San Gabriel Mountains appear in this shot, filmed looking slightly northeast (*right*), as Harold savors his happy encounter with Jobyna; a matching modern view appears to the middle, right.

East of the Disney lot, Lamer Street, which once ran for two blocks from Olive to Alameda, aligns directly with the identified star peak. Based on my study of early maps and photos, I believe the "T" intersection of W. Alameda and S. Lamer Street appears during the tree climbing scene as well (*right*).

LOBSTER PEAK

HAROLD'S COVE

Harold confronts the strongman aboard a derelict ship listing in a secluded cove. After several fight sequences, Harold subdues the thief by trapping him within a tower of life preservers. As Harold hoists the villain overboard (*left*), the distinctive profile of Lobster Point appears in the background.

These scenes were filmed on Santa Catalina Island, "26 miles across the sea" from the mainland, at the isthmus joining the two halves of the island, also called Two Harbors. Harold used the western harbor opening out to the Pacific Ocean. Buster Keaton filmed scenes from *The Navigator* (1924) at Gallagher Cove near Avalon on the east side of the island.

LOBSTER PEAK

HAROLD'S COVE

This evocative opening shot (*right*) employs a matte painting (or glass shot) to create clouds and sunbeams behind a V-shaped ridge line that does not, in fact, exist. The wagon trail overlooking the cove is clearly visible in the two modern views.

This frame below looks down on the general area where Buster Keaton and Stan Laurel would later be buried at Forest Lawn, unimaginable at the time of filming. The white box matches the panorama above.

Back on dry land, Harold races home with the thief (*left*). This spot sat at the south end the ranch, and appears in the back (*box*) when the medicine show arrives in town (*left, below*). The (N) points north in each image.

THE "OVERLOOK" SHOT OF THE WAGON WAS FILMED FROM THIS HAIRPIN TURN ON MT. HOLLYWOOD DRIVE IN GRIFFITH PARK

The town set was built at the south end of the ranch, close to the hills, far removed from the north end where most sets were built, apparently for the purpose of achieving this shot of the medicine show wagon overlooking the town (*above*). The back of the church set (*star, above*) compares to the front of the church (*left*).

The general area where Buster Keaton and Stan Laurel are buried (*oval, right*) appears in the movie frame to the middle left. Kim and E.J. Stephens hiked an hour up a dirt fire trail to capture this modern shot.

Another view of Harold's race home (*above*) looking west towards Cahuenga Peak (*star*), and the approximate area where the scene was filmed (*arrow, left*) as shown on a 1949 aerial view of the ranch. A modern view appears below.

A modern view of Forest Lawn and its neighboring landmarks.

The Forest Lawn and Mt. Sinai Memorial Parks to the north of Mt. Lee, former site of the Lasky Ranch, sit adjacent to the Hollywood Sign situated on the south face of Mt. Lee. Despite much controversy, the L.A. City Council approved the use of the former ranch as a cemetery site in 1948. Forest Lawn then immediately made six interments at the site, the minimum number to legally qualify the site as a cemetery. Despite litigation and an appeal, the cemetery-use permit was eventually upheld, and the memorial park opened March 4, 1952.

Speedy—Visions of New York

By 1927, New York had become the cultural and commercial center of the nation, if not the world. During the summer of 1927, Lloyd filmed throughout New York, including Coney Island and the locations indicated in this circa 1922 photo: 1) Yankee Stadium, which would open in 1923, 2) Hebrew Orphan Asylum, 3) Amsterdam Avenue, 4) 5th Avenue up to 57th Street, 5) Sutton Place, 6) Times Square/Herald Square, 7) Pennsylvania Station, 8) 5th Avenue starting at 16th Street, 9) Washington Square, 10) Union Square, 11) Williamsburg Bridge, 12) Fulton Street, 13) Brooklyn Bridge, 14) Coenties Slip, and 15) Battery Park.

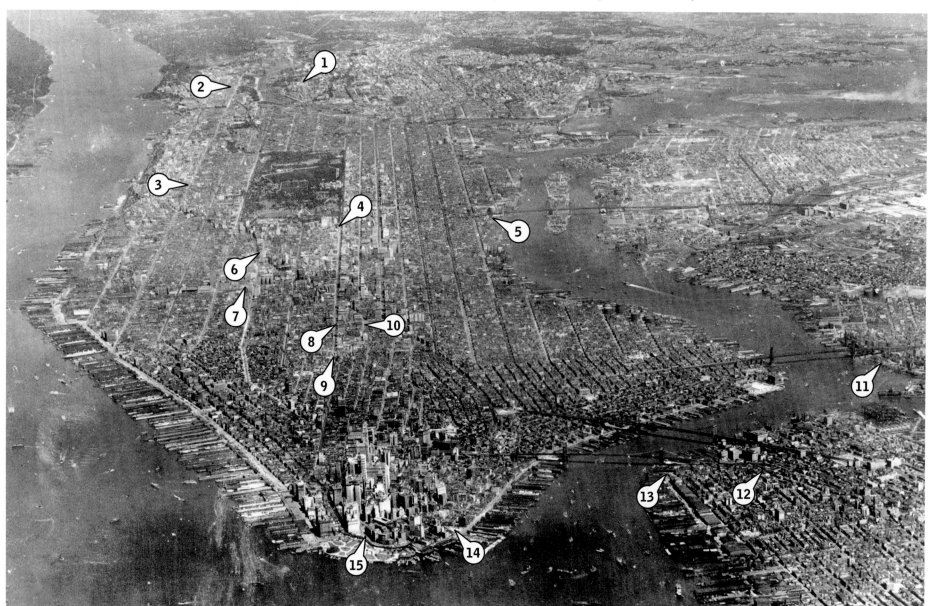

Overleaf: Lower Manhattan, December 1941.

Lloyd plays title character Harold "Speedy" Swift ("Speedy" was Lloyd's real-life nickname), who celebrates losing his soda jerk job by taking his girl, Jane (played by Ann Christy), to Coney Island for the day. Speedy's next job as a taxi-cab driver ends disastrously, but not before he takes Babe Ruth (in a cameo appearance) on a wild ride to Yankee Stadium. Jane's grandfather, Pop, operates the last remaining horse-drawn trolley franchise in New York. Shady developers wish to buy out Pop's interest, but when he refuses their low offer, they steal his trolley, as they know the franchise will expire if the trolley does not run at least once every 24 hours. Harold finds the stolen trolley, and in a wild cross-town chase arrives in time to save the franchise, which Pop then sells for a hefty sum.

The last horse-drawn trolley in New York (*below*) actually ceased operations in 1917, a decade before Lloyd came here to film.

This opening panning shot from *Speedy* of 1927 Manhattan viewed from Brooklyn, sets the stage. A modern view appears below.

New York celebrates
Charles Lindbergh's
arrival on June 13, 1927
(*right and below*).

Lloyd and company arrived in Manhattan mid-August 1927, for an intended four-week shoot, but ended up filming for 12 weeks instead. The movie presents the Big Apple in loving detail, and captures an especially exciting time in New York history, the summer of 1927. By 1927, the Great War was a memory, the Jazz Age was in full swing, and Manhattan's ongoing building boom crowded the skies, setting the stage for the iconic Chrysler and Empire State Buildings that were soon to come. In 1927, Duke Ellington began playing at Harlem's Cotton Club, *The Jazz Singer* premiered at New York's Warners' Theater, and Broadway's 71 theaters presented a record 264 new shows, including Jerome Kern and Oscar Hammerstein II's groundbreaking musical masterpiece *Show Boat*, premiering at the Ziegfeld Theater that had opened earlier the same year. After his historic trans-Atlantic flight starting on May 20, 1927, Charles Lindbergh was wildly celebrated on June 13th, by four million revelers with reportedly the largest ticker-tape parade in New York history (*left*), a tradition that began in 1886, following the dedication of the Statue of Liberty. Two weeks later, on June 26th, the wooden rollercoaster masterpiece, the Cyclone at Coney Island, began its 45-year reign as the world's fastest coaster. And the 1927 Yankees, arguably the greatest baseball team of all time, swept the Pittsburgh Pirates 4-0 in the World Series, capping their 110-44 wonder season that set scores of individual and team records, including Babe Ruth's monumental record 60 home runs.

Although the movie industry began in New York, and some Hollywood studios retained facilities there, Lloyd's production of *Speedy* was one of the few silent-era features to be filmed so extensively on location, and the only major production staged there by a leading comedy star. Lloyd was immensely popular, and encountered huge crowds everywhere he filmed, but New York's finest kept the onlookers in check. (Buster Keaton shot some scenes for his first MGM feature *The Cameraman* (1928) in New York, but logistics forced him to complete the project at home.) *Speedy* would prove to be Lloyd's final silent movie and arguably his last film triumph.

This title card (*left*) depicts vintage New York City landmarks as viewed from the East River. Beneath the "S" of "SPEEDY" stands the Singer Building, beneath the "PE" the Woolworth Building, and beneath the "Y" the Municipal Building, which similarly appear as the three tallest buildings (*below, left middle*) in this establishing panning shot from *Speedy* taken south of the Brooklyn Bridge. For some reason the Woolworth's immediate neighbor appearing to the left in the panning shot, the 44-story Transportation Building (completed in 1927), does not appear on the title card. The skyline was then changing so rapidly that perhaps the artist who painted the title card worked from an earlier photo (*bottom left*).

Completed in 1913, and standing 57 stories tall, the neo-Gothic styled Woolworth Building (*right*) was the world's tallest building until 1930. Frank Woolworth commissioned the building for his five-and-dime company's headquarters, and financed the construction in cash. Long known as the "Cathedral of Commerce," the building was never encumbered by a mortgage until it was sold 85 years later, in 1998. Its vaulted lobby is lavishly decorated with marble, mosaics, and carved caricatures of Woolworth counting his dimes, and architect Cass Gilbert cradling a model of the building. The Transportation and Woolworth Buildings have stood side-by-side at 225 and 233 Broadway for over 80 years.

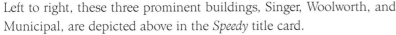

Left to right, these three prominent buildings, Singer, Woolworth, and Municipal, are depicted above in the *Speedy* title card.

The Municipal Building (1914) (*left*), stands at 1 Centre Street. Its upper floors were based on the Seville Cathedral's Giralda Tower in Spain. It was here that Buster and Natalie Keaton obtained their marriage license in 1921. The famous Wrigley Building in Chicago was influenced by this design. Stalin was reportedly so impressed by the Municipal Building that it served as the inspiration for several Stalinist towers built in Moscow. The 25-foot tall statue "Civic Fame" atop the Municipal Building (*left, center*) is Manhattan's largest, second only to the Statue of Liberty.

① ① ② ③ ④ ⑤

Completed in 1890, the World Building (5 *and below left*) on "Newspaper Row" housed the New York World newspaper, owned by Joseph Pulitzer. It was the tallest building in New York for several years. It was demolished in 1955 to expand the Brooklyn Bridge car ramp entrance.

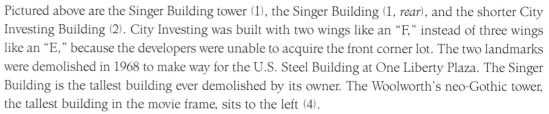

Pictured above are the Singer Building tower (1), the Singer Building (1, *rear*), and the shorter City Investing Building (2). City Investing was built with two wings like an "F," instead of three wings like an "E," because the developers were unable to acquire the front corner lot. The two landmarks were demolished in 1968 to make way for the U.S. Steel Building at One Liberty Plaza. The Singer Building is the tallest building ever demolished by its owner. The Woolworth's neo-Gothic tower, the tallest building in the movie frame, sits to the left (4).

Completed in 1899, the 29-story Park Row Building (3) was the tallest in the world until the Singer Building (1) was completed in 1908. The Singer held the record for only a year. New York would remain home to the world's tallest building until the Sears Tower in Chicago was completed in 1974.

A frame from *Speedy* (*middle, left*) compared to this circa 1920 view (*left*), which includes the 1916 Equitable Building (next page), but not the 1927 Transportation Building.

The Produce Exchange Building Tower (1) (razed) and the Standard Oil Building (2) near Battery Park (both discussed later) appear during the climax of *Speedy*. Across from the New York Stock Exchange, the 39-story Equitable Trust Company Building (3) (now Downtown by Philippe Starck) at 15 Broad Street, was built in 1927. Today, a massive rooftop mechanical system has replaced the two top tiers.

The pyramid-capped 41-story Banker's Trust Building (1912) (4) stands at 14 Wall Street. Its landmark tower was fashioned after the Mausoleum at Halicarnassus, one of the Seven Ancient Wonders of the World. To make room for the Banker's Trust site, the infamous 20-story Gillender Building was demolished in 1910, after just 13 years of service. Disproportionately tall for its tiny, narrow plot, the Gillender was never profitable, and at the time was the tallest building ever voluntarily destroyed.

Nearly adjacent to Banker's Trust stands the Equitable Building (5) at 120 Broadway. Configured like an "H," the massive 40-story building completely fills an entire one-acre block, with no setback, and casts a seven-acre shadow. Its 1.2 million sq/ft of office space is almost 30 times larger than its footprint. The public outcry following its completion in 1915 led to New York's 1916 zoning ordinance, requiring setbacks and reduced density to assure future construction would not completely block light and air to the streets below. The design for New York's elegant landmark spires, such as the Chrysler Building, was necessitated by this early law. The opening location footage to King Vidor's silent masterpiece *The Crowd* (1928) suggests the protagonist, "John," and his fellow corporate drones work in the Equitable Building.

A view of lower Manhattan from *Speedy* (*left*).

This view from *Speedy* looks north at Times Square. The 1927 feature film *Wings*, the only silent movie to win the Academy Award® for Best Picture (initially called Best Production), is playing at the Criterion Theater (*ellipse*). The arrow marks Harold's path (*below*) later in the film, beside the subway kiosk in each shot.

In this photo of Times Square (*above*), the Astor Theater, to the left, is showing *The Hunchback of Notre Dame* and across the way Loew's Theater is showing Mary Pickford's *Rosita*, both premiering in 1923.

Hollywood productions of stories purporting to take place in New York commonly include stock footage of Manhattan settings, such as this similar view (*above*) of Times Square appearing in the Harry Langdon comedy short *Feet of Mud* (1924).

Looking north at the Herald Building, north of Herald Square (*left*), as it appears in the movie, between Broadway and the former 6th Avenue elevated tracks. Macy's stands off camera to the left.

Founded in 1858, the Macy's at Broadway and 34th (*above*), opened in 1902 across from Herald Square. The red star tattooed on founder Rowland Hussey Macy's hand when he was a 15-year-old whaler became the store's logo. Macy introduced the one-price system, whereby all customers would be charged the same advertised price for goods.

A circa 1900 view of the New York Herald Building, designed by Gilded Age architect Stanford White for publisher James Gordon Bennett, with an Italian Renaissance arcade fashioned after the Loggia del Consiglio in Verona, Italy. The basement-level pressroom was visible from plate glass windows on the Broadway side, where large rolls of newsprint (*above*) can be seen standing on the sidewalk. The roof is ringed with electric-eyed bronze owls (*ellipse*). The rear half of the Herald was replaced with a 24-story tower circa 1928–1930, after *Speedy* was filmed, while the half facing Herald Square was replaced with a four-story building in 1940. The rooftop figures of Minerva and the bell-chiming blacksmiths Stuff and Guff (*square*), stand today as part of the Bennett Memorial in Herald Square Park (*above, center*). The elevated pre-electric trolleys were originally pulled by small steam engines (*rectangle*).

This establishing shot was filmed looking up 5th Avenue past 41st Street towards the intersection at 42nd Street. The New York Central Public Library stands off camera to the left. The square (*left*) indicates the correspondingly narrower view of the circa 1925 photo (*right*). The narrow white rectangle to the left marks the partially demolished remains of the historic Temple Emanu-El, built in 1868, on the NE corner of 43rd Street. The Postal Life Building at the SE corner of 5th and 43rd (*arrow*) still stands.

Looking north up 5th Avenue at the corner of 42nd Street, from the Central Library lawn. Temple Emanu-El (1868–1927) (*rectangle*) stands on the NE corner of 43rd. Over the years the neighborhood changed from residential to commercial use, leading, in part, to the Temple's relocation. The Postal Life Building (*arrow, below*) appears in the movie frame (*upper left*).

This November 14, 1868 article in *Harper's Weekly* depicts the recently dedicated temple. The building featured yellow brownstone, with an alternating red and black tile roof. The original congregation was formed in 1845 with 33 members, yet grew in prominence to finance the $650,000 construction soon after the Civil War.

Temple Emanu-El merged with Temple Beth-El in 1927, and together they raised the current Temple Emanu-El on 5th Avenue at 65th Street, across from Central Park, on the former site of John Jacob Astor's mansion. Dedicated in 1930, and seating 2,500 people (more than St. Patrick's Cathedral), Temple Emanu-El is the largest Jewish temple in the world.

In 1923, the Harold Lloyd Corporation bought the Westwood Location Ranch, bounded by Ohio Avenue, Manning Avenue, Santa Monica Boulevard, and Selby Avenue in West Los Angeles (*dotted lines, below*) as a possible studio site. Lloyd would continue production at the Hollywood Studio instead, but kept the property, building a private kennel there to house his many Great Danes. Lloyd built an extensive New York exterior set here for *Speedy*, fashioned after the Sheridan Square area of New York. Lloyd used this set again for his 1934 production *The Cat's Paw*, and rented it for other studio productions. Marc Wanamaker, whose Bison Archives provided this and many other photos in the book, discovered that Freddie Bartholomew's *Little Lord Fauntleroy* (1936) was filmed here as well. Over time, Lloyd sold the NW corner of the lot at Ohio and Selby to the Paulists, home to the St. Paul the Apostle Catholic Church and School (1), and the lot west of the New York set as the site for the Emerson Middle School (2). The remainder of the land was purchased by the Mormon Church in 1937, as the future site (*rectangle, below*) for the Los Angeles California Temple. The area landmark (*below right*) was the church's largest temple at the time it was dedicated in 1956.

WESTWOOD VILLAGE

UCLA

①

②

SANTA MONICA BOULEVARD

Below, Harold appears in an early scene from *Feet First*, filmed in Westwood Village beside the Janss Investment Company Building, the company that originally owned the Westwood Location Ranch property.

A partial view of *Speedy*'s elaborate old New York set (*below*). Its scale and detail are indicative of the quality and care Lloyd lavished on his productions. Immediately left is a portion of the *Speedy* set and how it appears in *Little Lord Fauntleroy* (center, below).

Lloyd's ranch was nearly adjacent to the Westwood Village Memorial Park Cemetery, located at 1218 Glendon Avenue. It is the final resting place for Marilyn Monroe, and for such other celebrities as Billy Wilder, George C. Scott, Donna Reed, Walter Matthau, Don Knotts, Gene Kelly, Jack Lemmon, Farrah Fawcett, and Fanny Brice. Joe DiMaggio arranged for Marilyn to be interred here to be close to the two women who had cared for her as a child. Though his marriage to Monroe lasted less than one year, DiMaggio sent roses to her crypt thrice weekly for 20 years.

Harold dashes north up 7th Avenue from the New York Times Building (*below*) during his failed effort to deliver flowers to his employer's wife. Lloyd was able to film location scenes such as this by hiding two cameras in a laundry truck. To the near right is an establishing shot from Harry Langdon's comedy feature *The Strong Man* (1926). Aside from a few stock-footage establishing shots, the Langdon feature was filmed entirely in Hollywood.

If you love looking at old photographs, you must visit Shorpy.com. With the slogan "History in HD," this fascinating website presents hundreds of vintage photos scanned from remarkably high-resolution 5x7 or 8x10 glass plate negatives, mostly from the Library of Congress. This towering 1905 view of the New York Times Building (*far right*) is but a small portion of the entire 154-MB high-resolution image available for download from the LOC. I first discovered this (and many other images in this book) at Shorpy.com.

Celebrating the official name change from Longacre Square, *The New York Times* held a 1904 New Year's Eve fireworks display at Times Square that grew into the annual festivities still held today. The first electric New Year's ball was dropped in 1907. Within 10 years, Times Square would grow into the premiere theater district in the country. After a decline beginning with the Great Depression, a post-World War II rebound, and then a further decline lasting into the 1980s, today the district is revitalized with family-oriented shops and theaters, and remains a landmark destination for tourists from around the world.

A detailed view (*below*) of the subway kiosk appearing beside Harold (*left*).

LADIES PARLOR AT
THE LION BREWERY

THE PACKARD MOTORCARS
DEALER AT 1540 BROADWAY
IS NOW A VIRGIN MEGASTORE
(*LOWER RIGHT*)

GEO. M. COHAN

ELECTRIC
HANSOM
WITH
PNEUMATIC
TIRES

Look at the details in this high-resolution photo. There are seven policemen wearing constabulary helmets, two to the left above, three in the far background (*ellipses, inset*), and two more to the right (*rectangle*, one behind the white horse). The New York Theater is hosting George M. Cohan in his 1905 production of *Little Johnny Jones* (*inset, above*).

On February 12, 1908, about three years after this photo was taken, six automobiles lined up in Times Square, the starting line for the *New York Times*-sponsored 20,000-mile Great Race from New York to Paris. Montague Roberts, driving a Thomas Speedway Flyer, led the American team to victory.

A rainy day in early 1943, dated by the Disney movie *Saludos Amigos* playing at the Globe (*rectangle, left*). The circle in the modern view (*right*) marks the Virgin Megastore at 1540 Broadway, the address for Packard Motors in 1905 (*above, left*).

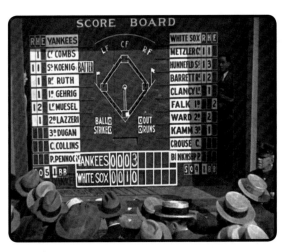

Harold plays a baseball-enamored soda jerk. He receives the ongoing score of the day's game from a buddy by telephone, and posts the score using donuts and pretzels to keep the kitchen crew apprised. Harold loses his job when he delays a delivery errand to watch the current score on an elaborate play-by-play scoreboard posted in a store window (*above*). In a few pages we'll see Harold climb atop a taxi for a better view of the board. The lineups for the New York Yankees and the Chicago White Sox presented in the film (*above*) appear to be accurate. The Yankees won 17 of their 22 games against the White Sox during the 1927 season.

Given the Internet and worldwide live media, it is nearly inconceivable that in bygone days baseball fans would line up at the local newspaper to keep track of the scores, updated by telegraph reports. This crowd in Washington D.C. (*above, center*) is assembled to "watch" the opening game of the 1912 World Series between the New York Giants and the Boston Red Sox, as represented on the scoreboard (*above, left*). A young lad (*ellipse, upper left*) sits poised to update the scores. The upper-right photo shows the crowd assembled in Times Square for news of the soon-to-be-infamous 1919 World Series, baseball's greatest scandal, when eight players on the superior Chicago White Sox threw the series in favor of the Cincinnati Reds.

This scene was filmed in Los Angeles, looking north up Flower towards 8th Street. Realizing he has lost his job, Harold crosses the street to buy a newspaper and searches the help-wanted ads while standing in front of the Women's Athletic Club Building (now razed) at 827 S. Flower Street (*below*). For some reason, Lloyd filmed nearly all of the Los Angeles shots for *Speedy* on Flower Street. Above Harold's head to the far right (*ellipse*) is a barely legible sign for the Golden State Electrical Co., confirming the Los Angeles location. This setting appears again during the film. The tall building to the right is the Los Angeles Gas and Electric Corporation (Southern California Gas Company) Building (see next page).

Harold stood by this lamppost (*rectangle, left*) beside the Women's Athletic Club.

Inscribed above the triple-arched entryway are the words "1867 Southern California Gas Company 1924." However, the company was acquired in 1929 by Pacific Lighting Corporation, a San Francisco company that owned the rival Los Angeles Gas and Electric Corporation, which explains the name change painted on the side of the building on the previous page. At the same

time, the city of Los Angeles had directly contracted to buy hydroelectric power produced by the new Hoover Dam, and refused to renew the combined company's gas franchise unless it sold its electric grid to the city. Since divesting its grid, the company has grown to become the nation's largest natural gas distribution utility, serving over 20 million customers.

Looking north at the 700 block of S. Flower Street towards Barker Brothers at the corner of 7th (*above*), a mother and child (*far left*) flag down Harold's taxi in front of the Parmelee Dohrmann Building. The left awning for the Myer Siegel & Co. store (*ellipse*) appears behind Harold (*center, left*). Harold will attempt to pick up his next fare (*star above*) in front of the Barker Brothers Building, the sole building in this photo to survive.

Harold struggles with the cab's sticky door in front of the Parmelee–Dohrmann Building. Looking south down Flower Street towards 8th Street we see the "ALE" of the Armondale Hotel marquee (1), the First English Lutheran Church (2) at the corner of 8th Street, the Gas Company Building (3), the Hotel Jean (4) at 840 S. Flower, and the Golden State Electrical Co. building (5) discussed previously.

Looking at the SE corner of Flower and 8th Street (*right*) at the First English Lutheran Church (2), built in the 1880s, when the street was still residential. The Gas Company (3) bought the church property in 1937, and built on the site in 1957. Today, the Gas Company occupies a 52-story tower on W. 5th Street across from the Biltmore Hotel.

A similar view looking down S. Flower towards 8th Street. Only the Gas Company Building (3) remains.

To the far right, Harold picks up his next fare a bit further up Flower Street. Although parked in front of the extant Barker Brothers Building, at the SW corner of 7th Street (*star on prior page*), you can see reflected in his windshield the extant Roosevelt Building (1922) (6) at the NE corner of 7th Street.

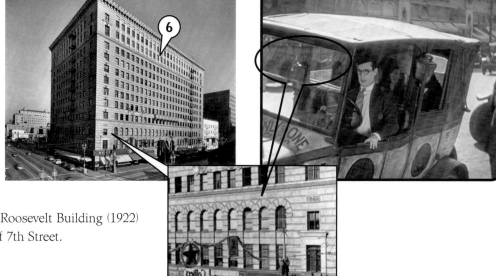

Harold's next customers hail his cab (*near right*) from in front of the Hotel Jean on the east side of Flower Street, this time nearly two blocks south from the Barker Brothers Building. With a bit of movie editing magic, Harold arrives to pick them up (*far right*) on the west side of the street, in front of the Women's Athletic Club, the same spot where Harold earlier crossed the street to buy a newspaper.

Looking up Flower Street from in front of the Women's Athletic Club we see above and below, the Roosevelt Building at 7th and Flower (6), the Armondale Hotel marquee (1), the First English Lutheran Church at the corner of 8th Street (2), the Gas Company Building (3), the Hotel Jean at 840 S. Flower (4) (below only), and the Golden State Electrical Co. building (5) discussed previously. A rectangle marks the hotel's small doorway sign (*below, and upper left*). Only (6) and (3) remain standing.

A view looking south at the 700 block of S. Flower Street in Los Angeles. The white callouts identify the places where Harold filmed. In the far background the Petroleum Securities Building (1) at the SW corner of Olympic, and the Hotel Ritz (Milner Hotel) (2) still stand. At the left is a similar view, today.

STATE NORMAL SCHOOL   JESUS SAVES   VIEW EAST DOWN 6TH ST.

SOUTHLAND HOTEL FIRE PROOF SAFETY FIRST

Harold's next botched taxi fare (*below*) stands in front of the Knights of Columbus Building at 612 S. Flower (*arrow, below right*). The "E" of a "CAFE" located next door at 608 S. Flower appears in the rectangle below. The predecessor to UCLA, the State Normal School campus stands at the future site of the Los Angeles County Central Library, built in 1926. The Bible Institute of Los Angeles (1914–1988) was known for years by its giant rooftop "JESUS SAVES" neon signs. Its 3,500-seat auditorium was larger than the current Kodak Theater in Hollywood. The Rosegrove Hotel at 532 S. Flower (*ellipse, above*) was the site of a tragic murder-suicide at about the time Harold filmed here. A separated couple, married only two months, decided to spend a week of happiness together here before the blonde showgirl bride returned to New York. The local artist

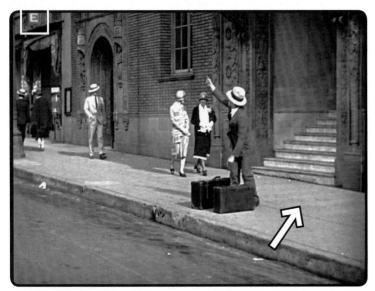

husband, distraught over losing his "golden girl," gazed at his estranged bride as she fell asleep listening to "All for Love" on the Victrola, then strangled her with a sheet before hanging himself with a bedspread.

During this hilarious scene, Harold awaits the outcome of a bare-knuckle brawl between an apparent landlord and his taxi-hailing tenant. Each time the tenant appears to be getting the upper hand, Harold places his luggage into the cab. As their fortunes reverse, Harold removes the tenant's luggage. The scene ends without resolution as a couple of New York cops commandeer Harold's cab for the first of three exciting chases through Manhattan.

The Rosegrove Hotel (*prior page*) appears in the upper-left corner (*rectangle*) of this movie frame (*right*). The arrow points to the Knights of Columbus doorway, as in the two images on the previous page.

Across the street is a storefront with the address "619" (*ellipse, above*). Because Harold had already filmed prior scenes on other blocks of S. Flower Street, I correctly surmised that these scenes were filmed on the 600 block of the same street as well. During the early taxi scenes, Harold jumps up and down Flower from the 800 block, to the 700 block, back to the 800 block, and finally to the 600 block.

A corresponding view of Flower Street today (*left*).

Speedy—Coney Island

Harold and Jane prepare to enter the Bowling Green subway station for their trip to Luna Park at Coney Island (*left*).

Harold's unseen foot gives Jane a good scare about her weight. The Standard Oil Building appears in the background to the right.

The Bowling Green subway kiosk Harold used was located on the SW corner of State Street and Battery Place. This corner (*above*) appears prominently later in the film. A modern view (*right*) shows the kiosk has been relocated to the Bowling Green plaza.

Harold and Jane arrive at the entrance of Luna Park (*left*), located on Surf Avenue in Brooklyn between W. 12th and W. 8th Streets. Look at the huge crowd swarming the entrance. The view to the right looks west down Surf Avenue, while the view below looks east. The Coney Island subway and elevated stations at Stillwell and Mermaid Avenues were just around the corner.

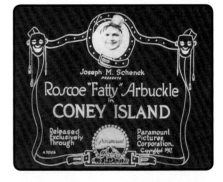

Roscoe "Fatty" Arbuckle and his sidekicks Al St. John and Buster Keaton filmed extensively at Luna Park for their 1917 comedy short *Coney Island* (*above*).

LUNA PARK & SURF AVE. B-19045
Coney Island
Copyright 1912 By
IRVING UNDERHILL, N.Y.

The Luna Park ticket concessions stands were built in the shape of Roman chariots. These chariots (*arrow, above right*) appear beside Harold and Jane (*right*), and beside a less-than-stone-faced Buster in *Coney Island* (*bottom right*).

An early photo of Luna Park (*above*) before colorful crescents and windmill circles covered the entrance. After failing to acquire the original 250-foot diameter revolving wheel designed by George Ferris for the 1893 World's Columbian Exposition in Chicago, George C. Tilyou built a smaller 125-foot diameter Ferris wheel on Coney Island in 1894. Tilyou later built Steeplechase Park in 1897, which remained a landmark Coney Island attraction until it was demolished in 1964. In 1902, Tilyou arranged for Frederic Thomson and Elmer Dundy to bring to Steeplechase Park their extremely popular "A Trip to the Moon" exhibition, built for the 1901 Pan-American Exposition in Buffalo, New York. Flush with this success, Thomson and Dundy opened their own Luna Park in 1903. The pair poured every dime they could scavenge or borrow into the park, and barely had enough cash remaining to make change for the opening day ticket sales. Nonetheless, the park was such a resounding success that they recouped their investment in only a few weeks. Thomson and Dundy would later build the Hippodrome, New York's largest theater, where massive pageants and spectacles were staged before audiences of up to 5,200 people.

STILLWELL STATION

SHOOT THE CHUTES

WITCHING WAVES

DRAGON GORGE

A TRIP TO THE MOON

ELEVATED TRACK

LUNA PARK

Luna Park, October 30, 1920. While the general layout remained the same, the park continuously replaced and relocated attractions. The two rides on the next page, filmed in 1927, were installed between 1920 and 1924. The sign on the "A Trip to the Moon" pavilion reads "LUNA PARK, Free Band Concerts, U.S. Battleship Recruits, Moving Pictures and Panorama, Free Dancing." The Dragon Gorge, an indoor scenic railway, featured sharp turns, waterfalls, and flames, as well as scenes of the Grand Canyon, the North Pole, and other exotic locales. The subway extension from Manhattan to Coney Island opened beneath the Stillwell elevated station in 1919, bringing millions to the beach for a nickel ride. Quite modest in size by today's standards, Luna Park drew a staggering 4,800,000 paid admissions its first May–September season, comparable, proportionately, to Disneyland's annual attendance.

For "A Trip to the Moon" (*above*), guests rode suspended indoor gondolas in the dark, past an unspooling panoramic painting showing first the liftoff from Luna Park, then the New York skyline, and then the Earth itself receding into the distance. Guests would disembark once reaching the moon, where they were entertained by costumed dwarfs while strolling through a faux lunar landscape. Guests were even offered bites of green cheese upon exiting. The ride was later upgraded to "A Trip to Mars," and replaced again with other attractions over the years.

The "A Trip to the Moon" pavilion appears in the background (*above*), as does The Bug ride (*below*), during Harold and Jane's spin on The Airplane Ride. The Airplane Ride and The Bug, shown in this 1932 photo (*left*), were newer attractions that do not appear in the 1920 aerial photo on the previous page.

The Bug ride (*right*) ran beside archways surrounding the Luna Park swimming pool, visible through the archway behind Harold (*left*).

Harold and Jane enjoy The Witching Waves, a ride where reciprocating levers under a flexible roadbed created traveling harmonic waves that propelled the carts forward. While Harold and Jane appear to be having a good time (*left*), Buster Keaton and Al St. John collide head-on (*bottom center*) in their film *Coney Island*.

The oval in this 1924 aerial photo (*right*) shows the location of the Airplane Ride and The Bug. The Witching Waves (*rectangle*) originally stood beside the Shoot the Chutes lagoon until after Lloyd filmed in 1927. By 1932, the ride had been relocated next to the Airplane Ride and The Bug.

Following a disastrous fire in 1907, Tilyou rebuilt his Steeplechase Park bigger and better than ever. The enormous Temple of Fun enclosed nearly three acres of amusements, attracting customers rain or shine. The

Chanticleer Carousel (*right*) featured ostriches and giant chickens instead of ponies, while a three-tier animal menagerie carousel stood inside. Despite public cries to preserve the Temple of Fun as a historic landmark, the new owner, real estate developer Fred Trump (The Donald's father), quickly demolished it after the park closed in 1964.

Lloyd also filmed a few scenes at Steeplechase Park on its world famous racing-horse ride. The view of Harold and Jane on the center horse (*below*) was filmed looking west along the beach. The prominent Half Moon Hotel (*squares, below*) appears in the background. The view to the lower right shows the enormous crowds drawn to the beach on a typical summer's day.

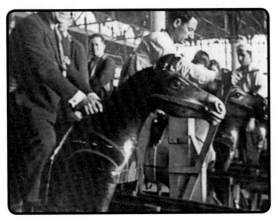  

The Steeplechase Horses carried riders around the exterior perimeter of the Temple of Fun, across a lake, through a tunnel, and over a series of dips. Tilyou explained one reason the ride was so popular was that men and women always enjoy an excuse to hold one another. The funhouse attractions also gave the sexes a chance to get cozy as they mixed and tumbled with one another.

The Steeplechase Temple of Fun contained dozens of indoor rides and attractions (*above*). In the foreground, guests swing past on chairs attached to a revolving center post. In the background, guests sit on The Hoopla, a giant wooden ring attached to a center post, pushed around by burly attendants like a multi-directional see-saw. Created in 1891, and rebuilt after the 1907 fire, The Hoopla often exposed a woman's ankles (or more!).

Tilyou knew a little titillation was good business. Patrons exiting the horse ride had to pass through the Insanitarium–Blowhole Theater, a public stage where they were subjected to electric shocks, revealing blasts of air, and other indignities. No one minded much, and once initiated, guests could sit on benches to view the next round of victims.

An original Steeplechase horse on display at the Coney Island History Project Museum.

The iconic Shoot the Chutes ride, pictured here, was a vestige of the former Sea Lion Park that Thompson and Dundy acquired as the site for their Luna Park. They built a slight upturn in the track just as the boat enters the lagoon, causing the boat to rise up and bounce roughly upon the water. As seen here, guests would ascend in the boat, disembark at the top so the boat could be repositioned, and then re-board for a thrilling ride down.

Roscoe Arbuckle seems to be getting a little more action on his descent (*right*) than Harold does with Jane (*left*).

A clown, horseback rider, and group of exotic performers entertain the crowds as another boat splashes down beneath Luna Park's landmark 200-foot tall electric tower.

Comedy styles change over time. Everyone safely exits the boat in Harold's movie. A decade earlier, Roscoe and Buster Keaton (doubling for the girl) exit their boat a bit more unceremoniously (*below*).

Aside from shots of Harold and Jane on various rides, the exterior park scenes were likely all filmed at the Abbot Kinney Pier in Venice, California, where Harold had filmed before, or the Ocean Park Pier nearby. The "Some Kick" roller coaster sign and the curved, striped awning on the Venice Pier (*right*) can be seen in this frame (*upper left*) from the Laurel and Hardy short *Sugar Daddies* (1927), and below at the far right. Charlie Chaplin used the Venice Pier, including the Noah's Ark attraction (*left*) for several scenes in *The Circus* (1928). As explained on the following page, the Venice Fun House (*box, below*) was not used for the movie's fun house interior scenes.

This 1925 aerial view looks south at the Abbot Kinney Pier in Venice.

After noticing that wet paint has ruined his suit, Harold flips himself the bird (right). Considering the unclear motivation for his gesture, and that the "digitus impudicus" had far greater shock value during the 1920s than it does today, I am intrigued as to how and why this scene appeared in the movie.

The funhouse interior scenes were filmed at the Jones Fun Palace on Ocean Front Walk, on the north side of the Ocean Park Pier. I knew Lloyd did not film at the obvious spot, the Steeplechase Pavilion of Fun in Coney Island, because none of the elements of that funhouse match the movie. As is often the case, clues from another movie solved the mystery. Known as one of the leading sex symbols of her era, Clara Bow, the "It" girl, played her signature role as the Cinderella shop girl who falls for her wealthy boss in *It* (1927). During that movie, Clara takes her boss (Antonio Moreno) for a day of fun at "Coney Island." As seen here and beyond, Clara and Harold obviously filmed their respective sequences at the same place. Notice the identical "SKOOTER" sign appearing behind Harold (*lower left*) and Antonio (*below*). I knew *It* was a Hollywood production, as some scenes were filmed in Los Angeles across from the Biltmore Hotel. Since it made no sense that Clara and Antonio would travel to New York just to film a fun house scene, I knew that the fun house Clara and Harold used had to have been close to Hollywood instead. Other views of the revolving drum appearing in *It* show that the drum was rather long. The trick to crossing through it was to walk "diagonally" into the spin.

The Human Roulette Wheel, or Social Mixer, at the Jones Palace of Fun appears with Harold (*left*) and with Clara (*right*). The wheel was built flush with the floor sitting within a bowl. The distinctive indoor Parker Carousel stands behind Harold, and was likely off camera to the right of Clara.

The Steeplechase Park wheel at Coney Island (*left and lower left*) clearly does not match; it had a raised center section and a perimeter fence. The Venice California Fun House wheel (*right*), as featured in Hal Roach comedies such as *On the Loose* (1932), was available for Harold to use in 1927, but it was clearly much too small. Harold used another small wheel in his early short *Why Pick On Me?* (1918) (*lower right*). This 1918 wheel was likely found at an earlier incarnation of the Venice or Ocean Parks Piers, and was thus likely destroyed when the piers completely burned in 1920, and in 1924, respectively. At a similar Steeplechase attraction, the Human Pool Table (*below*), guests would attempt to traverse a floor covered with 24 discs spinning in opposing directions.

Harold, Clara, and their respective dates enjoy the double-dip giant slide at the Jones Ocean Park Fun Palace (*above*), which can be viewed behind the Parker Carousel in this postcard (*far right*). The Coney Island Steeplechase Park giant slide had many smaller dips, and thus could not have been the slide appearing in the film. The edge of the Parker Carousel appears in the upper-right frame (*oval*).

I would have saved a lot of trouble if I had first read Jeffrey Stanton's wonderful book, *Venice California, 'Coney Island of the Pacific,'* where he correctly wrote that Lloyd filmed at the Jones Fun Palace. This confirmatory photo from Jeffrey's book (*right*) shows the distinctive carousel matching the one appearing with Lloyd below, as well as the dips of the Fun Palace giant slide to the back.

Searching for other funhouses in the area besides the Venice house, I found this ad (*right*) for the Ocean Park Fun Palace, which opened on July 2, 1925, about 18 months after the prior Ocean Park Pier had burned down. I knew I was on the right track because the ad shows a double-dip slide in the lower right corner. The Fun Palace, which was clearly grander than the Venice House, does not appear in many movies because it was converted into a skating rink in 1929, just four years after it opened.

The shorter Venice giant slide was divided into separate tracks. The Venice slide appears here in *On the Loose* (1932) (*right*). This same Venice four-track slide stood in for Coney Island during the fun-house scenes in King Vidor's Oscar® nominated masterpiece *The Crowd* (1928).

This 1924 aerial photo depicts, clockwise from the upper left: the Stillwell Avenue elevated station; the Witching Waves; Shoot the Chutes; the front entrance to Luna Park; the 1924 site of the Giant Racer roller coaster, replaced in 1927 by the historic Cyclone (*bottom right*) that reigned for decades as the world's fastest coaster; the large turn behind Steeplechase Park; and the front of the park.

As Harold and Jane's fun-filled day draws to an end, we see glimpses of Luna Park's dazzling electric display (*right*). The park was reported to have over one million lights.

At the turn of the prior century, when leisure time and disposable income were in short supply, the great Coney Island parks provided one of the few sources of inexpensive mass entertainment. While most New Yorkers were unable to afford vacation or travel, factory workers, recent immigrants, and other socially disadvantaged groups could still save their nickels and lose themselves for a day at Coney Island. As other entertainment options captured the public's attention, including the movies (and later radio), amusement parks lost their preeminence during the 1920s. Luna Park was hit hard by the Depression, went bankrupt for a time in 1933, and struggled thereafter for years until closing in 1944, following a disastrous fire. Low-income apartments now stand on the Luna Park site.

The box in the panorama below shows an unusual Luna Park attraction, the Infant Incubators. At a time when most hospitals were unable to care for premature babies, pediatrician Dr. Martin Couney and a team of nurses cared for them in his specially designed incubators. Dr. Couney financed operations by charging the public admission to see the babies put on display, which continued as a park attraction until 1943. The doctor is credited with saving the lives of thousands of babies.

Speedy—Midtown

We return from Coney Island back to Harold's misadventures as a New York cabbie. While parking his car, Harold accidentally locks bumpers with a parked moving van. When the van departs, it tows Harold's cab away (*above*).

Harold chases after the van, but a pothole shakes the cab loose before Harold can catch up with it (*above right*). This setting is 12 Sutton Place South at E. 56th Street (*right*). Noticing the open air between the two buildings in the movie frame, I sensed this shot may have been close to a river. I knew Harold filmed other scenes at Sutton Place along the East River, so I scouted the area using Google Street View and quickly found the spot while sitting at home in California. The elegant apartment was built around 1925, on property formerly used as a brewery and coal yard.

Overleaf: A 1933 view north from the Empire State Building showing 5th Avenue (*center*) leading up to Central Park.

PENNSYLVANIA STATION (1910–1963)

A pair of police detectives hijack Harold's cab, demanding a quick ride to Pennsylvania Station. Moments after the detectives dash inside, a traffic cop arrives to give Harold a speeding ticket (*above*).

THE 150-FOOT TALL ROOF TO THE GIANT MAIN WAITING ROOM

W. 33RD STREET, LOOKING WEST

NORTH UP 7TH AVENUE

These women and children (*left*) are taking a break from drying the wash to peek at the passing scene. There appear to be ten other people on the apartment rooftops in the foreground.

A gentleman holds his companion's side (*right*) as they wait for the cop with the constabulary helmet to wave them across; the car is driving past the north carriage drive. The Pennsylvania and Long Island Railroads occupying the station each had a private drop-off drive for their customers.

The scene to the lower left is easily identifiable as being filmed along the front (east) side of Pennsylvania Station, looking north up 7th Avenue from W. 31st Street. However, the ticket scene (*left*) was not filmed at the front of the station, but along W. 33rd looking east toward 7th. The corner of the extant Hotel Pennsylvania (*right*), where Glenn Miller and other big bands played during the '30s and '40s, appears in the background (*rectangles, left and right*). The hotel's exchange telephone number, "PE6-5000," was the inspiration for one of Miller's greatest hits, "Pennsylvania 6-5000." First opening in 1919, the hotel claims its phone number is the oldest continuing use phone number in New York.

At the time of completion in 1910, the eight-acre Pennsylvania Station covered more territory than any other building ever fabricated at one time, constructed with 550,000 cubic feet of pink granite freighted in from Milford, Massachusetts. The 7th Avenue façade, conceived as a monumental city gateway, was designed by architects McKim, Mead & White as a Roman Doric colonnade supported by columns 35 feet tall. The station culminated a much larger project undertaken by the Pennsylvania Railroad Company that began in 1903, with the construction of massive railroad tunnels under the North and East Rivers leading into town. Train ridership peaked after WWII, supplanted by freeways and jet travel. As ridership and revenues declined in the late 1950s, the financially strapped Pennsylvania Railroad could not afford even basic maintenance, and the station fell deeper into neglect and disrepair. In the end, the company sold the air rights to the property for construction of the current Madison Square Garden in exchange for a 25 percent ownership interest, and a smaller modernized station situated completely underground. Preservationists were shocked that no laws prohibited the 1963 demolition, leading to the enactment of preservation laws that would save Grand Central Station a few years later. Today, the current Penn Station is busier than ever, and funding has been approved to reconfigure the neighboring 1912 Farley Post Office Building, nearly as massive and grand, into the station's "new" home.

Similar views looking north up 7th Avenue from W. 31st as seen in the film (*left*), and shortly before the station was demolished in 1963 (*right*). Only the front (east) side of the station was lined completely with Doric columns. The right rectangle marks the movie frame's point of view. The station's demise is arguably New York's greatest architectural loss.

The grand waiting room (*left*) ran north-south for nearly two blocks, and was the largest public space in New York, comparable in scale to St. Peter's nave in Rome. Clad in honey-colored travertine marble, the room was flanked by 60-foot tall Corinthian columns, straddling a 40-foot wide grand stairway, beneath barrel-vaulted ceilings 150 feet high. Clerestory windows on all sides bathed the room with natural light. These views were taken in 1910 and 1962.

Until the first blow fell, no one was convinced that Penn Station really would be demolished, or that New York would permit this monumental act of vandalism against one of the largest and finest landmarks of its age of Roman elegance.... [W]e will probably be judged not by the monuments we build but by those we have destroyed.

—"Farewell to Penn Station,"
The New York Times,
October 30, 1963

Harold drops off the detectives (*above*) beside the Grand Concourse entrance on W. 33rd Street, where the ticket scene (*prior page*) was filmed. The car is parked on the sidewalk.

A modern view of the Penn Station 7th Avenue entrance (*below*).

Similar views looking north across the grand concourse towards 33rd Street taken on April 24, 1962 (*lower left*), and prior to opening in 1910 (*below*).

Believing the policemen are still in his cab, Harold speeds east down E. 34th Street from the corner of Madison Avenue, terrifying the innocent passenger who, unbeknownst to Harold, entered the cab in place of the cops. The five rectangles on this page each mark the same awning on 34th Street.

This modern view looks west towards Madison Avenue. The former Altman Department Store, running the length of E. 34th Street between 5th and Madison Avenues, now houses the City University of New York (CUNY) Graduate Center and a branch of the public library. The parapet roof of 45 E. 34th Street, evident in the movie frame, still appears today (ovals).

Harold filmed several speeding shots along E. 34th Street between 5th and Madison, and edited them into the movie in scrambled order. These two shots above were taken before and after the cab crossed Madison Avenue, showing the length of the former Altman Department Store Building in the background to the right.

A matching modern view looking west from Madison towards 5th Avenue along the side of the CUNY Graduate Center.

The Empire State Building (*right*) stands on the site of the former Waldorf-Astoria Hotel.

This speeding shot (*left*) was taken heading east down E. 34th Street from 5th Avenue. Behind the cab to the left is the ground floor of the Waldorf-Astoria Hotel (*upper left*), and behind the cab to the right is the corner of the Knickerbocker Trust Company (*upper right*).

The squares above and left mark the corner of the Waldorf-Astoria Hotel, current site of the Empire State Building.

Modern view looking west at 5th Avenue from E. 34th Street; the Empire State Building is to the left. The buildings appearing in the top center photo are all still standing, though their façades have been "improved" and several stories have been added to the corner building.

Harold again speeds past the traffic cop (*above*) traveling north up 5th Avenue past the prow of the Flatiron Building. The trolley behind Harold (*oval, above*) is situated in nearly the same spot as the trolley marked with an oval below.

BROADWAY

LOOKING WEST DOWN 23RD

HAROLD'S PATH UP 5TH AVENUE

Looking south (*right*) at the iconic prow of the Flatiron (Fuller) Building, Broadway is to the left and 5th Avenue is to the right. Although in some photos the building appears razor thin, its footprint is actually a right triangle, with its 5th Avenue and 22nd Street sides meeting at a right angle, and its long hypotenuse side running along Broadway. When viewed from Broadway, the face of the building appears like a giant freestanding wall (*bottom left*). The arrow (*bottom right*) marks where Harold traveled north up 5th Avenue, crossing W. 23rd Street.

The Flatiron sits on a small corner, isolated from its neighbors, and conspicuously situated across from Madison Square. New Yorkers witnessed the construction of the 22-story landmark with great fascination. The building was one of the city's tallest when it opened in 1902, and remains New York's oldest skyscraper.

Harold drives by the Flatiron Building a second time a bit later in the movie.

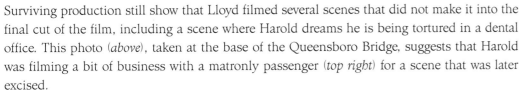

Surviving production still show that Lloyd filmed several scenes that did not make it into the final cut of the film, including a scene where Harold dreams he is being tortured in a dental office. This photo (*above*), taken at the base of the Queensboro Bridge, suggests that Harold was filming a bit of business with a matronly passenger (*top right*) for a scene that was later excised.

The Queensboro Bridge (or 59th Street Bridge) opened March 30, 1909. At the time the west span of the bridge between Manhattan and Blackwell (now Roosevelt) Island was the fourth longest span in the world, bested only by the Brooklyn and Manhattan Bridges, and the Firth of Forth Bridge in Scotland.

A modern view of E. 59th Street and Sutton Place (*right*).

The traffic cop finally waves Harold over for another ticket (*above left*) at the SE corner of Sutton Place looking west down E. 58th Street. Once ticketed, Harold takes a break at the same corner to read the newspaper (*above, right*). I located the ticketing corner by reckoning from the Ritz Tower at Park Avenue and 57th Street in the background as a landmark. The newspaper reading corner was easy to find due to the legible street sign appearing in the studio photo to the right. Only after reckoning from the Ritz Tower did I realize both shots were filmed at the same spot.

Notice the tremendous crowds gathered to watch the filming (*right*). Such difficulties forced Buster Keaton to return home to finish his Manhattan-based film *The Cameraman* (1928), but Lloyd owned his own studio, and could afford to stay in town for as long as necessary.

Built in 1925, the Ritz Tower (*left*) was the first residential skyscraper in New York.

Today, none of the buildings visible during the scene and in the studio photo remain (*left*), while vintage buildings do remain along the east side of Sutton Place.

This view (*left*) shows the SE corner of Sutton Place and E. 58th Street, looking south. Harold was pulled over for a ticket in the shadow of this building (*prior page*). The car is in the same spot as in the prior studio photo showing the large crowds. The same corner as it looks today (*above*).

After reading this "news" story (*left*), Harold learns Babe Ruth is making a public appearance nearby and rushes to see him. This fake story is interesting in several respects. First, Babe visited the real-life Hebrew Orphan Asylum (HOA) in Hamilton Heights to film scenes for the movie. Although this worthy charity would likely have benefitted from the publicity, the story appears to have been "sanitized" by replacing the word "Hebrew" with "City."

Next, the fake story states Babe's 58th home run "has beaten his home run record up to date," even though Babe had hit a record 59 homers in 1921. Since this fake story was prepared well after the season ended, it is unclear why they would mix up the facts. Ruth filmed at the HOA on Thursday, September 15, 1927, after hitting homers 51 and 52 during a September 13th double-header, and would hit home run number 53 the next day. Babe hit his record-breaking 60th home run on September 30, 1927.

Lastly, Babe had a very busy time the week of Sunday, September 11th, to Saturday the 17th. To begin, Ruth played a total of eight games that week, including double-headers on Tuesday and Saturday. On Monday, his only day off, Babe appeared in court to address charges he had allegedly assaulted a man on the street, and was cleared of the charges that Friday. On Thursday, Babe not only filmed at the HOA, and various other scenes for the movie, but also found time to squeeze in a game that afternoon.

LAST MINUTE NEWS

The busy Babe Ruth is to spend the noon hour at the City Orphan Asylum on First Avenue giving signed baseballs to his young admirers. Not only has the Bambino beaten his home run record up to date but he is busy as ever giving help and cheer wherever he can. Yesterday was his 58th and with a double header today George Herman should make it an even sixty.

A crowd gathers in front of the Hebrew Orphan Asylum (HOA) (*left*).

The HOA first opened on Amsterdam Avenue and W. 136th Street in 1884, and in time would house up to 1,750 children. When the Child Welfare Act passed in 1915, destitute widows began receiving allowances sufficient to resume caring for their children, and New York's orphan population, including the HOA's, dropped dramatically. Long considered the nation's premier orphanage, the HOA's institutional approach became increasingly outdated compared to child care models based on small group homes and foster care. The HOA had planned to build a new "cottage style" campus on rural property it owned in the Bronx in the 1920s, but these plans depended on selling the Amsterdam site to the New York Yankees for their new stadium. Despite numerous newspaper accounts confirming the deal, in February 1921, the Yankees decided to build on a much larger site in the Bronx instead. After the Yankee sale fell through, the HOA had no choice but to stay put. The HOA closed the Amsterdam facility in 1941, which thereafter housed junior officers studying at City College across the street under the Army Specialized Training Program. Following WWII, the building served as a dormitory (Army Hall) for the college until it was demolished by the City Parks Department in 1955, as the site for the Jacob H. Schiff Playground. Humorist Art Buchwald lived at the HOA as a child for several years.

Babe tosses autographed baseballs to some lucky fans (*left*). Upon learning of Babe's filming at the HOA, one can imagine someone in Yankee management telling Babe "Yeah, we almost bought the joint." The HOA children must have had a memorable summer, as newspaper accounts report they also participated in Lindbergh's wild ticker tape parade held in June. The corner of the Trinidad Apartments at 501 W. 138th Street appears behind Babe and in this modern view (*right*).

Built in 1884, the HOA on Amsterdam Avenue acquired new neighbors when the City College of New York campus, the first free public institution of higher education in the United States, was built in 1906. The 6,000 seat Lewisohn Stadium, directly across from the HOA, was dedicated in 1915, and served the community for nearly 60 years, until it was demolished in 1973. Mrs. Charles Guggenheim organized inexpensive summer concerts there starting in 1918, an outdoor Carnegie Hall for working stiffs that attracted crowds approaching 25,000 to listen to the New York Philharmonic Orchestra and leading concert performers. George Gershwin performed his *Rhapsody in Blue* here during that magic New York summer of 1927. In later years, greats such as Duke Ellington, Frank Sinatra, Marian Anderson, Louis Armstrong, and Leonard Bernstein, to name a few, would perform here as well.

Babe crawls into Harold's cab (*left*) as a trolley rolling down Amsterdam appears to the right edge of the cab. The movie frame and view below both look north up Amsterdam Avenue towards W. 138th and the City College Harris Hall (*rectangles*).

Researching vintage maps, I was struck by the Dickensian names of the various charitable institutions I had found, including the Hospital for Ruptured and Crippled Children; the Home for Respectable Aged Indigent Females; and Saint Zita's Temporary Home for Friendless Women.

> *"I swing big, with everything I've got. I hit big,*
> *I miss big. I like to live as big as I can."*
> *—Babe Ruth*

Two of the most beloved celebrities of the 1920s, Harold Lloyd and Babe Ruth. The two sold more tickets, in their respective fields, than any other comedian or athlete of the decade.

Babe Ruth is arguably the greatest, most popular, and most iconic athlete in American history. At a time when baseball was far more popular than football or any other sport, and hero-worship flourished, Babe completely dominated the game, shattering scores of records, many of which still stand today. In 1920, Ruth, batting alone, hit more homers than the totals for every other major league team save one. His record 60 home run season in 1927, accounted for 14 percent of all home runs in his league, comparable to hitting 340 homers today. He hit two home runs in a single game 72 times, an unbeaten record, and is the only player to hit three homers in a World Series game on two occasions. Ruth's career slugging percentage of 0.690 (total bases divided by total at bats) remains the highest in baseball history. Aside from his batting prowess, Ruth pitched a shut-out for the Boston Red Sox in the opening game of the 1918 World Series, was the winningest left-handed pitcher from 1915–1917, and for more than 40 years held the record for most consecutive scoreless innings pitched in the World Series at 29 2/3. Known for his affable charm, insatiable appetites, and rotund physique, the larger than life player reached a mythic status we will likely never see again.

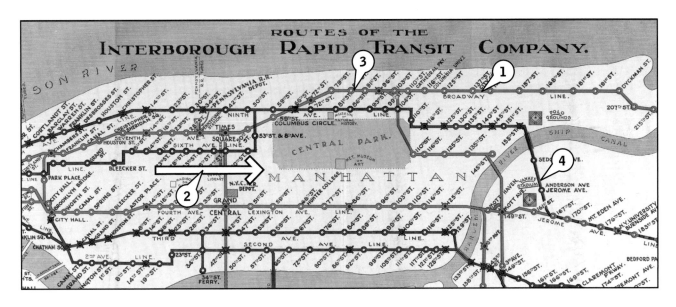

ROUTES OF THE
INTERBOROUGH RAPID TRANSIT COMPANY.

Using maneuvers that would terrify veteran cabbies, Harold speeds Mr. George Herman Ruth from the orphan asylum in Hamilton Heights (1), along random stretches north up 5th Avenue (2), and then back up to Amsterdam Avenue (3), before arriving at Yankee Stadium (4).

Mr. Ruth's Wild Ride

During the wild ride, they travel up stretches of 5th Avenue in random sequential order as marked in alphabetical order below.

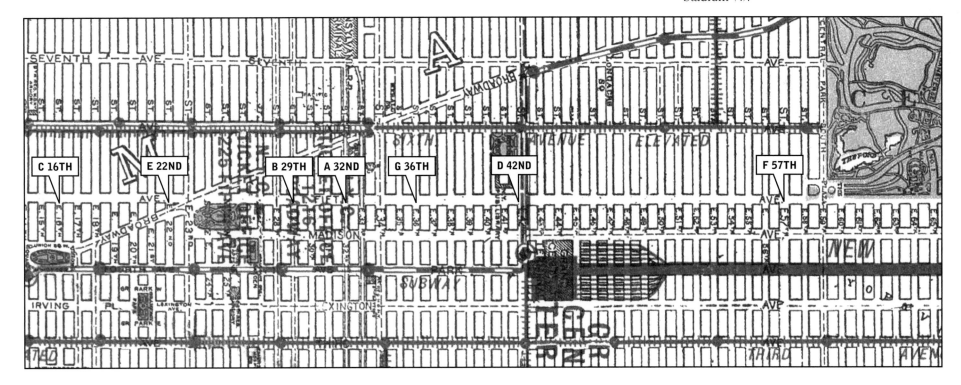

Although presented in nearly random order during the film, Harold and Babe's trip up 5th Avenue will be presented here in geographic order, south to north, beginning with this shot (*above*) taken approaching the NE corner of W. 16th and 5th. The order of the scenes as presented in the movie are indentified on the map (*preceding page*). The round arched doorway to 85 Broadway was home to publisher Houghton Mifflin. Its neighbor to the left, Marshall Field & Co., occupied 87-89 Broadway (now a Banana Republic).

Swerving to the west, the car approaches the broken pediment entry (*rectangle, above left*) of the Merchants Exchange Building (now another Banana Republic) at the SW corner of 17th, and to the rear, the former home of the J. L. Mott Iron Company (now a Gap) at the NW corner of Broadway.

FIFTH AVENUE BUILDING

BRUNSWICK BUILDING

FIFTH AVENUE BUILDING

BRUNSWICK BUILDING

CLOCK AND OBELISK

Skipping ahead a few blocks, the cab races up 5th Avenue towards the SW corner of Madison Square Park. In the background is the Fifth Avenue Building and the Brunswick Building at the corner of 26th Street. The rectangle above marks the Worth Memorial obelisk in Worth Square, and the oval above marks the sidewalk clock tower beside the Fifth Avenue Building at 200 5th Avenue. By suddenly turning right onto W. 22nd Street (see next page), the cab turns at the back of the Flatiron Building before reaching Madison Square.

Above, looking south down 5th Avenue towards the Flatiron Building from the Fifth Avenue Building Clock Tower (*also oval at top*). The clock was installed in 1909, and designated a city landmark in 1981.

This circa 1910 photo (*right*) looks north towards Worth Square (*below center*). Erected in 1857, the monument marks the grave of General William Jenkins Worth, for whom Fort Worth, Texas, is named. It is the second oldest monument in New York, and the only official grave set within a city street. Broadway runs to the left, 5th Avenue to the right.

Left, a modern view of the Worth Monument and the Met Life Building.

FIFTH AVENUE BUILDING

BRUNSWICK BUILDING

When Harold and Babe suddenly turn sharply to the right at 22nd Street (*arrow, left*), we can briefly glimpse the back of the Flatiron (Fuller) Building rush by. The single-story glass atrium "cowcatcher" at the prow of the building (*oval left, right, and left middle*) can be seen.

The arrow (*left*) marks where Harold and Babe turned east (*right*) off of 5th onto 22nd.

This panorama below looks east at Madison Square Park along 5th Avenue (*dotted line, below*). In 1909, the Metropolitan Life Insurance Building tower, fashioned after the Campanile of San Marco in Venice, supplanted the Singer Building as the tallest building in the world. The Woolworth Building would claim the title in 1913. The original Madison Square arena stood opposite the NE corner of the park. On May 5, 1925, Jewish boxer Sid Terris, the East Side "Galloping Ghost of the Ghetto," beat the "Scotch Wop," Italian-American Johnny Dundee, a 14-year veteran of 400 bouts, in the final event held at the arena before it was demolished.

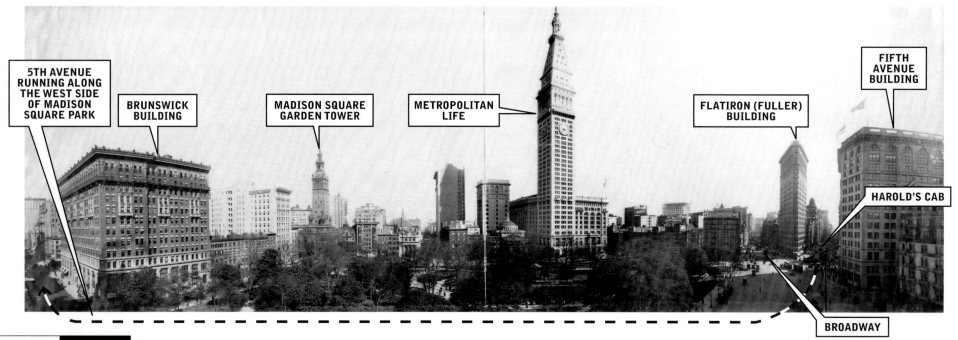

5TH AVENUE RUNNING ALONG THE WEST SIDE OF MADISON SQUARE PARK

BRUNSWICK BUILDING

MADISON SQUARE GARDEN TOWER

METROPOLITAN LIFE

FLATIRON (FULLER) BUILDING

FIFTH AVENUE BUILDING

HAROLD'S CAB

BROADWAY

MARBLE CHURCH | WILBRAHAM | HOLLAND HOUSE

MARBLE CHURCH | HOLLAND HOUSE | WILBRAHAM | WALDORF

The cab (*above, left*) next approaches the corner of W. 29th Street and 5th Avenue, site of one of New York's historic churches.

Marble Collegiate Church (*right*) is the oldest Protestant organization in North America, in continuous service since 1628. When the present church building was dedicated in 1854, it was surrounded by dirt roads, as it was outside the city limits which ran up only to 23rd Street. The cast-iron fence surrounding the church was intended to keep stray cattle off of the property! The neighboring Holland House Hotel (with flag) remains essentially unchanged, although upper floors have been added. The Wilbraham Building next up the street also appears unchanged since this 1901 photo.

Viewed today (*far right*), the Empire State Building dwarfs its southern neighbors.

HOLLAND HOUSE | WILBRAHAM

Approaching W. 30th towards the Wilbraham Building, built in 1888–1890 (*above, left*), and a modern view (*above, right*). The building originally housed bachelor apartments, meaning none of the units had kitchens. Instead, an eighth-floor common dining room served all of the cooking-impaired male tenants.

Crossing 30th Street, the taxi whisks past the multiple arches of the Textile Building (*above*) occupying the entire east side of 5th Avenue between E. 31st and E. 30th Streets.

WALDORF-ASTORIA HOTEL

WALDORF-ASTORIA HOTEL

The cab approaches the Reed & Barton Building at the corner of W. 32nd Street (*above*), then heads farther north towards the east side of the former Waldorf-Astoria Hotel on W. 33rd Street (*upper right*).

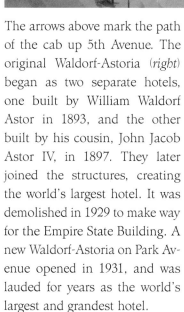

A modern view (*above*) of the Reed & Barton Building at W. 32nd Street.

The arrows above mark the path of the cab up 5th Avenue. The original Waldorf-Astoria (*right*) began as two separate hotels, one built by William Waldorf Astor in 1893, and the other built by his cousin, John Jacob Astor IV, in 1897. They later joined the structures, creating the world's largest hotel. It was demolished in 1929 to make way for the Empire State Building. A new Waldorf-Astoria on Park Avenue opened in 1931, and was lauded for years as the world's largest and grandest hotel.

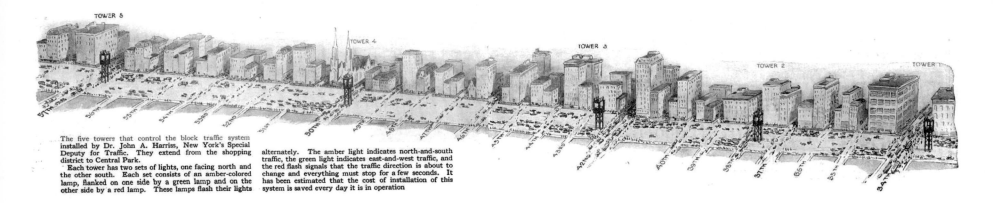

The five towers that control the block traffic system installed by Dr. John A. Harriss, New York's Special Deputy for Traffic. They extend from the shopping district to Central Park.

Each tower has two sets of lights, one facing north and the other south. Each set consists of an amber-colored lamp, flanked on one side by a green lamp and on the other side by a red lamp. These lamps flash their lights alternately. The amber light indicates north-and-south traffic, the green light indicates east-and-west traffic, and the red flash signals that the traffic direction is about to change and everything must stop for a few seconds. It has been estimated that the cost of installation of this system is saved every day it is in operation

© Underwood & Underwood

The master signalman in his tower at the corner of Fifth avenue and Forty-second street. He controls the lights in all the five towers, signaling the other towermen by means of an electric bell system

This same view of the Waldorf-Astoria (*right*) also shows the 5th Avenue traffic signal tower located at W. 34th Street (*arrow*). Experimental towers were installed along 5th Avenue in 1920, in order to control traffic, using the block signal system originally developed by the railroads. Situated at the intersections of 34th, 38th, 42nd, 50th, and 57th Streets, the five 5th Avenue towers were replaced with permanent bronze towers in 1923. By sending electric signals to control men located in each tower, the master signalman at 42nd Street could control the lights allowing all 5th Avenue traffic to move at the same time. Despite its initial success, the tower islands blocked the road, and were removed in 1929.

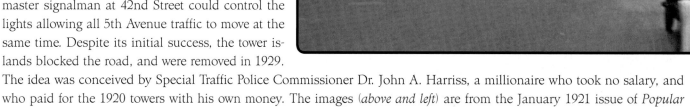

The idea was conceived by Special Traffic Police Commissioner Dr. John A. Harriss, a millionaire who took no salary, and who paid for the 1920 towers with his own money. The images (*above and left*) are from the January 1921 issue of *Popular Science* magazine.

Harold and Babe approach W. 36th Street, the final view of 5th Avenue to appear during their taxi sequence (*right*). The rectangles in the vintage and modern views mark the onetime location of Tiffany & Co. at 393 5th Avenue. The arrow marks the W. 38th Street traffic tower.

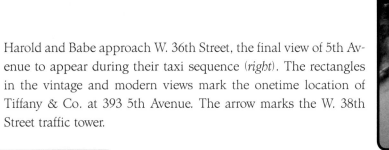

Harold's cab now reaches 42nd Street (*left*), confronting the master traffic control tower and the former Bristol Building at the NW corner of 5th Avenue. This broader view from 1922 (*lower left*) shows the main branch of the New York Public Library, which does not appear in the movie, standing across from the Bristol on the opposite corner. At the time, the library was the largest marble building in the world. It officially opened on May 23, 1911, instantly becoming one of the world's largest libraries with over one million volumes. The iconic lion statues guarding the front entrance were named "Patience" and "Fortitude" by Mayor Fiorello LaGuardia as a Depression-era inspirational gesture.

Views of the bronze 5th Avenue traffic towers (*below*).

BRISTOL BUILDING

First Publication of Design of New Bronze Traffic Towers

Handsome Traffic Tower for Fifth Avenue Unveiled

Harold and Babe approach W. 57th Street and the northernmost of the five 5th Avenue traffic towers (*near right*). The corner is the site of Bergdorf Goodman under construction. The rectangle (*right*) shows a painting of how the completed building will look, and the small arrows (*right and far right*) mark the site of the Pulitzer Memorial Fountain, diagonally across from the SE corner of Central Park. The Bergdorf Goodman stands on the site of the former Cornelius Vanderbilt mansion (*far right and below*) that was demolished in 1927, some time prior to filming. The bold arrow shows the relative direction of the taxi in each image.

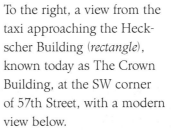

To the right, a view from the taxi approaching the Heckscher Building (*rectangle*), known today as The Crown Building, at the SW corner of 57th Street, with a modern view below.

A view of the Vanderbilt Mansion before it was demolished to make way for Bergdorf Goodman, looking south down 5th Avenue from W. 58th Street. The mansion appeared briefly in Buster Keaton's debut feature film *The Saphead* (1920) (*inset*).

BELNORD   WEST PARK PRESBYTERIAN CHURCH

Modern views approaching W. 81st Street (*above*) and also W. 83rd Street (*below*).

The action suddenly jumps from 5th Avenue to the Upper West Side, where the taxi travels north up Amsterdam Avenue from between W. 81st Street (*above*) to W. 83rd Street (*below*). In the far background stands the extant Belnord Apartments and West Park Presbyterian Church, both on W. 86th Street.

The action jumps again, this time to the Macombs Dam Bridge approaching Yankee Stadium. Babe reacts on cue to the various near-misses (right). Babe was no stranger to movies, having already starred playing himself in *Headin' Home* (1920) and in *Babe Comes Home* (1927), the latter directed coincidentally by Ted Wilde, the credited director of *Speedy*. Wilde would be nominated for an Academy Award ® for Best Comedy Direction of *Speedy* in 1928, the sole year the honor was bestowed.

This scene (*right*) was likely filmed while traversing the Macombs Dam Bridge (notice the bridge girders at back), as Babe sat in a prop taxi-cab, cut in half, driven around on a trailer. The sunlight streaming through the "roof" clearly reveals this bit of movie magic. The rear projection technique for filming interior shots within traveling cars was not commonly used before the arrival of sound movies.

The Macombs Dam Bridge heading east over the Harlem River towards the now de-molished original Yankee Stadium.

The Yankees sold well over a million tickets during Ruth's inaugural 1920 season with the team, more than double the sales of any other club. At the time the Yankees had been subleasing playing time at the Polo Grounds from the New York Giants under a long-term lease. When the Giants snubbed the Yankees by refusing to offer another long term lease, the Yankees looked to build their own park. Although management nearly acquired the site of the Hebrew Orphan Asylum (discussed previously) for their new park, they acquired a much larger site in the Bronx, just across the river from the Polo Grounds. The resulting Yankee Stadium, nearly twice as big as any other park for its time, was rightfully hailed "The House That Ruth Built." The photo at right was taken April 3, 1923, two weeks before the grand opening.

Above and below, scenes showing the front ticket booths at Yankee Stadium.

Yankee Stadium opened on April 18, 1923, before the largest crowd then ever assembled for a baseball game. As if pre-ordained, Babe christened the park by hitting its inaugural home run in the bottom of the third inning, a savage 3 RBI homer smashed into the right-field bleachers. The Yankees won that day, beating the Boston Red Sox 4-1. The stadium was home to the Yankees from 1923 to 1973, and following major renovations, from 1976 until the final game played there on September 21, 2008. The stadium was demolished and is now the site of Heritage Park. The adjacent new Yankee Stadium opened on April 16, 2009.

An aerial view showing the Polo Grounds field in Upper Manhattan, home to the New York Giants (now San Francisco Giants) from 1911 to 1957, and temporary home to the Yankees from 1912 to 1922 (*left*), and the new Yankee Stadium just across the Harlem River in the Bronx (*right*).

This scene from the film, taken from the front of Yankee Stadium, offers a view of the Macombs Dam Bridge (*right*).

Speedy—Brooklyn

Left to right, three prominent towers as viewed from Brooklyn in this circa 1927 photo (*left*) and behind Harold (*oval, right*): the Transportation Building, the Woolworth Building, and the Municipal Building.

Thugs hijack Pop's trolley car, hoping to put him out of business. Harold intercepts a note saying the car is hidden at Kent Avenue. As he arrives on the scene in the opening shot, pondering where to look, a street sign reading "KENT AV.—S 8 ST" is fully visible.

The stolen trolley was hidden at an old ferry dock (*inset*) at Kent Avenue and S. 8th Street in Brooklyn, near the base of the Williamsburg Bridge. The site is now a small parking lot. The white quad towers of the Brooklyn Edison Company appear in this circa 1927 photo and movie frame (*rectangles, above*).

Overleaf: Looking north up Everit Street towards the Brooklyn and Manhattan Bridges.

Harold prepares to take off with the trolley (*above*). Looking west down the East River we see the aligned steel and masonry towers of the Manhattan and Brooklyn Bridges, respectively (*oval, above*).

Below, this October 1991 aerial view shows the ferry pier (*arrow*), near the base of the Williamsburg Bridge (foreground), and the alignment of the Manhattan and Brooklyn Bridge towers (*oval*), corresponding to the view above.

The ferry site piers (*rectangle, above*), at the end of S. 8th Street, are still visible in this 1988 view, looking east.

Viewed in this circa 1910 photo (*right*), the Williamsburg Bridge is the longest span suspension bridge over the East River, exceeding the older Brooklyn Bridge span by five feet. With its double-deck design, the new bridge nearly trebled the older bridge's transport capacity. Amid cannon fire and the unfurling of giant United States flags from its twin towers, the Williamsburg Bridge formally opened on the afternoon of December 19, 1903. That evening, immense crowds on both sides of the river witnessed the bridge's illumination, a shimmering pyrotechnic display, and a maritime pageant hosting a fleet of 140 vessels.

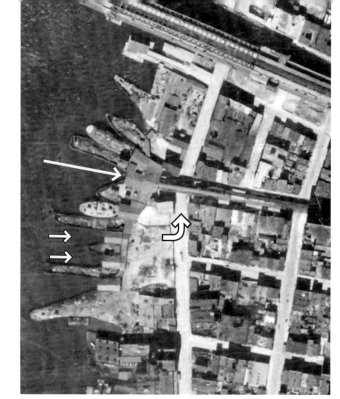

Earlier, as the crooks lead the stolen trolley into the ferry yard, you can see the pitched roofs of two small ferry buildings (*arrows, left*) corresponding to the buildings marked with twin arrows on this 1924 aerial view (*right*). The long arrow (*right*) marks the BMT elevated station and tracks running east along Broadway into the heart of Brooklyn. The heavy diagonal across the top of the photo is the Williamsburg Bridge. The curved arrow (*right*) corresponds to the path Harold takes out of the ferry yard onto Kent Avenue (*below and below left*).

In this movie frame (*above*), Harold begins the race home, turning out of the ferry yard, north onto Kent Avenue, approaching the corner of Broadway. While the corner buildings have been demolished, the rectangle marks 409 Kent Avenue, visible at the right edge of the frame, and in the corresponding modern view (*right*). An elevated train sitting on the now-demolished Broadway tracks appears at the top of the frame.

Left to right: the Transportation Building, the Woolworth Building, and the Municipal Building.

This 1927 photo looks northwest from Brooklyn towards lower Manhattan. After 13 years of construction, the Brooklyn Bridge was finally completed in 1883. Spanning the East River, it was the longest suspension span in the world until the previously mentioned Williamsburg Bridge opened nearby in 1903. The third East River span, the adjoining Manhattan Bridge (*right edge, above*) was completed in 1909. The gentrified Brooklyn neighborhood near the bridge is called "DUMBO," an acronym for Down Under the Manhattan Bridge Overpass. Lloyd filmed the race home near the base of both bridges and near the Brooklyn Bridge elevated station (*ovals*).

The race home switches from the foot of the Williamsburg Bridge to the foot of the Brooklyn Bridge (*upper left*), as Harold speeds north up Everit Street towards the elevated tracks running along Old Fulton Street, which block the Brooklyn Bridge from view. The matching view to the left was taken in 1922. The doorway in the modern view (*rectangle above*) can be seen in the movie frame on the next page, as can the convertible within the oval of the upper left still. The back of the Eagle Warehouse & Storage Co. building (1893) appears prominently in the matching view below. The arched front entryway to the warehouse appears on the next page.

All four images on this page look north up Everit Street towards the corner of Old Fulton Street.

This reverse-angle view (*above*) of Harold racing north up Everit Street under the Old Fulton Street elevated tracks was filmed by a second camera at the same time as the shot on the preceding page. The rectangle above corresponds to the rectangle doorway in the modern view to the right, and in the modern view on the preceding page. The oval above marks the arched front entryway to the Eagle Warehouse & Storage Co. building to the right. The convertible at the far-right edge above (*arrow*), appears within the movie frame oval on the prior page. By filming the scene twice from different angles, Harold created two shots for the price of one stunt.

The thugs pursue Harold along the same path (*above*), north up Everit Street, crossing Fulton Street, and continuing onto Water Street. The E.W. Munns Kalsomine Co., at the left end of the above panorama, was the initial clue leading to the other Brooklyn Bridge discoveries. Kalsomine is a form of whitewash. There were many paint and white lead businesses in this neighborhood.

A modern view (*above*) of the corner of Water Street and Fulton Street in Brooklyn.

This scene (*right*) was likely filmed in Brooklyn at the base of the Manhattan Bridge. The Frank L. Burns Coal Co. had a coal yard at the north end of Adams Street immediately east of the bridge. While many vintage buildings in the area remain, a few were demolished, precluding a positive ID. The convertible in the foreground is the same car mentioned in the prior two pages.

In this panning shot (*above*), Harold races west from under the Brooklyn Bridge on Prospect Street (P), past the Main Street underpass (M) (which runs north—its left side is obscured), and then turns right past the corner Prospect House (*rectangle*), heading northwest onto Fulton Street (F *and arrow, below*), beneath the elevated tracks running along the street. The intersection above was a bewildering array of elevated stations and tracks, street-level tracks, and tracks running on the bridge. The block of Fulton to the left, along with the Fulton elevated tracks, has been completely demolished. A glimpse of where Harold made his turn past the Prospect House appears to the lower left (*inset and arrow*) in this circa 1910 photo taken from the bridge's elevated station. The east side of the previously mentioned Eagle Warehouse appears as well.

THE EAGLE WAREHOUSE

A modern view of the Main Street underpass (M) and the Prospect Street underpass (P) to the Brooklyn Bridge. Due to modern street reconfigurations, Main Street, which used to run under the bridge from Plymouth Street south to High Street, now ceases at Front Street, two blocks north of the bridge. The arrow marks Harold's path from Prospect onto Fulton.

The filming now jumps back and forth between New York and Los Angeles. Harold stops at William N. Snowden's stables at 403 Aliso Street in Los Angeles (*above*) when he notices his horse has started to limp. The wooden board with "Blacksmith" painted on it is a prop, a visual cue added by Lloyd's staff. Mr. Snowden sold and boarded horses and mules, a thriving business before the automobile age.

Los Angeles had dozens of horse and mule stables east of downtown, especially near the former Chinatown, situated within the dashed line below. Nearly all of the structures in the foreground below were demolished to make way for the Union Passenger Terminal, which opened in 1939. The oval below marks the Snowden stables, while the rectangle identifies the Plaza de Los Angeles and New High Street, areas where Lloyd filmed extensive scenes for *From Hand to Mouth* (1920).

The Snowden stables (*oval, above and right*) were situated close to City Hall and the Hall of Justice (*box, above and right*).

While Harold leads his horse to the blacksmith, an oncoming trolley pushes Harold's unattended trolley car away down the street (*above*). We are now in the Upper West Side of Manhattan, looking at the SW corner of Amsterdam Avenue and W. 106th Street. I found this spot by looking up the address to the Gristede Brothers grocers sign visible during the scene.

Without a horse, Harold continues to make his way home by tying the trolley to the bumper of a car (*lower left*). Harold is now up in Hamilton Heights, traveling south down Amsterdam Avenue from W. 145th Street. The corner building with the amazing optician sign (*oval, left*) still stands (*below*) and the oval below marks where it was located. The corner building at W. 146th Street (*rectangle, far left, and inset, left*) has survived as well.

Harold continues his free ride hitched to the car (*above*), this time traveling north up Amsterdam Avenue approaching W. 143rd Street. The tree marked with an oval stands in Hamilton Square.

A modern view north up Amsterdam Avenue towards W. 143rd Street.

In this view, the car and trolley turn left from Hamilton Place onto W. 143rd Street, traveling east towards Amsterdam Avenue. The tree (*oval, above*) is the same tree marked in the frame above.

A modern view of W. 143rd, Hamilton Place, and Hamilton Square.

After Harold cuts free from the car giving him a tow, he spots this pair of horses (*above*) that might come in handy. We now jump to Hollywood, where these scenes were filmed on Santa Monica Boulevard, between Flemish Lane and North Oxford Avenue. The vertical sign for the Signal Apartments at 5425 Santa Monica Boulevard appears in the background.

A modern view of the Signal Apartment Building.

An apartment on Flemish Lane appears behind the horses in the shot above.

A modern view of the apartment building on the NW corner of Santa Monica Boulevard and Flemish Lane.

The action now jumps to South-Central Los Angeles, a few miles south of downtown. A mannequin dressed in police garb (a promotional prop for a fictitious movie, *The Traffic Cop*) falls to the street, blocking Harold's path (*right*). Harold retrieves the dummy and places it standing guard at his side, fooling the police into granting Harold leeway as he

A modern view looking north up South Broadway towards 45th Street.

continues to speed home. This scene was filmed on South Broadway, looking north at the corner of 45th Street. I suspect Harold filmed many other scenes at this point in the movie in this neighborhood, but so much today has been demolished that it is no longer possible to make a match.

The stretch of Broadway running through South-Central L.A. was originally called Moneta Street. The awning for the Moneta Hardware Co. at the corner of Broadway and 45th Street appears to the left. In later scenes, this policeman will chase Harold on horseback for a few blocks along what I suspect to be adjoining blocks of South Broadway.

A modern view looking south down South Broadway towards 45th Street.

At this point during the race, the action jumps back and forth between Manhattan and Brooklyn several times. This scene (*above, left*) looks west down Plymouth Street in Brooklyn as Harold races east towards Adams Street. The scene below, appearing later in the film, is the identical shot filmed from an opposite point of view, looking east down Plymouth. It appears that every vintage building in both shots is still standing. Notice how the position of the cars in each shot is the same (and that nearly every window in the 1927 view below is broken). I figured out the bottom location once I had noticed the cameramen (*inset*) standing off to the side during the scene. The foreground shade in both images below is provided by the Manhattan Bridge.

This scene above, appearing later in the race, was filmed in Brooklyn, traveling north up Furman Street. The warehouse to the left of the movie frame still stands, but is today covered with tarps and scaffolding, preventing a full matching shot.

A modern view looking up Furman Street toward the Brooklyn Bridge's east tower. The Brooklyn Railroad Company Building, built in 1860–1861, appears in both images above (*oval*).

Notice the crowds watching from over the fence and along the sidewalk. The elevated station in the back was the starting point for the elevated line running east down Fulton Street.

This 1988 aerial overview shows all of the Brooklyn shots relative to one another.

Speedy—Downtown

The race home continues now mostly through lower Manhattan. Above, Harold races through Greenwich Village and down 8th Avenue from Jane Street, towards Abingdon Square. The corner buildings (*rectangle*) near Jane Street have been demolished, creating a tree-filled informal park or garden. Notice the people watching from the third-floor windows. Lloyd stated he filmed scenes near Sheridan Square in the Village. I found this location on Google Street View by looking at nearby streets that used to have trolley tracks.

Harold steers south past the Hotel Astor at the corner of W. 44th and Broadway (*far left*), at the north end of Times Square. The landmark hotel, which opened in 1904, was demolished in 1967. The Capitol Theater (*oval*) appears on the next page. Notice the similar traffic tower (*above, left*) that stood in Times Square.

Overleaf: Circa 1937 view of Battery Park and the beginning of Broadway.

When Lloyd and company returned home from New York, they realized that they lacked certain shots for Harold's race home. They had long shots of the trolley driven by Harold's stunt double, and close-ups of Harold in the front cab, but they did not have medium shots showing Harold driving the horses. Rather than return to New York to shoot the few needed scenes, Harold decided to film them using process shots, in which New York street scenes were composited to the background of studio shots of Harold and the running horses (apparently on a treadmill) filmed in Hollywood. Although these few process shots serve their purpose, they contrast sharply with the otherwise naturalistic scenes filmed in New York.

To the right, Harold races past the Wintergarden Theater where the marquee heralds "*A Night in Spain*, starring Ted & Betty Healy," a musical revue that ran for six months in 1927. Ted Healy (*left*) was a popular comedian, vaudeville performer, and film actor who wrote some of the music and lyrics for the show. Healy is best remembered today as the impresario for the Three Stooges. Ted was an established vaudeville performer when he asked childhood friend Moe Howard to join his show in 1922. Moe's brother Shemp joined in 1923, and Larry Fine joined in 1925. Shemp left the act and was replaced by brother Jerome "Curly" Howard in 1932. The Three Stooges worked with Healy, on and off, until 1934.

A Night in Venice, a sequel revue starring Ted Healy, ran in 1929, featuring songs by Oscar Hammerstein II and choreography by Busby Berkeley. The cast included Larry, Moe, and Shemp (*below*).

Harold rides south on Broadway towards W. 50th Street, between the Capitol Theater (*oval, above*) and the Wintergarden Theater to the right. The box in both images (*above*) shows the corner transition between the stone façade and brick side of the 12-story building adjacent to the theater.

Harold continues racing south down Broadway towards E. 17th Street, as shown in the movie frame and the modern view above. The police are parked at the NW corner of Union Square. I found this location by noticing the Worth Monument and Commodore Criterion Building in the far background (*inset and lower left*), and working backward down Broadway with Google Street View until hitting 17th Street.

A modern view of Worth Square on Broadway, adjacent to Madison Square, showing the Worth Monument and the remodeled Commodore Criterion Building.

An early view looking north at Union Square (*right*). The white box corresponds to the movie frame (*upper left*).

BACK OF FLATIRON BUILDING

METROPOLITAN LIFE BUILDING

Harold races past the policemen, unaware that the police mannequin at his side is now thumbing its nose. The outraged police captain (*right*) returns the greeting. Behind him are the extant Everett Building and the Guardian Life Insurance Company of America Building, situated on the NW and NE corners, respectively, of E. 17th Street and Park Avenue South. A modern view of the buildings appears above.

The oval above marks the location of the policemen's car at the SE corner of Broadway and E. 17th Street.

Admittedly, this spot was easy to find. Harold races south from 5th Avenue through the Washington Arch Memorial into Washington Square Park (*left*). At the time, and until 1964, 5th Avenue traffic could traverse the park through the archway and then split south onto either Thompson Street or West Broadway (now LaGuardia Place). The modern view below was taken by Alan Cordova on September 27, 2007, showing supporters arriving early for a Barack Obama campaign rally held there that evening. It was described by *The New York Times* as "one of the largest campaign events of the year."

Washington Square has long been considered the heart of Greenwich Village. The park site was acquired by the City Council in 1797 for use as a Potter's Field (common burial ground). Historical records suggest that burials were never removed from the site, and that the remains of as many as 20,000 people were left behind when the land was filled in and paved over for use as a public park in 1827. It was here in 1835, that Samuel Morse, a professor at the adjacent New York University, hosted the first public demonstration of

the telegraph. Dedicated in 1895, the Washington Arch was designed by architect Stanford White, who fashioned it after the Arc de Triomphe in Paris. Construction of the arch was delayed in 1890 when human remains, gravestones, and an intact coffin were found while digging the foundation.

5th Avenue buses in Washington Square.

On two occasions, Harold races beneath different parts of the S-shaped elevated tracks of the Coenties Slip, part of the mile-long South Ferry Branch of the Third Street elevated line running between the Battery and Chatham Square. The elevated line served the community from 1878 until 1950. The oval in the right frame above marks the corner street sign at Water Street. The prominent doorway cornice in the right frame above appears in the modern view below, just left of the street lamp. The tracks curve from the near corner of Front Street (*above left*) to the far corner of Pearl Street (*above right*).

The tower of the Produce Exchange Building (*square, left and top left*), stands over the curved tracks of the Coenties Slip. The slip was an artificial inlet in the East River for loading ships that was land-filled in 1835. The aerial view (*left*) was taken in 1927, the year Lloyd filmed there.

Harold steers west from State Street onto Battery Place, racing past the Washington Building towards the elevated train station on the corner of Greenwich Street. The Woolworth Building stands tall in the background above the arrow, while Bowling Green Park and the Standard Oil Building appear at the far right. The oval to the far right marks the back of the subway entrance where Harold and Ann Christy enter the subway on their way to Coney Island (*bottom right*) earlier in the film.

A modern view of the corner of State Street and Battery Place.

A circa 1937 aerial view of Harold's turn from State Street onto Battery Place.

SIGN READING: "LINCOLN FIREPROOF STORAGE"

While filming another pass under the Battery Place elevated station (*above, left*), the stuntman swerved to avoid an oncoming car and smashed into one of the support posts. Fortunately, no one was hurt and Lloyd and his gag men cleverly incorporated the real-life accident into the story. In the film, Harold is crestfallen to discover the accident has broken a trolley wheel in two. Harold then notices a nearby manhole cover, appropriates it for a repair, and is soon back on his way. The manhole scene (*above*) was filmed in Los Angeles, on the corner of N. Spring Street and Alpine Street, by the Lincoln Fireproof Storage Company building, a few blocks north of the Plaza de Los Angeles.

A modern view of the corner building (*right*), and a 1933 aerial view of the Plaza de Los Angeles (*far right*). The manhole still sits in the intersection.

In another process shot (*above*), Harold travels south down Broadway past W. 33rd Street and along Greeley Square, to the left (the southern counterpart to Herald Square, to the north), and the McAlpin Hotel, to the right. The 34th St./ Herald Square elevated station appears behind Harold overhead, blocking the view of Macy's up the street. This setting was one block east from the Pennsylvania Station discussed previously. The oval above marks the sign for W. 33rd Street, covered by scaffolding in the modern view.

For the second time, the trolley races around the corner from State Street onto Battery Place, as the following appear in the background from left to right: the Standard Oil Building on the NE corner of Broadway and Beaver Street; Bowling Green Park; the Produce Exchange Building on the SE corner of Beaver Street (originally completed in 1884 and replaced with a glass office tower in 1959); and the U.S. Customs House (1907) to the south of the park.

The statue of Abraham de Peyster (mayor from 1691 to 1695) (*above and right*) was placed in Bowling Green Park in 1896, and removed in 1972 to accommodate park and subway renovations. It was relocated to nearby Hanover Square in 1976, but is currently in storage awaiting a new site. Bowling Green is New York's oldest park. It was here, on July 9, 1776, that the Declaration of Independence was received and read in New York, that protesters toppled a gilded lead equestrian statue of King George III standing in the park, and later melted down the lead to make bullets. The protesters had planned to parade the king's head around on a pike, but Loyalists captured the head and returned it to England. While records show it arrived safely, the head has not been heard of since.

To the left is one of New York's greatest early buildings, the Produce Exchange Building at the east side of Bowling Green. The tower (*box*) appears a few pages back in the photos showing the Coenties Slip.

One of the delights of finding high-resolution vintage photos is spotting the details of daily life. I count 14 window-washers working all over the building, but only three women on the street. Below, a mustachioed street peddler pushes his banana cart.

A 1908 view of the recently completed U.S. Customs House (*far left*) at the south end of Bowling Green. The 1924 aerial view (*below*) shows the proximity of Bowling Green (*left*) and the Coenties Slip (*right*).

The front steps of the U.S. Customs House (*above*) are guarded by four groups of allegorical figures (sculpted by Daniel Chester French) representing, from left to right: Asia, America, Europe, and Africa, symbolizing the building's role as point of entry for the world's goods. The figure of America appears in the foreground of this scene (*upper right*), depicting the annual Policemen's Day Parade from Buster Keaton's *Cops* (1922). The former building at the NE corner of Broadway and Beaver Street (*rectangle, above*) was reconfigured and amalgamated into the Standard Oil Building in 1923. The inset above points to the subway entrance appearing earlier in the film.

The figure of America (*oval, above*) appears in the background of Harold's race home. The dark red brick of the Produce Exchange contrasted sharply with the Custom House's white stone. The Produce Exchange was built on an iron skeleton a year before the world's first skyscraper—the Home Insurance Building in Chicago (1885)—was built with this technique. The Exchange's vast second-floor main hall measured 220 by 144 feet, with 47- to 60-foot high ceilings.

A modern view of the glass tower that replaced the Produce Exchange in 1959, with the figures representing America in the foreground.

Above, Harold races from Grove Street and 4th Street, past the Christopher Street Sheridan Square subway entrance, towards 7th Avenue. The row of sunlit apartments on the left is Grove Street, and the row of sunlit apartments in the background to the right is Christopher Street. The photo above identifies St. John's Lutheran Church at 81 Christopher Street, built in 1821. The above scene is the final location shot appearing in the movie.

In the end, Harold returns the trolley in time, Pop Dillon sells the franchise for a fortune, and Harold and Jane contemplate wedding plans. So ends Lloyd's final silent film, and our journey through silent-era New York. Constantly evolving and changing, the city that doesn't sleep will never pause long enough to pose for a formal portrait. Yet Harold Lloyd captured remarkably vivid impressions of New York during an era when it rightfully boasted the biggest and the best of all things, and held sway over the nation and the world with more bravado and assurance than perhaps at any time before or since.

THE END

Vintage and modern views of the city's continuously changing skyline.

The Transition to Sound

Feet First (1930)

The "boy meets girl" opening scenes from *Feet First* were filmed in 1930, in Westwood Village, south of the recently opened University of California at Los Angeles campus, where classes first began in 1929. Below, Harold peers around the corner of the Janss Investment Company Building (2), built in 1929 at the corner of Broxton Avenue and Westwood Boulevard, while the arcade entrance to the University Professional Building (3), on the corner of Broxton and Kinross Avenue, appears behind him. At left, a traffic altercation takes place at the corner of Westwood and Le Conte Avenue (1). Although many original buildings within the village remain, modern high-rise apartments and office towers now encroach on this charming neighborhood.

Overleaf: Harold Lloyd's magnificent 16-acre Green Acres estate. The family moved into the 32,000 square foot, 44-room mansion during August of 1929.

This view looks up Broxton towards the tower of the Fox Westwood Village movie theater on the left, where Hollywood premieres are often held, and up Westwood Boulevard towards the Holmby Building tower on the right. *Feet First* is likely one of the first movies to use Westwood Village as a movie location. Lloyd's Westwood Location Ranch (discussed in the *Speedy* chapter) was located just a few blocks away. The buildings within the square (*above*) correspond to the movie image at the bottom left.

The tile roof overhang has been removed from the side of the Janss Building (*below*). To the right, Harold is so love-struck that his face has been blurred on this publicity still. The Holmby Building tower appears in the background.

Harold's troubles begin when he stows away on an airplane in an air-mail sack. The sack is misplaced, and eventually becomes entangled on a city high-rise scaffold (discussed in the prior *Thrill* chapter). During this brief scene, Harold's plane lands at Mines Field, the predecessor to the vast Los Angeles International Airport (LAX) complex. The former hay field was used as an airfield for several years, and was officially dedicated as Los Angeles Municipal Airport on June 7, 1930. Mary Pickford reportedly made the formal dedication.

The original east hangar building, appearing in this movie frame (*top left*) and photo (*top right*), still stands at the SE corner of LAX at what is now Aviation Boulevard (1) and W. Imperial Highway (2), a bit west of N. Douglas Street. The long, straight stretch of Atchison, Topeka & Santa Fe rail tracks running north-south, parallel to Aviation Boulevard (1), was frequently used for silent-era railroad chase sequences. The east hangar appears to the left in the inset photo.

Movie Crazy (1932)

During this opening scene, Harold appears to be riding in the back of a convertible limousine. The shot widens to reveal he is hitching a ride alongside the limousine on his bicycle, before turning into the driveway at 690 E. Villa Street in Pasadena. Captain Lee Nelson (Ret.), a reader born in 1917, contacted me to share a childhood memory of watching Harold Lloyd film scenes on East Villa Street near his home in Pasadena, while holding onto the side of car from a bicycle. Using Bing Maps Bird's Eye View and Google Street View, I prowled the area remotely from my home in Northern California. I was delighted to report back to Captain Nelson that the picture he saw being filmed was called *Movie Crazy*, and that the homes along the street have barely changed.

Above, Harold rides past 674 E. Villa Street. Below, Harold on the driveway of 690 E. Villa.

Movie Crazy is widely considered to be Lloyd's best talking feature. Harold plays a Kansas boy who is invited to Hollywood for a screen test in response to his application, which innocently contains another man's photo. The movie provides fascinating behind-the-scenes peeks of Hollywood movie-making, and of the United Artists Studios in particular. In the story, Harold meets both a young blond actress, and the raven-haired Spanish señorita character she plays, without realizing they are, in fact, the same person. In the end, Harold wins the girl and a studio contract.

To the left, Harold's movie frame aligns seamlessly with a modern view of 690 E. Villa Street in Pasadena.

Unlike *Girl Shy*, where Harold "arrives" at the Santa Fe Depot, and yet enters town from the Southern Pacific Depot a few blocks away, Harold's arrival in *Movie Crazy* provides detailed views of both the back *and* front of the Santa Fe station. Above is a circa 1900 view of the passenger shelter along the back of the station. The oval, above and to the upper right, marks the same shelter post. Below is a view of the station taken during filming, looking south from the First Street Viaduct.

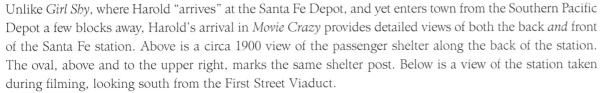

The same arch and/or circular Western Union sign appears within the box in Snub Pollard's 1928 short *Once Over* (top), in Harold's scene from *Movie Crazy* (middle), and in Laurel and Hardy's 1929 comedy *Berth Marks*.

Southern Pacific held monopoly power over Los Angeles rail transport until the Atchison, Topeka & Santa Fe began competing there in March 1886, greatly accelerating the influx of newcomers to the area. The exotic Moorish-style Santa Fe Depot was built in 1893, and stood between E. 1st and E. 2nd Streets, facing downtown along Santa Fe Avenue. The Union Station Passenger Terminal that opened in 1939 (built upon the site of the original Chinatown), consolidated the Santa Fe, Southern Pacific, and Union Pacific passenger lines into a common station, obviating the need for individual stations. The Santa Fe depot was damaged from the 1933 Long Beach earthquake, and was reported to have been demolished in early 1942. The gas storage tank stanchions (*oval, above*), are from the same facility where Lloyd's stalled car was hit by a train in *For Heaven's Sake*.

The square archway behind Harold is identified to the left, and is the same archway at the bottom left.

When Harold arrives at the Santa Fe Depot, he comes upon a crew filming a movie. As Harold watches an actor apply make-up, a square archway with the Santa Fe logo appears in the background (*box, top left, and above*), the same arch appearing behind Snub Pollard in *Once Over* (*above, right*). My first clue that Lloyd filmed *Movie Crazy* at the United Artists Studios was the equipment with "U.A. CORP" stenciled on the side passing by in the background (*far left*).

Harold is about to bump into a temperamental studio boss (*above, middle*) beside the depot's front entrance, which appears directly above in the 1919 Stan Laurel comedy *Hustling for Health*.

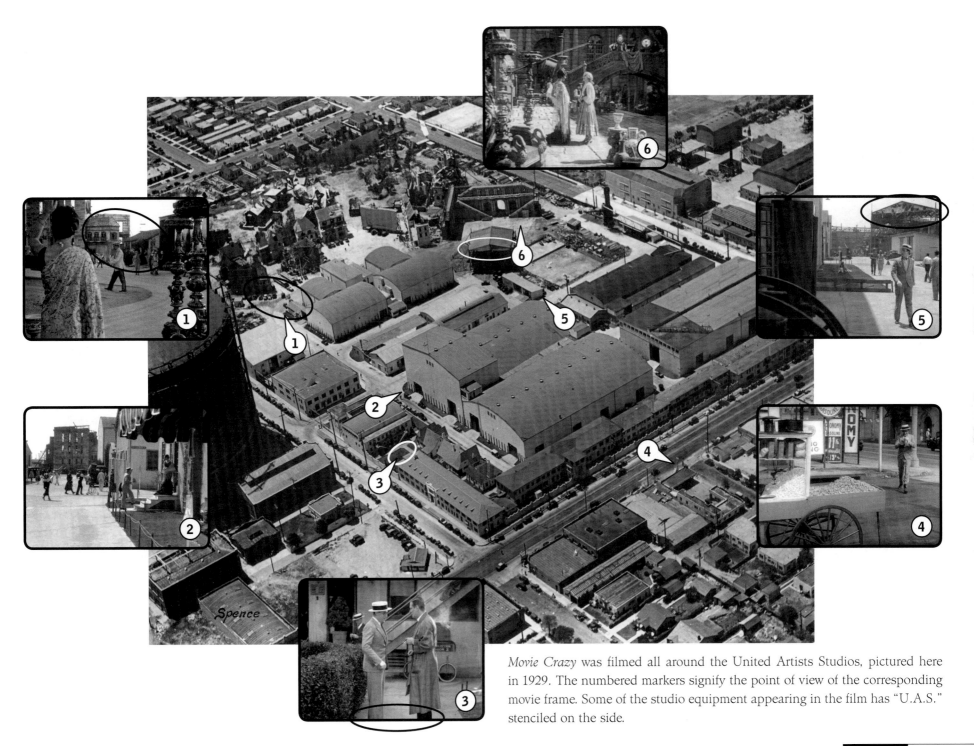

Movie Crazy was filmed all around the United Artists Studios, pictured here in 1929. The numbered markers signify the point of view of the corresponding movie frame. Some of the studio equipment appearing in the film has "U.A.S." stenciled on the side.

This aerial detail shows Harold's path crossing N. Poinsettia Place and the long row of imposing studio offices behind him. The inset to the right shows a United Artists emblem still capping the doorway (*oval*) behind Harold. United Artists was formed in 1919, when actors Charlie Chaplin, Douglas Fairbanks, Mary Pickford, and director D. W. Griffith formed their own movie production and distribution company. The Pickford-Fairbanks Studio on Santa Monica Boulevard between N. Poinsettia Place and Formosa Avenue became the United Artists Studios, and later the Samuel Goldwyn Studios. The studio is known today simply as "The Lot."

Below, one stage from the 1932 movie (*lower left*) remains identifiable today.

Harold is about to lose a special piece of small jewelry in the vast heap of peanuts before him. He is walking from a gas station at the NE corner of the "T" intersection where N. Poinsettia Place intersects Santa Monica Boulevard. The oval behind him marks an entrance to the United Artists Studios, now closed off (*below*). This gas station played a role in Buster Keaton's 1925 feature *Seven Chances* (see next page).

During *Seven Chances*, Buster Keaton flees a mob of jilted brides by sprinting east down Santa Monica Boulevard (*white arrows, left*) past the same corner gas station appearing in *Movie Crazy*. The black arrows show Harold's path.

The stores Buster passes appear in this aerial detail (*left*), from the photo below, showing the sets for the Douglas Fairbanks fantasy epic *The Thief of Bagdad* (1924).

Not only did Harold and Buster cross paths, they did so in the shadow of this legendary Hollywood studio. The oval in the movie frames (*top right*), photo (*above*), and aerial detail view (*left*) all mark the same doorway at 7211 Santa Monica Boulevard, across the street from where dozens of classic movies were filmed.

Harold Lloyd, Charlie Chaplin, and Douglas Fairbanks, relaxing in the sun.

Photo Credits

HAROLD LLOYD images and the names of Mr. Lloyd's films are all trademarks and/or service marks of Harold Lloyd Entertainment Inc. Images and movie frame images reproduced courtesy of The Harold Lloyd Trust and Harold Lloyd Entertainment Inc.

The author would like to give particular acknowledgment and thanks to Suzanne Lloyd, Kevin Brownlow, Marc Wanamaker, Rich Correll, Christina Rice of the Los Angeles Public Library, Dace Taube of the USC Regional History Center, Special Collection, and Olivia Morales of the Brooklyn Public Library.

Marc Wanamaker—Bison Archives: cover all; 1 all; 3; 6; 8 top; 13 ul; 14 ul; 37; 38 cl, bc; 46 ll; 55 ul; ll; 56 lr; 57 ur; 59 ll; 60 ul; 61 bc, ur, lr; 62; 68 top; ll; 69 cr; 71 ur; 72 r; 73 ur, lr; 74 lr; 76 ul; 82 ul; 83; 88; 89 all except bc; 94 top c; 95; 96 c; 97 cl; 98 ul; 99 lr; 104 lr; 106 l; 108 ul, ur; 110 c, ur, lr; 113 l; 117 ul; 118 lr; 120 l; 122 lr; 126 ul; 135; 136 ul, lr; 146 cl; 148 ll; 155 ll; 156 cl, ll; 159 l; 168 ll; 174 ll; 179 ll, lr; 187 lr; 188 ul, lr; 189 ul, cl; 191 ur; 192 ul; 203 ul, ll; 204 ur, ll; 227 ur, b; 228 ll; 241 ul, ur; 242 lr; 243 ul; 297 ll; 299 c; 300 ul; 301 cl, ll; 304.

Suzanne Lloyd: 5.

Luke's Movie Muddle (1916), *The Nonskid Kid* (1922), *Sold at Auction* (1923)—*American Slapstick* (All Day Entertainment, Mark Roth, ReelClassicDVD.com): 8 bc; 32 bc; 143 ul, bc-l.

Library of Congress: 11; 86 ur; 193; 194; 196 top; 197 ur, ll, lr; 198 all; 199 all; 201 ur, ll; 202 ll; 205 r, b; 206 top, ll; 207 ll, bc; 216; 218 ur, ll; 219 l, ur; 220; 221 ul; 225 ul; 226 ll, r; 232 b; 233; 235 all; 236 lr; 237 ul, top c, ll, bc; 239 ul, top c, ll; 240 ll, r; 246 r; 249 lr; 250 cl, b; 251 ll; 253 c, lr; 255 ll; 256 ur, ll; 258 lr; 260; 261 ll; 262 all; 264; 265 lr; 268 cl, ll; 276 c; 277; 280 lr; 281 b; 282 ur, lr; 283 ul, ll; 284 ll; 286 ur; 287 cr; 288 ul, ur, cr, ll; 289 ul; 291 ul; 297 ul.

California Historical Society, Title Insurance and Trust Photo Collection, Department of Special Collections, University of Southern California: 12 l; 15 ur, cr, lr; 16 top c, lr; 17 ll, ur; 20 ll; 21 ul, cl; 26 ur, lr; 27 top c, ur, cr; 28; 34 ul; 43 ur; 47 bc; 49 ll, cr; 50 ur; 51 ll; 52 ul; 63 all; 66 cl; 67 l; 74 ll; 75 ur, b; 76 b; 77 ll, bc; 78 cr; 79 ul, cl; 81 lr; 82 ur, lr; 84 ll; 86 cr; 90 ul; 91 ul, bc; 92 lr; 93 lr; 99 ul, bc; 100 ur, ll; 104 ll; 105 ul; 106 ur; 108 ll, lr; 109 ur, 110 ll; 112 l; 113 bc; 115 bc; 123; 125 (1), (2), (4), lr; 128 lr; 133 cr (C), cr (B); 134 ur; 137 cr; 138 ul; 140 top c, cr; 141 lr; 144 r; 148 cr; 155 ur, lr; 157 ur; 171 cl, c, lr; 174 top c; 185 cr; 202 ur; 208 ll; 213 lr; 214 top, lr; 269 ur, ll, lr; 294 t; 295 cl; 298 ul.

Security Pacific National Bank Photograph Collection/Los Angeles Public Library: 13 ur; 15 top c; 21 ll, lr; 22 ll; 23 ur; 24 ll; 32 cr; 33 ur; 34 ll; 45 cl; 46 bc; 52 ll; 64 cl; 65 all; 70 lr; 72 ll; 80 c; 90 lr; 93 ll; 94 ll; 98 b, ur; 101 ll; 109 ll; 125 (3); 129 c; 133 ur; 134 ll; 139 top c, bc, lr; 141 top c; 154 cl; 155 top c; 158 top c; 163 cr; 166 ll; 170 ur; 176 ur; 184 c, lr; 185 ul, top c; 208 r; 212 b; 293 ur.

By the Sea (1915), *Work* (1915), *The Bank* (1915), *Police* (1916), *Easy Street* (1917), *The Adventurer* (1917)—*Chaplin's Essanay Comedies Collection and The Chaplin Mutual Comedies Collection* (David Shepard and Film Preservation Associates): 13 cr; 16 cl; 23 lr; 24 lr; 43 cl; 71 lr; 81 cl, ll.

Bliss (1917), *By Sad Sea Waves* (1917), *Be Reasonable* (1921)—*American Slapstick 2 Collection* (All Day Entertainment, David Kalat): 14 ur; 78 ur; 80 lr.

Are Crooks Dishonest? (1918), *Just Neighbors* (1919), *His Royal Slyness* (1920)—*The Harold Lloyd Collection Slapstick Symposium* (Eric Lange and Serge Bromberg, Lobster Films): 14 cr; 15 ul, c; 16 ur; 86 c, bc, lr; 86 c, bc, lr 143 ll; 218 cr, lr; 219 lr; 222 ll, bc, 225 ur, cr, lr; 226 cl, c.

The Hayseed (1919), *Coney Island* (1917)—*The Best Arbuckle Keaton Collection* (David Shepard, Film Preservations Associates, Lobster Films): 40 top c; 41 (1B); 143 ll; 218 cr, lr; 219 lr; 222 ll, bc, 225 ur, cr, lr; 226 cl, c.

David Kiehn: 14 ll.

Whittington Collection, Department of Special Collections, University of Southern California: 15 cr; 60 ur; 92 ll; 134 lr; 162 lr; 210 ur; 211 c, bc; 293 ll.

The Bancroft Library, University of California, Berkeley: 17 c; 22 cr.

UCLA Air Photo Archives, Department of Geography, Spence Air Photo Collection: 18 r; 19 c, lr; 285 ur, lr.

Mystery of the Leaping Fish (1916), *When the Clouds Roll By* (1919)—*Douglas Fairbanks: A Modern Musketeer Collection* (David Shepard, Film Preservation Associates, Jeffrey Masino, Flicker Alley LLC): 19 bc; 22 ur; 138 cl.

A Dog's Life (1918), *Shoulder Arms* (1918), *The Idle Class* (1921), *The Circus* (1928), *City Lights* (1931), *Modern Times* (1936) (Roy Export Company Establishment/Bubbles Incorporated SA): 20 c; 51 cr; 52 c; 87 ur; 96 lr; 101 lr; 173 ll; 174 cr, lr; 187 ll; 227 cl.

El Pueblo de Los Angeles Historical Monument: 22 lr; 23 top.

The Scarecrow (1920), *Neighbors* (1920), *The High Sign* (1921), *The Goat* (1921), *Cops* (1922), *The Love Nest* (1923), *Three Ages* (1923), *Sherlock Jr.* (1924), *Seven Chances* (925), *Go West* (1925), *College* (1927)—*The Art of Buster Keaton Collection* (The Douris Corporation, David Shepard, Film Preservation Associates, and Kino International Corporation): 23 c; 24 ur, cr; 44 ul; 45 ur; 66 ul; 68 lr; 69 ll, lr; 81 c; 84 c, bc; 87 ul, cr; 92 ul; 93 bc; 96 cr; 132 ul; 133 bc; 136 ll; 139 ur; 151 lr; 166 ul; 171 cr; 180 lr; 256 c; 289 ur; 301 ur.

Frauds and Frenzies (1928), *Hold Your Breath* (1924), *Hot Foot* (1924), *Christmastime* (1922), *Help Wanted* (1928)—*The Slaphappy Collection* (Larry Stefan and Richard M. Roberts): 23 ll; 91 lr; 94 ur; 117 ll; 133 ll; 152 ll; 162 ur.

Seaver Center for Western History Research, Los Angeles County Museum of Natural History: 23 top.

The Janitor (1919), *The Prodigal Bridegroom* (1926)—*The Silent Comedy Mafia* (Christopher Snowden, Unknown Video): 23 bc-l; 47 c, cr.

Pictometry International: 25 lr; 116 ll.

Tillie's Punctured Romance (1914)—*Chaplin at Keystone Collection* (© Lobster Films for the Chaplin Keystone Project): 26 cr; 61 cl; 122 cr; 148 top c.

This Rebel Breed (1960) (aka *Black Rebels* and aka *Lola's Mistake*) (© 2005 Something Weird Video, Inc.): 30 ll; 32 cl; 36 bc.

California History Room, California State Library, Sacramento, California: 31 c, bc; 32 ll; 33 cl; 35 ll, bc; 36 c; 51ul; 64 ll; 116 top c, ur; 209 ur; 211 ur.

Act of Violence (1948), Metro-Goldwyn-Mayer—*Classic Collection Film Noir Vol. 4* (© Turner Entertainment Co.): 36 ll.

Hop to It! (1925), *Should Sailors Marry?* (1925)—*The Oliver Hardy Collection Slapstick Symposium* (Eric Lange and Serge Bromberg, Lobster Films): 36 top c; 98 ul.

Free Wheeling (1932), *Boxing Gloves* (1929), *Fish Hooky* (1933), *Bouncing Babies* (1929)—*The Little*

Rascals: The Complete Collection (© Hal Roach Studios, Inc., RHI Entertainment Distribution LLC): 41 ul, c; 56 ll; 147 cr, ll.

Big Red Riding Hood (1925), *Jeffries, Jr.* (1924), *Jus' Passin' Through* (1923)—*Becoming Charley Chase* (© 2009 All Day Entertainment, Looser Than Loose Publishing and Silent Cinema Presentations, Inc.): 41 cr; 53 c; 87 lr.

Old Gray Hoss (1928), *Die Kleinene Stroiche 1927–1929* (© Hal Roach Studios, Inc., Kinowelt GmbH): 42 top c, cr, lr; 147 top c.

Fool's Luck (1926)—*The Forgotten Films of Roscoe "Fatty" Arbuckle* (Laughsmith Entertainment, Inc.): 44 cl.

The Suitor (1920)—*Larry Semon: An Underrated Genius* (Looser Than Loose Publishing): 44 cr.

Google Maps, © Google, Inc.: 46 c; 158 lr; 163 lr; 273 ur, lr.

Fire Fighters (1922) (Turner Entertainment Co.): 53 top c.

Pulp Fiction (© 1994, Miramax Films): 54 cr.

Laurel & Hardy: *Wrong Again* (1929), *Liberty* (1929), *Duck Soup* (1927), *We Faw Down* (1928), *Sugar Daddies* (1927) (Hal Roach Studios, Inc., Richard Fenner and Company, Inc., and Hal Roach Studios [Trust]): 58 cl; 105 ur; 146 (B1), cr; 185 ll; 227 ul.

The Academy of Motion Picture Arts and Sciences: 59 ul; 89 bc; 120 top c, ur; 127 ul; 177 ur; 217 ur.

The Cook (1918) (Milestone Film & Video): 64 cr, lr; 66 bc; 72 lr.

Historical Society of Long Beach: 66 ur.

Los Angeles Fire Department Historical Society Archive: 69 ur, bc.

Santa Monica Public Library Image Archives: 70 ll; 71 ll; 165 ul, ur.

Men O' War (1929), *Berth Marks* (1929), *On The Loose* (1931) (Hal Roach Studios, Inc., CCA): 72 cl; 140 ll; 229 cr; 230 lr; 297 lr.

Jeffrey Stanton: 74 ur; 230 cr.

Why Pick on Me? (1918): 75 ul, center row; 76 ur, cl, cr; 77 cl, cr; 78 lr; 79 ur; 80 ul, ur, ll; 81 ul; 229 lr.

The Southern Pacific in Los Angeles, 1873–1996 (Larry Mullaly and Bruce Petty): 84 c; 86 cl, ll.

North by Northwest (1959) (Metro-Goldwyn-Mayer, Turner Entertainment Co.): 85 bc.

Ralph Melching Collection, Pacific Railroad Museum/Pacific Railroad Society, San Dimas, California: 87 top c.

The Setup (1949) (RKO Pictures Turner Entertainment Co.): 94 ul.

Kevin Brownlow: 96 ll; 107 top c, bc, cr, lr; 114 ul; 122 ul.

Annette D'Agostino Lloyd: 111 ul; 118 ur.

Moonlighting pilot episode (Picturemaker Productions, ABC Circle Films, American Broadcasting Companies, Inc.): 114 ll, bc; 118 ll; 122 ll.

The Cameraman (1928) (© Turner Entertainment Co.): 131 cr.

Bruce Torrence Historical Collection: 131 lr; 132 lr; 148 ul; 166 cr.

Mother's Joy (1923)—*The Stan Laurel Collection Slapstick Symposium* (Eric Lange and Serge Bromberg, Lobster Films): 138 ur.

Hustling for Health (1919)—*The Stan Laurel Collection Slapstick Symposium Vol. 2* (Eric Lange and Serge Bromberg, Lobster Films): 143 cl; 298 lr.

Three Little Pigskins (1934), *Pop Goes the Easel* (1935), *Hoi Polloi* (1935), *False Alarms* (1936)—

The Three Stooges Collection, Volume One (© Columbia Pictures Industries, Inc.): 148 ur; 161 ul; 180 c; 181 cl, c; 186 ll.

Hollywood Sanborn fire insurance maps, © 1919 Sanborn Map Company, EDR Sanborn, Inc.: 149 ll; 153 ur.

The Watson Family Photography Archive: 151 ul, cr.

Soldier Man (1926), *Saturday Afternoon* (1926), *His Marriage Wow* (1925), *The First 100 Years* (1924), *Feet of Mud* (1924)—*The Harry Langdon Collection Lost and Found* (All Day Entertainment and Lobster Films): 158 ur; 160 ul; 161 cr; 162 cl; 200 ll.

Rudolph's Revenge (1928), *The Big Shot* (1928), *Once Over* (1928)—*Weiss-o-rama* (Kit Parker, Richard M. Roberts, Kit Parker Films, and Blair and Associates): 161 c; 180 c; 297 ur; 298 bc.

Southern Pacific Lines, John R. Signor, Southern Pacific Historic & Technical Society: 168 ur.

Pacific Electric Stations, John Heller, Electric Railway Historical Association of Southern California: 168 lr.

Courtesy of the Robert E. Ellingwood Model Colony History Room, Ontario City Library: 169 ur, ll, lr.

Test footage from *The Birth of a Nation* (1915) (Film Preservation Associates): 187 ur.

Shutterstock: 195 lr; 197 c; 291 lr.

Little Lord Fauntleroy (1936) (United Artists): 204 c.

The Strong Man (1926) (© 1926 First National Pictures, Inc., © renewed 1954 Warner Brothers Pictures, Inc.): 205 top c.

New York Public Library: 222 r; 231 c; 245 top; 259 ur; 261 ur; 263 ur; 288 lr.

Brooklyn Museum: 223 ur.

Selected archival movie frames from *Coney Island: A Film by Ric Burns* (© 1991 WGBH Educational Foundation and Steeplechase Films, Inc.): 223 lr; 224 ul, top c, ur, ll, bc; 229 cl, ll, bc; 231 ul.

It (1927) (Paramount Pictures Corporation): 228 cr, lr; 229 ur; 230 top c, ur.

Popular Science Magazine, Vol. 98 – No. 1, January 1921, Vol. 102 – No. 4, April 1923: 254 top, cl; 255.

Brian Merlis / Brooklynpix.com: 265 ll.

Paul E. Gierucki: 279 lr.

National Register: 295 ur.

All remaining photos were taken by the author or are from the author's collection. The author apologizes for any oversights or omissions in supplying appropriate credits, and will make every effort to provide appropriate acknowledgments in subsequent editions of the book.

Author Blog: Chaplin – Keaton – Lloyd – More

For tours of silent film locations, videos, PowerPoint lectures, new discoveries, and trivia regarding Charlie Chaplin, Buster Keaton, Harold Lloyd, and other silent comedy stars, visit the author's blog http://SilentLocations.WordPress.com.

Also by John Bengtson: *Silent Echoes: Discovering Early Hollywood Through the Films of Buster Keaton* (Santa Monica Press) and *Silent Traces: Discovering Early Hollywood Through the Films of Charlie Chaplin* (Santa Monica Press).

Parting Shot

The world at his feet, Harold Lloyd relaxes high above the city he knew so well. Lloyd's unprecedented streak of hit comedies dominated the box office throughout the 1920s, making him one of Hollywood's most popular and successful stars. Decades later, silent visions of that bygone era are preserved forever in the background of Harold Lloyd's classic films.